THE FORTUNATE ISLES

The Fortunate Isles

A Study in African Transformation

Basil Davidson

Africa World Press, Inc.

P.O. Box 1892
Trenton, New Jersey 08607
(609) 695-3766

Africa World Press, Inc.
P.O. Box 1892
Trenton, New Jersey 08607

First American Edition 1989

Typeset by Input Typesetting Ltd, London

Library of Congress Catalog Card Number: 88-83119

ISBN: 0-86543-121-3 Cloth
0-86543-122-1 Paper

Cape Verde and its people

As for the old Discoverers, I think my name should be added to theirs, and with better reason if modesty allows. For they discovered a handful of desert islands. But in those islands I have discovered a world.

The celebrated writer José Saramago,
after a visit of 1986

This book is
dedicated

To those who began
and
To those who continue

Contents

Preface	ix
Acknowledgements	xi
Part One Where and Why?	1
Part Two The History of Silence	21
1 Birth of a people	23
2 A system of ruin	34
3 'But a day will come . . .'?	48
Part Three Against the Odds	61
4 Beginnings	63
5 The struggle in the islands	93
6 The challenge of 1974	109
Part Four Continuing Cabral	127
7 From the bare ground	129
8 Launching participation	143
9 Woman's place is . . .?	167
10 Land: trees: green renewal	178
11 A country at peace	195
Appendix 1 Independence documents	202
Appendix 2 Mass participation	205
Notes on sources	207
References	210
Thematic Index	218

Preface

On 12 December 1962 a lone and lean young man from a cluster of remote islands, an unknown spokesman of an unknown people, appeared before the Fourth Committee of the General Assembly of the United Nations, and, to much surprise, expected help.

Amílcar Cabral told the United Nations that he had not come to ask for troops to free his country, Cape Verde, from colonial rule, but for diplomatic and political support. 'Perhaps we should be able to ask you for troops. But we think that unnecessary, because we are sure we can do it for ourselves.'

Rhetoric or bravado? What David was going to be able to evict the Goliath of a powerful European dictatorship from its ancient control of an archipelago in mid-Atlantic?

The same dictatorship killed Cabral in January 1973. But in July 1975 Cabral's successor, Aristides Pereira, could stand in the midst of Praia, the capital of Cape Verde, and tell a listening multitude that independence was theirs: 'the outcome of a long struggle, of a long resistance'.

And peace came, a gentle and a mutual peace. How could this have happened? And what came after?

Acknowledgements

This book has drawn on a personal experience which began for me in 1960 when the late Amílcar Cabral first came to London and we formed a friendship unbroken till his death in 1973. But if I became interested in 1960 in Cabral's two countries of Cape Verde and 'Portuguese Guinea', as it then was, or Guinea-Bissau as it has since become, it was not until 1974 that I could begin visiting the archipelago. That initial visit led to others in 1976, 1980, 1983, 1986 and 1987.

My acknowledgements and thanks therefore go to many persons over many years, and especially to all those who, as my references make clear, have helped me with oral or documentary evidence, memoirs, discussions and hospitality. I also wish to thank José Saramago for allowing me to quote from one of his articles, Christopher Fyfe for his helpful critical reading of my initial text, and Augusta Conchiglia for her photographs.

Indispensable financial aid was given me by the Swedish International Development Agency and the Scandinavian Institute of African Studies, and my warm thanks go to their generous and disinterested support.

Basil Davidson

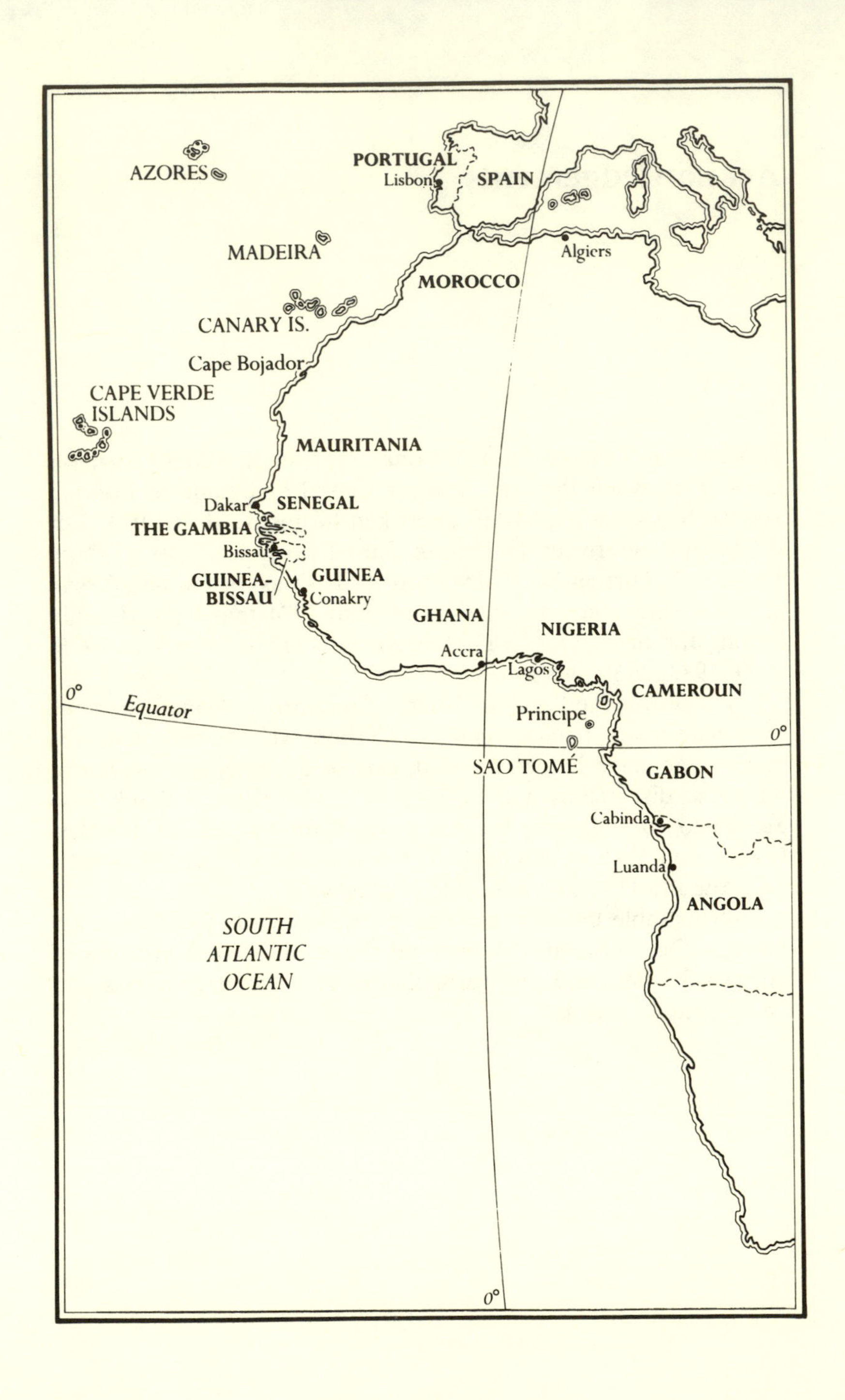
AZORES
PORTUGAL
Lisbon
SPAIN
MADEIRA
Algiers
MOROCCO
CANARY IS.
Cape Bojador
CAPE VERDE
ISLANDS
MAURITANIA
Dakar
SENEGAL
THE GAMBIA
Bissau
GUINEA-
BISSAU
GUINEA
Conakry
GHANA
NIGERIA
Accra
Lagos
CAMEROUN
0°
Equator
Principe
0°
SAO TOMÉ
GABON
Cabinda
Luanda
ANGOLA
SOUTH
ATLANTIC
OCEAN
0°

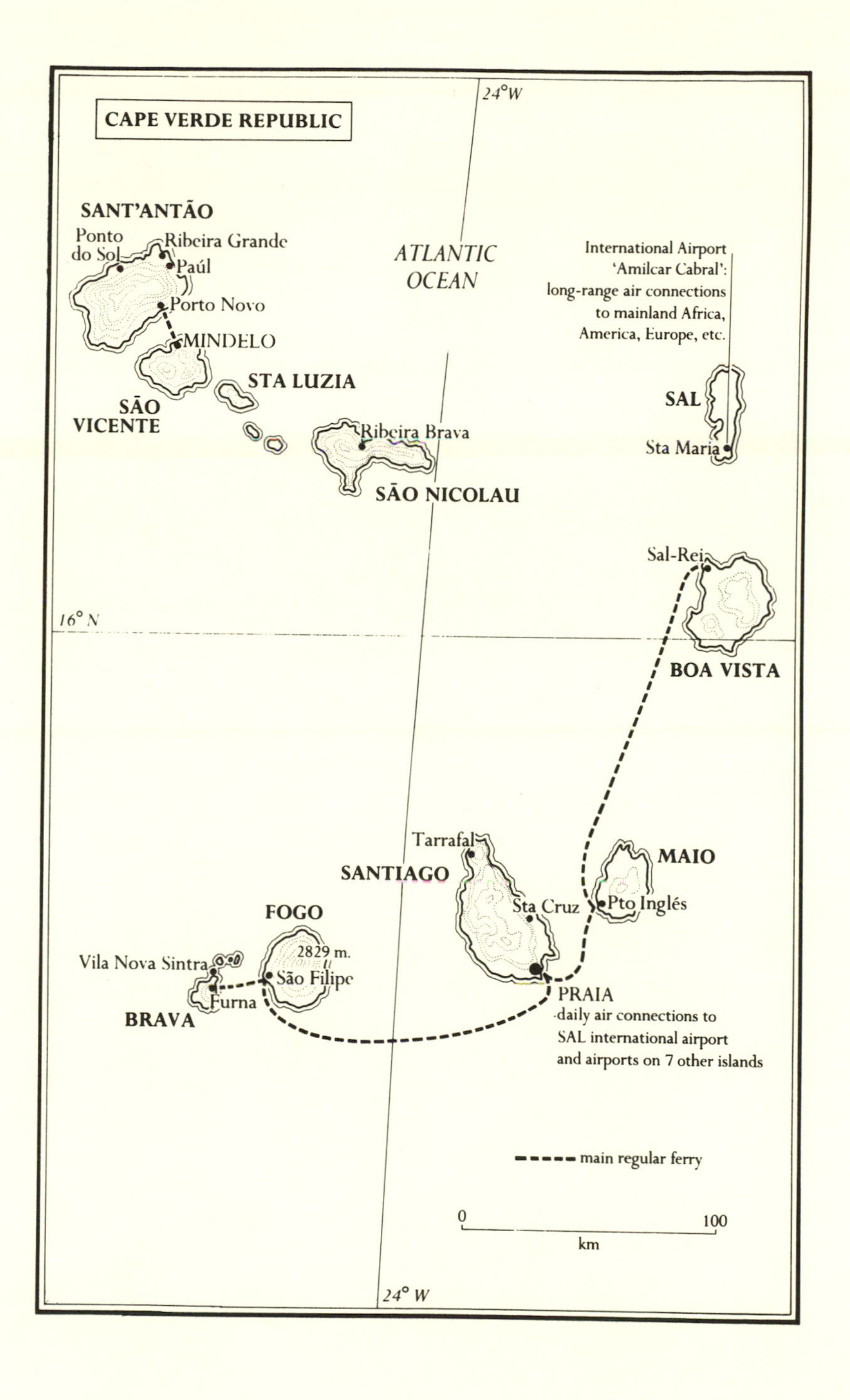
CAPE VERDE REPUBLIC
24°W
SANT'ANTÃO
Ponto do Sol
Ribeira Grande
Paúl
Porto Novo
MINDELO
SÃO VICENTE
STA LUZIA
ATLANTIC OCEAN
Ribeira Brava
SÃO NICOLAU
International Airport
'Amilcar Cabral':
long-range air connections
to mainland Africa,
America, Europe, etc.
SAL
Sta Maria
Sal-Rei
16° N
BOA VISTA
Tarrafal
SANTIAGO
MAIO
Sta Cruz
Pto Inglés
FOGO
2829 m.
Vila Nova Sintra
São Filipe
Furna
BRAVA
PRAIA
daily air connections to
SAL international airport
and airports on 7 other islands
main regular ferry
0
100
km
24° W

Part One

Where and Why?

Ilhas perdidas
no meio do mar
esquecidas
num canto do Mundo
– que as ondas embalam
maltratam
abraçam . . .

Islands lost
in the midst of the sea
forgotten
in an angle of the World
– where the waves cradle
abuse
embrace . . .

Jorge Barbosa, poet of Cape Verde

Cape Verde Republic:
Atlantic archipelago

N 17° 22′ to 14° 48′
W 22° 44′ to 25° 22′

Prevailing Wind   North-East Trades

I

On journeys up and down the world I have heard it said that these are islands – there may be twenty of them, counting uninhabitable rocks, but nine with people – which came out of the sea in the famous year of 1975. A less credible version is that they are not, in fact, islands but a grass-green cape on the coast of western Africa; while many good folk, I also know, have simply denied all awareness of their existence. If such islands really existed, these otherwise well-informed persons say, then people would have heard of them but people have not heard of them.

All the same, the islands of Cape Verde are certainly there. A long way south of the Canaries and some 450 kilometres to the west of Africa's wide western bend, they are out there to be found, anchored somewhere in the grey and blue Atlantic where petrels dabble their feet upon the waves and fish leap past on arrowed wings. Heading from the mainland a day before, an average diesel-driven ship will raise them in a silver dawn; and that is when these legendary islands do indeed come out of the sea as you peer into the western void and perceive that it is not a void. Tipped with morning light, their peaks and hem-stitched edges shoulder from the violet haze at ocean level, hugely rising, hard to believe, their tallest summit almost three thousand metres above the Atlantic: a landscape of looming cliffs and knife-carved rocks like nothing else the world can show.

They are most solidly there, tough volcanic cores and solitary mountains in an oceanic archipelago which has a land surface measuring 4033 square kilometres – the islands of Cape Verde, the Fortunate Isles.

When not confusing them with the Canary Islands to the north, the ancient world knew of them as the Islands of the Blest where sumptuous nymphs of Hesperus, four by some reports or seven

This is a land long stripped bare by nature and by men, where, they say, it is the goats that have taught them 'how to eat stones'. The donkeys, too . . . (Photo copyright Augusta Conchiglia)

by others, lay in fabled gardens guarded by a dragon beyond the skyline of the western seas, and fed on golden apples and domestic bliss. Times have evidently changed, for while there are a few apples to be found on Cape Verde there is none that is remotely golden; and if there is domestic bliss in reasonable quantity there is no single trace of a dragon. Yet the sequel will show in due course, and however improbably, that it may be right to call these islands fortunate.

Improbably: for this in truth is a barren land where people, as their poets say, have learned to feed on stones: the goats have taught them how. Here are stones in a surrounding ocean which leads everywhere else, but everywhere else remains immensely out of sight, far distant, the destination of exiles yearning for home. Here is a people that was planted by the indifferent greed of history but somehow has survived, clinging to their rocks, defying the seas that divide them from everywhere else. The islands of Cape Verde, the Fortunate Isles: no one knowing them will fail to return . . .

II

Airlines connect them nowadays with Africa and Europe and America – by big jets to the international airport named after their hero, Amílcar Cabral, on the island of Sal, and small jets from Sal to the national airport of Praia on the island of Santiago, and then on to other airports on other islands. But the surrounding ocean in its immensity is lost to the blind traveller by air. Even when suffering the stomach-twisting wallow of Atlantic rollers, the traveller by sea has a better introduction.

Some 320,000 people by a count of 1986 live here on nine islands: on five islands to the windward or *Barlavento* and four to the leeward or *Sotovento*, named like this because the prevailing wind blows north-easterly, at times a zephyrous breeze but as often a gale. Two islands are relatively large, being some fifty miles or so across although a long way out of sight of one another. These are Santiago and Sant'Antão, so high and steep in their volcanic cliffs and peaks that each can seem, when you stand somewhere in their midst, as though it were a continent of mountains: until, that is, you climb the next peak and see, dizzily beneath your feet, its necklace of Atlantic surf.

Next to Sant'Antão is São Vicente, practically a desert island save for its city of Mindelo with a superb natural harbour, and next again Santa Luzia where no one lives, and then São Nicolau. Much further again and far out of sight is Sal, the airport island where some 7000 people live, and after that, coming round to leeward on a long haul, there is Boa Vista next to Maio, flattish islands with vivid histories of their own – but each of these islands insists upon a vivid history of its own – and then within sight there are the lofty peaks of Santiago, which is the biggest island and where, in the olden times, slavery took its firmest hold.

Tucked into a useful harbour on the southern side of Santiago, Praia is the capital of these Fortunate Isles; and from Praia on a clear evening the haze lifts to reveal, some fifty miles away, the mighty flanks of Fogo, *The Fire*, its volcanic peak rising to an altitude of 2800 metres in a sky–aspiring cone which still grumbles deep in its interior and last erupted, though in quite a friendly way, killing nobody, in 1951. More even than its neighbours, Fogo is an island of most startling aspect which needs really to be seen to be believed and then is unforgettable. Beyond Fogo and close to it, there is the little land of Brava where the old whaling masters from New Bedford and Rhode Island, Captain Ahab and company, used to find their best and bravest harpooners; or so they affirm on Brava, and quite possibly it is true. Beyond Brava there is no more land until, some 14,000 kilometres away, you reach the cliffs of the Antarctic.

I went to Brava, again by sea, on a February morning of 1986 with the wind carving troughs and deeps between Atlantic waves. Soon you can go by air, but then you had to go by sea. You had to go from the capital of Fogo, which is São Filipe, a pleasant townlet perched on cliffs that lately received a good stone harbour mole. But a gale of 1982 swept away the outer length of the mole, not yet rebuilt in 1986; and so if you go by sea you go on board the ferry by being carried through the surf on the shoulders of men who do this work, and then by rowboat to the ferry moored near the sea-drenched mole. The ferry is a Danish diesel built for the rollers of the Kattegat, which is just as well: because the channel between Fogo and Brava, as someone remarked at the time, *é terrivel* in its pitching and rolling, a sleeve of ocean an hour across that is well-respected for its challenge to the stomach.

Across this channel, with the peak of Fogo drawing back above you, there is the hump of Brava beneath a frown of rainless cloud, and below it a sheltered port in a narrow bay, the port of Furna. The ferry buckets into this bay with Furna town spread along its hillside in ranks of toylike houses ranged on terraces above the quay. Seen from the deck, these huts and houses look as if painted there by a stay-at-home hand, blue and pink and neatly small with rooms windowed on either side of a door, as though in a world of their own: which, in fact, they largely are. Yet Brava people are travelling folk, and here in Furna harbour the echoes of the heaving seas are those of departure for America the Golden, as almost anyone in these parts will confirm if asked.

The Cape Verde islands have long been an archipelago of emigration for reasons anything but fortunate, and Brava perhaps more than any other. Drought and famine have driven the people away, and even now, when nobody dies of hunger here, on Brava they are 'waiting to depart' so that, while cheerfulness keeps breaking in, there is an air of sorrow to the place. Yet Brava emigrants, like other Cape Verdeans, also return: from America or Holland, Portugal or Senegal or half a hundred distant lands where a living can be found. They return with cars and radios and fashionable garments and the various garbage of foreign parts, while those who have made their pile build houses for retirement where, in the meantime and it may be a long time, aged aunts or female cousins reside as solitary custodians.

The ferry casts anchor near the quay and people get ready to be rowed ashore. Here beside me is a prosperous Brava emigrant who makes a living in New England but comes home every year with the idea that what Brava needs is the spending of money by Brava men with incomes or pensions earned abroad. He too is about to build for his retirement, and already has an eye on the delectable village of Fajã d'Agua nesting at the foot of cliffs where German engineers, now in 1986, are helping to build Brava's airport. Strong on island history, this emigrant tells of times past when the port of Furna could be so full of rigged ships and schooners that 'you walked across the bay from deck to deck'.

Furna is the port from which the ever-praised *Ernestina* made her voyages, the last of the great emigrant schooners – for nowadays the people go by air from Sal – and a famous skipper of the *Ernestina* was this emigrant's great-uncle. 'They used to race across with our emigrants and back again with food and stuff. My great-uncle made it once from Rhode Island to Furna in twenty-two days. Wasn't anyone else who ever did it that fast.'

And here beside him on the deck, chatting, is a Cape Verdean who will never be an emigrant, Carlos Tavares, one of the extraordinary young men who freed the islands from foreign rule in 1975, rising forty now and pleased that his friend from New England should be planning to build at Fajã d'Agua. Carlos stands on the deck as though standing on his own firm ground, which is what in a real sense he is doing, for the building of an independent country against the odds, tremendously against the odds, is the dream and vision that Carlos and his friends have made come true.

Contradictions: quite a few though seldom obvious. Above the quayside, 50 yards away, huge letters in black paint celebrate the name of Aristides Pereira, President of this secular republic born in 1975; and yet Aristides Pereira, the vividly loved leader of this new state, is the twelfth child of the former vicar of Boa Vista, a most Catholic and respected clergyman with whom the Bishop of Cape Verde, half a century ago, was glad to take his dinner while asking fondly after the children. For the Cape Verdeans of those days, though it seems not since, expected their clergymen to create their own families and thought it wrong, or at least unneighbourly, when they did not.

Since then there is also family planning. But today on the quayside awaits a brown-robed priest from Italy, the shepherd of a Brava flock, whose Capuchin Order follows Pope Woytyla in most strenuously demanding that priests must be celibate and women refuse to kindle the fires of Hell by indulging in the sins of contraception. On this the secular republic of Cape Verde thinks otherwise, insisting that women must be free to choose and that the population, as a practical matter, will, without contraception, double in number in the next fifteen years or so. That being the case, the return of famine may be the real alternative to birth control.

The Cape Verdean Republic accordingly promotes family planning with clinics for that purpose, and has a striving organization of Cape Verdean women for defence of the rights of women, including the right to choose or reject motherhood, and when to choose. 'We may not be able to change the attitudes of men,' Maria das Dores, who leads this organization of Cape Verdean women, remarked to me the other day, 'but at least we can change the attitudes of women.' She is not hopeful about the attitudes of men. And here on the deck of the Brava ferry is an admirable Swedish midwife and health worker who works on Brava, and she, if possible, is still less hopeful about the attitudes of men.

This Swedish nurse considers, professionally, that the pill is the most appropriate form of contraception, or else the coil, and tells me as the ferry jibs and heaves on the surges of the Brava channel that the trouble here is precisely the trouble with the attitudes of men. 'The men are mostly very backward, they can be bullies afraid of losing the upper hand if women get protection. So women come to me in secret. Oh yes, they come all right, openly or in secret, they know their need.' As for the exhortations of the Capuchins from Italy, we leave them on one side. We are going ashore in the rowboat and another of the passengers, it appears, is the editor of a Catholic periodical published in São Vicente and rather oddly entitled *Terra Nova*, which writes most vehemently against the teachings of the new Republic and in favour of the teachings of Pope Woytyla. Carlos Tavares cannot admire this editor and does not speak to him, but will not quarrel with him either. There is nothing wrong with tolerating an opposition paper, even if you find it sorely mistaken in its views and offensive in its editorial tone; but you do not have to like it.

After we have climbed from the rowboat to the quay, Carlos and the Italian brown-robed priest shake hands with diplomatic warmth, and there is no problem. This is Carlos's own island, after all, and the Church of Cape Verde begins to be a patriotic church, a Cape Verdean Church, for the Portuguese hierarchy which used to reign here went home after independence, or was sent. As for family planning, that is what the women want and mean to get, no matter if Roman priests may not feel able to approve; and it is the women, who stay at home while men depart, who form the real if unadmitted backbone of society here.

There is bustle on the quayside, greetings between friends, a great shifting and dumping and lifting of bundles; and in any case the ferry's arrival is a day's news. This diesel ferry is another innovation of recent years; in Portuguese times before it, an aged boat from Fogo or from Santiago might arrive once in a fortnight or even, with contrary gales, not at all. Carlos tells how they used to climb to a high point and watch for that aged boat, and, when at last they saw it coming, cry out 'Sell-o! Sell-o!', a Cape Verdean version of the old English *Sail-ho!*

Cars arrive and depart. One of them takes us spiralling and twisting up the cliffside to the capital of Brava, Vila Nova Sintra, somewhere in the darkness of a night with stars. I have not before visited Vila Nova Sintra but there has to be a first time and Vila Nova Sintra, among other matters of interest to the historian, was the birthplace of a local renowned poet, Eugenio Tavares, as well as of modern patriots of valour such as Carlos Tavares who would never claim such eminence, although he certainly deserves it.

There are lights across the hollow which holds the town ahead of us, somewhere in this tropical night-time on the top of Brava's hump; and people are sitting at their gates or strolling in roadways scented with hillside thymes and lavenders. We come to a halt outside a house which neighbours on the town's central plaza. More friends arrive, many friends; and food. Brava listens to the news, and tells its own.

III

The news from Cape Verde has been seldom good: whenever, rather seldom, it has come at all. Famine from cyclical drought has composed a great deal of the news for anyone outside who happened to be listening, and from as early as the first recorded famine of 1580–83 when 'many died and others departed'.

'Some were found dead in the streets, others in their houses', recorded Father Balthazar Barreira of the famine of 1610, because they had eaten wayside plants or poisonous trash for want of better, 'or else they died after their last crust of bread'. And so on down the years. 'I can remember the last famine, the famine of 1947', in our own time recalls Luis Fonseca of the island of Sant'Antão, 'when I was a small child, and saw the corpses carried on stretchers of bamboo for burial in trenches, the cemeteries could no longer hold the dead.'

History here has been a monotony of death by hunger. Why then should people have tried to make a living in this unfortunate land, and why, still more surprisingly, should they have persisted? It may be that humanity grows stronger in confronting sorrow; but history can add some other reasons. Several Portuguese sailed here first, in the 1460s, and found no people. Almost at once they began to bring in captives from the West African mainland to work as slaves at growing crops of whatever could be made to grow. Becoming aware of periodical drought, few Europeans followed, but many captives were Mandjak, Mandinka, Fula, Balante or their neighbours, bought or beaten into slavery by merchants or marauders along the ocean creeks of the 'Rios de Guiné' which became known, at least by the sixteenth century, as the 'Rios de Cabo Verde'. Most Cape Verdeans, in short, came here in the first place because they could not help it.

But the profits from this island system of slavery ensured that the system should continue, at least by the erratic force of its own momentum. It continued slowly, chiefly on Santiago and Fogo. But gradually the numbers grew in much the same relative proportions: a handful of white or near-white Europeans, counted in scores rather than in hundreds; a great majority of Africans, tens of thousands; and in between, with their number continually enlarged by the force of nature, a people neither white nor black but ranged in many variants of brown: a notably handsome people as such origins can often form. Across the years this became a stable population and even, in fact though not in any theory, a unified population.

Unified in fact: because slave revolts and slave evasions went together with diminishing imports of fresh captives from the mainland, until the great majority became effectively free persons. And again unified in fact: because the few Europeans were increasingly absorbed into the brown population, and the browns into the blacks, so that the indigenous but African heritage increasingly took dominant place and influence. Thus there came about, perhaps by 1700 or so, the creation of a Cape Verdean people, Creole in its destiny and language, which was no longer a mulatto people, nor a *mestiço* or a mongrel people such as could belong anywhere else, but a people of its own, specific and original to its place.

At the same time this people was not unified and could not be unified according to the usage of those days. As in other Creole communities, whether in the West Indies or elsewhere, the mentality of slave-owning introduced what the modern world knows as racism and its categories. As indispensable weapons of exploitation in a slave-dependent society, these categories divided people into free and not-free but still more, when that particular division blurred at last and fell away, into gradations of skin colour.

Crudely, there were three such gradations: white and brown and black; but in practice, as this society unwound its complexities of claim on power or privilege, there were many more gradations. With 'pure whites' extremely few, the small number of near-whites claimed the highest rung on the ladder; then came those, rather more numerous, who were the children of near-whites and browns, next the abundant children of the browns and browns, next below the likewise abundant offspring of browns and blacks, and last of all but far the most, the families of blacks and blacks. Sanctified by time and custom, with lesser divisions in between, these categories of skin colour became in all instrumental ways the guide and monitor of social power and possession: with comparatively much of both at the top of the ladder but less and less of either as the rungs descended until, at the bottom, there was no power and no possession.

So long as colonial rule held firm, this astonishing contradiction between the realities of nature and the realities of the 'system' could not be questioned. Every subjectivity of privilege derived from its fountainhead in Europe, in this case in Portugal, while the requirements of colonial rule ensured that law and order, government and social position, rights and duties and all the stars and planets in the racist firmament of life, should remain as fixed as in the universe before Copernicus and Galileo. Even today, when the categories of racism have lost their strength or been driven underground, men's private thoughts can still retain them. Even today, years after colonial rule has gone, the blacks of West Africa can still be capable of condemning, as somehow being less than real people, the browns of Cape Verde or other Creole communities. And the browns of Cape Verde can still nourish the thought, in return, that the blacks of the mainland have yet to find their way to civilization. May it not be better, strictly between ourselves, to be a second-class citizen of Europe or America than a first-class citizen of Africa? The question has at times been poignant, and even painful.

But the facts of nature are stronger than the 'system' and its cultural hangover, while recent history has made them stronger still. Notwithstanding all the junk and drivel of an inherited racism, the people of Cape Verde were obliged to liberate themselves from the rule of Europe, not from the rule of Africa; and it is Africa, not Europe, that has saved them. No matter what the power of old habits of prejudice, the great drama of this liberation has reinforced the sense of Cape Verdean identity as being an African identity.

The development of language has provided another unifying factor. Through the early years the captives brought as slaves from the mainland must have retained their mother tongues, but gradually, with the needs and conditions of slave employment, they began to speak their mother tongues mixed up with Portuguese; and in this way a much modified Portuguese became their common language. This Creole or Crioulo has flowered in island variants, and is not entirely standardized even today when Crioulo has long become a literary vehicle. Yet these variants were mutually comprehensible. Cape Verde, in short, could come to nationhood with its national language well established.

Other influences have gone in the same unifying direction. The musical culture of Cape Verde, for example the characteristic *morna* cycle of tunes and songs, comes neither from Portugal nor from Africa but offers its own contribution; yet the music is closer to Africa than to Europe, while anyone who comes here from Africa will recognize the rhythm of the *batuque*, and some other Cape Verdean dances of antiquity, as descending from the cultures of the mainland. Again, if 95 per cent of Cape Verdeans are devoutly or nominally Roman Catholic and most of the rest are adherents of one or other Protestant congregation, the old beliefs of the mainland can still be found in consultations about witchcraft and in places that lately were, and sometimes still are, shrines to ancestral spirits. At a village amid the canyons of Sant'Antão, in 1980, I found the elderly judges of a people's court at solemn work in measuring a case concerned with the casting of a malevolent spell upon a lady who resented it; and the case was and is not rare in its kind. As on the African mainland, sick persons in Cape Verde find a modern doctor if they can, but nobody will be surprised if they should consult a traditional doctor: the *mestre* or master of spells and counter-spells.

This people taken out of Africa was placed in a land of precipice and canyon, and presented with a destiny no less abrupt and stark. Once upon a time there were many trees on these islands: 'but the tree-cover dwindles year by year and the springs dry up', while 'the rains fail and the land produces nothing, and thousands die of hunger'. That was written by a visiting agronomist, Henrique de Arpoare, in 1881, but could as well have been written many years earlier or many years later. Much of the archipelago degraded into desert before modern times; and modern times, till 1975, did nothing to prevent this degradation.

But slavery also dwindled. Pirates from the high seas made assaults and uproars in the little towns of the archipelago; and slaves escaped to the hills and preferred to remain there, factually free, building thatched huts on cliffsides or lost in canyons where no access looked possible and little was attempted. A new quality of life could be wrested from misfortune. Slaves seized their freedom, especially on the big island of Santiago where, even now, the layout of solitary homesteads far up the mountainsides or niched in high and pathless gullies still bears witness to the freedom that was seized.

Many slave revolts certainly occurred even if few are recorded in such archives as remain; but in this the history of Cape Verde varies from that of other islands, like Jamaica, where plantation slavery was also the norm of economic life. Slave owners here were too few to be able to mount expeditions bent on recapture, while the import of captives to be retained as slaves for local use fell away much earlier than in the Caribbean.

Facing each other across their racist grid, slaves or former slaves and slave-holders were left to get along together as they could. There arose a *convivencia* of a kind, a community of tolerance, that might be rough in its emotions and uneasy in its attitudes but was none the less made permanent by the force of circumstance. And out of this *convivencia* there came as the years proceeded a sense of loyalty to place: to canyon or mountain, island or even archipelago; and it is this, together with a shared culture, that has shaped the magnet of identity with which *Caboverdeanidade*, 'Cape Verdean-ness', has acquired its force.

There were new arrivals from outside. Towards 1800 New England whalers began sailing east and south on two-year cruises and found additional crewmen in Atlantic islands, at first in the Azores and then in the Cape Verdes. So useful were the Cape Verdeans who sailed in American whalers that a United States consulate was opened in Praia as early as 1818, and endured for eighty years which also saw the beginnings of Cape Verdean settlement in New England. Then, with the 1860s, iron ships driven by steam as well as sail began to displace the wind-driven ships. Thrusting Welsh and English coaling companies sent out agents from Cardiff and Newcastle-upon-Tyne until the harbour of Mindelo on São Vicente could offer bunkers for the world's shipping. That was a local boon which also saw the opening of a golf course and an English club to the point that São Vicente became the glass of Cape Verdean fashion. 'Everyone likes to say they come from São Vicente', as one still hears it said. But coal gave way to oil late in the 1920s.

After the coal, it must be said, an utter silence fell once again. The closing of the epoch of coal was also the opening of an epoch of stiff dictatorship in Portugal: a half-century of rigid colonial subjection epitomized on São Vicente by its most prominent building, a square-blocked *fortinho* on an eminence above the harbour. My friend Luis Fonseca was one of those who spent some time as a 'political' in that *fortinho* during the 1960s. He has taken me to see it. The roof is falling in and the locks no longer lock, but the cells remain useful to families without other accommodation.

Cape Verde in those years sank altogether out of sight or hearing of the world. Nothing was known about the islands save in fragmentary rumour or official report until the times did alter: which, in this case, began to occur in 1956. That was the year which was marked – but who else marked it? – by the launching of an independence movement under the lead of the unknown man who was going to address the United Nations in 1962, Amílcar Cabral: 'We have not come to ask you for troops to free our country, because we are sure that we can do it for ourselves.'

Brave words indeed: but the Portuguese dictatorship in 1962 was powerful and intact, engrained in Portuguese life by decades of confident supremacy. Its chief figure, António de Oliveira Salazar, suffered neither from doubt nor weakness, and could and did depend upon the ample aid and sympathy of every major military and industrial power west of the USSR. Those who were 'sure that we can do it for ourselves' were a small company, a mere handful, with nothing to aid them but their own intelligence and will. If such qualities were going to be enough, much would have to happen first.

IV

Much happened, sometimes foreseen but as often not; and the drama of this liberation of Cape Verde from the fetters of its past is surely among the strangest scenarios in all the tangled process of decolonization.

The history of Africa's emergence from colonial rule has been approached in various ways whether constitutional, sociological, anthropological or politico-scientifical. The persons in the drama, or so it has seemed to me, have been less noticed. So it has tended to be a limping disembodied history of things instrumental or statistical, programmatical or economical, rather as though the persons in the drama were charismatic symbols of Destiny – in the usual prosopography, a strictly male affair – or hapless figures carried on a flood of things. Yet the persons in the drama, the persons who counted in those years, the men and the women who made this history were what is truly memorable. They had little to call on save their intelligence and will. But their intelligence and will were after all decisive.

A 'picture gallery' of the liberators of Cape Verde is scarcely feasible if only because abstraction would disfigure what was always a comradeship, a community of friends, a pooling of intelligence and will. That kind of iconography is inappropriate to what these men and women worked and struggled for. They themselves would probably reply that they followed the teaching and example of Amílcar Cabral as well as they were able; and yet an iconography of Cabral is also inappropriate. If he was outstanding among them – and he would have been outstanding in any company – his 'portrait' has still to be set among that same community of friends and comradeship in an often desperate enterprise which, before the end, took his life away. I think from a long acquaintance that Cabral was a marvellous human being, and I have seldom had the fortune to meet his equal. Even his faults and failings could seem a reassuringly human compensation for his irresistible superiority of mind and character: one was grateful for his faults and failings, along with the laughter by which he excused them. No icon could do him justice.

The crucial persons in this drama came in fact to be quite many; and the same is true of them as well. Only a few can be mentioned in these pages for every obvious reason. Behind Cabral were those who followed him from the first and took over from him after the dictatorship had killed him in January 1973: Aristides Pereira, Abilio Duarte, Fernando Fortes, his brother Luíz and others; and then the younger ones, Pedro Pires, Honorio Chantre, José Araújo, and others again; but behind these there were many more, women as much as men. And again behind all these were the people whom they led, the people with their memories and hopes. Back through the generations behind them, a long procession, there peer from doubt and frustration the ideas and intentions of rebellious slaves, of countless exiles, of sailors on a thousand foreign vessels, and of those who were poets, song-makers, pioneers of protest and self-affirmation. All this belongs to the picture; all this is part of the story. All this: and the nature of the enterprise.

Much happened after 1956, and much, in hindsight, can have seemed to be a pathway to disaster. The plan for armed landings from the sea was among what happened. 'We trained in Cuba, thirty of us in two fighting units, one for the landing on Santiago, the other for Sant'Antão. We practised getting ashore against simulated enemy defences. We were young and very fit, our morale was high . . .'

It is Olivio Pires recalling the plan programmed for 1967. Olivio in 1986 is an elder of authority in this country of the young. He is just turned forty, and a centrally responsible cadre of the independence party of Cape Verde, the PAICV. A man of Sant'Antão, he is otherwise a lean and lithe walker on the hills who appears to move by levitation, a knack and power which many Cape Verdeans apparently command at will. He is also a man of savourous humour, and tolerant of weaker brethren. I know all this because I have toiled behind him on his hills, and watched his bearded smile look back for me forgivingly.

He is thinking now of 1967: altogether a curious year. The number of US troops in Vietnam was moving towards its first half-million, and the giant bombers were warming for their work of mass obliteration. In Britain Prime Minister Harold Wilson was about to confer with the Rhodesian settler rebel, Ian Smith, on the British warship named, so absurdly in that context, *Fearless*. The following year was to be Human Rights Year according to the Universal Declaration of the United Nations; while Great Britain, according to official spokesmen, was concentrating on 'the promotion of inter-racial understanding', whatever that might be thought to mean. In the Portuguese Empire, meanwhile, the armies of the dictatorship led by Dr Salazar were concentrating on their civilizing mission to Africa by dropping napalm on the natives, as I myself, walking in that same year through zones of 'Portuguese Guiné' held by its African movement of independence, was obliged to observe.

A curious year, yes: but a painful year. Nigeria was engulfed in civil war. Latin America was reeling under the impact of political disasters in Peru, Bolivia and elsewhere. Students in Europe were gathering their strength to wrench away the paving stones of Paris and other sites of contestation. A new age was on the way: or not.

And in Cuba thirty Cape Verdeans were looking for a ship to sail them back to fight the enemy in their homeland.

All this, too, is somewhere in the picture.

The oral and archival sources of the history in this book are chiefly Cape Verdean, partly Portuguese, and in small degree from other origins. Notes and references at the end of the book say more about them. Documentary sources for periods of settlement and social formation are comparatively rich in reports, memoirs and occasional commentaries by sea captains, traders, administrators; and much of this material is accessible in anthologies and collections put together by Portuguese historians, notably Barcelos. In this respect a special acknowledgement is due to a modern Cape Verdean historian, António Carreira, whose books, notably his *Cabo Verde: Formação e Extinção de uma Sociedade Escravocrata*, are unique and indispensable.

Portugal's brief years of parliamentary republican rule, from 1910 to 1926, unleashed a fruitful if often tumultuous tide of argument and disputation in which Cape Verdean writers, along with others from other African colonies of Portugal, had their share; and the records for this period are usefully rich in the jousting of political journalists, whether professional or amateur. Writers from 'Portuguese Africa' then had their first real chance to speak for their peoples or claim to speak for them; while the Republic even saw an early congress in Lisbon of the Pan-African movement. Several Cape Verdean newspapers of this period are valuable in respect of the origins of what was to become, after the Second World War, the crystallization of a Cape Verdean nationhood.

In 1926 the parliamentary Republic of Portugal went down in melodramatic confusion to military 'saviours' who, in the manner of Iberian generals, lacked even the imagination to perceive their inadequacy. Steered by a Catholic hierarchy of medieval loyalties, however, they opened the way for an ideologist of what the world already knew as fascism – initially of Italian generation and afterwards of German – and Salazar began his almost half-century of personal rule. An intelligent paternalist with a strong if antique sense of Portuguese history, Salazar set about binding Portugal into the contradiction of a modernizing programme couched in terms of the past. Given the nature of the country and its largely peasant majority, the product had to be both painful and apparently permanent.

After the generals' coup of 1926, accordingly, but more than ever after the early 1930s when Salazar introduced a 'New State', *Estado Novo*, which closed down all political freedoms and declared them wicked and perverse, the archives become faulty or worse. There were no more large and fearless inquiries into the state of the Portuguese empire such as those of Lopes de Lima in the 1850s; and, save for one or two courageous dissenters from within the regime such as Henrique Galvão after 1945, there were no more grand disclosures or confessions. The reader will therefore bear in mind that the Portuguese record of the modern history of Cape Verde, at least from 1930 down to 1974 when the dictatorship and the *Estado Novo* were overthrown, remains partial and inadequate. Access to recent State archives is difficult in Portugal today, not least because the bulk of those most relevant to the colonies are closed to inspection and in any case dispersed in the cellars of various ministries or deposited in heaps of uncatalogued files and folders; while the same is reliably said to apply to materials older than the legal fifty-year limit for public access. Happily, for the events of 1974–75 in relation to Cape Verde, General Vasco Gonçalves and some others who overthrew the dictatorship have generously come to my aid with unpublished writing.

The Cape Verdean records for recent times are by contrast rich and various in oral testimony, and to a smaller but still useful extent in written evidence. A definitive history of Cape Verde through the last half-century will be the work of Cape Verdean historians; but much may be attempted in the meantime.

The core of what follows here consists of the history of two periods. One of these is the period from about 1940 to 1974, essentially the birth and development and vivid experience of the struggle for independence; and this is Part Three. Part Four inspects 'the history of the present', essentially the first decade of Cape Verdean independence; and here the central theme is the launching and construction of the politics of mass participation which embody so much of the originality and, as it appears to me, the interesting success which has attended that difficult enterprise.

Briefly, Part Two offers a view of the historical backcloth against which this people has emerged.

Avoiding footnotes in my text, I have listed sources by page number at the end of the book.

Part Two

The History of Silence

Quato ora di madrugada
Djentes São Vicente em pe
Ta grita ta tchora
Spera largada di ses fidjo
Pa São Tomé

Four o'clock in the dawning
São Vicente folk are there
To cry their sorrow
For sons who are sent away
To São Tomé

Mindelo lament

1 Birth of a people

I

West African coastal sailors are said to have found these islands in a distant past, probably at the time of the empire of Mali during the thirteenth century. If so, they decided not to settle here. North African sailors, though competent mariners, went no further south than the latitude of the Canary Islands: going further was believed to be an invitation to disaster.

Shortly before 1400, the North African historian Ibn Khaldun summarized the maritime experience of those times. Sailing beyond the latitude of the Canaries – beyond Capes Não or Juby or Bojador on later maps – ships would be blown out of sight of land and lost infallibly. And the great Catalan Atlas of 1375, compiled by Abraham Cresques from largely North African information, had already shown in touching detail the little Catalan galley of Jaime Ferrer, pictured far down the forbidden coast in Ferrer's 'search for gold', only to note that he and his crew never returned.

Probing southward, the medieval Portuguese long obeyed the rule. The 'capes' in question might be no more than curves or spits of rock protruding from an otherwise featureless Saharan coast, but it would be death to go beyond them:

> Quem passar o Cabo Não
> Ou tornera, ou não . . .

Any who failed to turn back at the level of Não or Bojador would be swallowed by devils or driven ashore or simply drowned; but the sailors' real reason for turning back was more prosaic. So far as I know this reason was first explained in modern times by Raymond Mauny in 1960. He pointed out that the always prevailing wind to the south of Não or Bojador blows from the northward. So it was easy to sail onward to the south but

The people of the Cape Verde Islands have always had to face a life of difficulty. Far out in the Atlantic, the seas around them have no helpful 'continental shelf': their navigation, like their fishing, has had to meet the ocean in its vastness and its furies. But ever since they joined the old whaling crews from New England, and became famous for their skills at sea, these people have known how 'to join their islands to the main'. (Photo copyright Augusta Conchiglia)

impossible to come back save by rowing against the wind. Until, that is, the adoption of sailing rigs capable of making way against the wind, together with direction-finding instruments, notably the astrolabe, that could steer a course when out of sight of land.

This new technology, initially of Chinese invention and use, began to reach the Portuguese in the 1430s, but already in 1434 Gil Eannes took a single-masted *barcha* south of Bojador and came safely home again. All the decisive maritime discoveries flowed from this. Within fifty-four years the Portuguese were to round the Cape of Good Hope, while Columbus, going westward, discovered the islands of the Caribbean.

In this great penetration of the seas, the Cape Verde archipelago was sighted in 1460 or possibly a few years earlier, and received its first small settlement of Europeans in 1462. This was mainly on Santiago Island, and of a feudal nature 'donated' by the King of Portugal. Portuguese or Spanish or Genoese, these few dozen early settlers found a hard land. Striving to bolster this settlement for strategic reasons, the Portuguese crown gave it rights denied to other Portuguese settlements. Of these rights the most valued consisted in a trading monopoly along the West African coast between Senegal and Sierra Leone: effectively, along the creeks and shores between the River Casamance and the Islands of Los. So it was that this reach of coastland came to be known as 'the rivers of Cape Verde', taking the title not from 'the green cape' in western Senegal but from the distant islands of that name.

Meanwhile it was found that the islands themselves could grow sugar, maize and some other useful crops if only a labouring population could be brought in to do the work. The solution was obvious. The Turks had already found it on the Mediterranean island of Cyprus where they prospered by using European slave labour to grow sugar. Portuguese settlers on the south Atlantic islands of São Tomé and Principe were about to follow suit with captives enslaved from Angola and other equatorial regions. The Cape Verdean settlers applied to their 'rivers of Cape Verde'. They went to the mainland and seized or bought captives for enslavement in their archipelago.

The system, if one may call it a system, grew slowly but implacably. By 1582 on the islands of Santiago and Fogo – then the only Cape Verdean islands of any settlement – there were one hundred white men and some 13,700 African slaves of both sexes, together with a few hundred Africans who were not slaves. By 1600 it appears that on the same two islands were about 1500 free persons and some 14,000 slaves.

Several factors made their contribution to the originality of this people. Few Europeans came to join the descendants of the early settlers, for other destinations proved less arduous and more profitable. No greater quantity of slaves for use in the islands was now required save in replenishment for those who died, but the slave trade to the west remained valuable. After 1600, most captives brought from the mainland were destined for onward transit to Brazil or the Caribbean, once they had been taken through a period of 'seasoning': once, that is, the captives had acquired the habits and acceptance of slavery, and some kind of language relationship had been built between them and their masters. Slavery persisted in the islands, but the islands primarily became a relay-station in the network of the Atlantic trade.

The archives have yielded some numbers thanks to the pioneering work of António Carreira. In the four years 1609–12, for example, 1468 captives were landed on Santiago from the 'rivers of Cape Verde' – also known as the 'rivers of Guinea' in a label then coming into use – but 8110 'seasoned' slaves were exported from Cape Verde to Colombia, Mexico, the Canary Islands, and Seville in Spain. Slave trade studies may eventually tell us how many Africans reached the New World by transit through Cape Verde; as matters stand today, one may think that they must have totalled tens of thousands from first to last.

This meant that the bulk of the long-term population of the islands, whether slave or free, acquired the characteristics of permanence. High on the list of these characteristics, as we have seen, was a continuous mixing of the 'races' which, given an almost total absence of white females, nothing could prevent. This bothered the authorities in Lisbon. A royal order of 1620 decided that white females in Portugal hitherto exiled to Brazil, for whatever offence, 'should now be exiled to Cape Verde, so as to extinguish the race of mulatos as much as may be possible'. It made no difference. A Cape Verdean population of mixed origin, although overwhelmingly of mainland African origin, was already in formation.

Exploiting their rights of trade monopoly, free settlers had prospered whether or not they were white, and in defiance of recurring drought. A report of 1549 to the Portuguese monarch could claim that 'apart from Lisbon, no other cities of the Kingdom yield as much as Ribeira Grande', then the little capital on Santiago Island but now, long in ruin, known as Cidade Velha; and this claim, though an exaggeration, was not without some substance. A Portuguese pilot one year later could wax almost lyrical on the comforts of Ribeira Grande, 'with its handsome houses inhabited by an infinity of Portuguese and Castilian gentlemen'. Six years later the bishop of Cape Verde began building a cathedral there, and in 1570 the King consented to the founding of a seminary.

II

But no seminary was founded, and ruin was already on the way. Ruin was provoked partly by the system of monopoly which, as elsewhere, induced a powerful defiance in those shut out from the system. The court in Lisbon might imagine that the King's governor in Cape Verde would maintain law and order, not only in the islands but also along the coast of the rivers of Guinea – the old 'rivers of Cape Verde' – where the governor's writ was supposed to run as well as in the islands. But no such control of the coastland proved possible. Smuggling soon flourished. Cape Verdeans went ashore on the mainland and set up independent trading posts along creeks where no royal servant could reach or stop them.

For decades and whole generations these *lançados* or *tangomãos* – sometimes white men, much more often brown or black – dealt with all who came, whether *dyula* and other traders from the West African interior or maritime speculators from Europe. Physically little or no different from the peoples among whom they dwelt, they acted as valued intermediaries with the 'outside world', and evolved their own form of Crioulo as a trading language which, with time, has become a genuine language.

But the success of the *lançados* was of course at the expense of 'legitimate' traders from the archipelago. Many of the latter found they could not compete with the smuggling trade and preferred to join it. Discouraged by drought and deepening poverty, others departed for Europe or Brazil. Then pirates came to hasten these departures. 'Privateers' like Francis Drake and Jacques Cossard might be the laurelled heroes of England and France: seen from the other side, they were monstrous agents of disaster. No part of this Atlantic seaboard was free of their depredations; and Cape Verde suffered even more than the rest. For upwards of 150 years the little island towns were time and again robbed or sacked by assault from the sea.

The French appear to have begun first, in 1537, boarding and looting six or possibly seven ships in Cape Verdean waters, and more thereafter. But 1562 brought England's turn. John Hawkins took and looted six ships in that year, and eleven more in 1565; in 1566 Lovell plundered five ships and Hawkins, back on the coast, another nine. In 1585 an English squadron under Drake anchored off Santiago Island and sent 600 men-at-arms ashore. 'Driving the defenders before them,' in the words of a contemporary account, these 'entered the City (of Ribeira Grande, now called Cidade Velha) almost without resistance, where they sacked houses and destroyed them. The authorities fled to the hills and the English, carrying away their spoil, departed to Cartagena and San Domingo' in the Caribbean.

Next came a Flemish invasion in 1598 and at later dates. And so it continued, with a new assault every few years. In 1655 the Dutch sacked the town of São Filipe on Fogo Island in a violent four-day spree. Finally it was the French who made a thorough job of ruining the old capital of Ribeira Grande. A veritable fleet of twelve fighting ships under Cossard is said to have taken loot worth more than £3 million in the money of those days, truly a huge extraction of Cape Verdean wealth, and one from which Ribeira Grande was never to recover.

'Most of our houses and our ancient buildings' including the cathedral, reported the once confident Municipal Chamber of Commerce of Ribeira Grande in 1743, 'are in ruins, without our being able to repair them, while most of our farms are lost by reason of there being no slaves to labour on them.' No more than twenty whites remained in the archipelago, 'mostly so poor and wretched as barely able to survive'. More important for the future, these uproars offered slaves the chance to slip away from bondage and escape to the inland hills of Santiago where no avenging hand could reach them. Far up on steep hillsides or lost in hidden gulleys, these 'maroons' of Cape Verde – the Jamaican term was never used, but might have been – built their isolated huts, their *funcos*, and lived to themselves. You can see the same pattern of habitation to this day.

Then came the nineteenth century and the gradual ending of

the maritime slave trade; still more gradually, slavery also began to vanish from the islands. A rough count of 1834, according to the prudent Lopes de Lima writing a few years later, gave a total of 51,854 free or freed persons, but only 3974 slaves. No more were coming from the West African mainland, and only a trickle from Europe: in 1807 a census had enumerated 1752 whites, but only 919 in 1869. Those who did come from Europe were nearly all *degredados*, convicts sentenced to hard labour and exile for crimes ranging from theft to political dissidence: between 1802 and 1882, according to incomplete Lisbon records, as many as 2433 *degredados* were shipped to the islands. They were at once absorbed into a population increasingly homogeneous in its culture and way of life, if notably various in the colours of its skin.

As to language, Portuguese was the official tongue but little used and still less understood, while the original languages of the slaves from the mainland – languages mostly of the Mande and Fula groupings – were likewise gone except in stray words and phrases. The language of the islands had become Crioulo in a number of insular variants, and this Crioulo continued to develop flexibility and strength. By the end of the nineteenth century all the islands, including the remote and precipitous Sant'Antão, were the home of stable populations, even while communications between them remained few and difficult.

Joined by their island destiny, this people evolved a specific and distinctive culture among all the range of Creole cultures which emerged from transatlantic slavery and settlement. In Latin America, for example, the whites and near-whites were numerous enough to impose a culture which they derived from Europe, while the blacks were left in limbo and the truly native populations, Indios, were consigned to an effective non-existence. In Cape Verde there had been no native population, while whites and near-whites were never enough to impose more than a formal and official culture taken from Portugal. Coming out of slavery, the blacks had lost their original cultures but acquired another of their own; and this Cape Verdean culture was what could and did survive. But was this culture finally dependent on Europe or on Africa? Or was this merely a mulato or mixed population of divided loyalties? The questions were important, but they would long wait for an answer.

III

'Colour prejudice' has clearly been a subject of enormous interest to all 'mixed' communities, however factually homogeneous they might really be; and colour prejudice had long become a social regulator by the time that an indigenous Cape Verdean people emerged from the mingling of many African peoples with a relatively tiny number of Europeans.

'Distinction by skin colour' seems in time to have reached an almost pathological condition. A census of 1856, for example, solemnly listed no fewer than seventeen distinctions of skin colour ranging from various shades of 'very dark' to 'almost white'; and it appears to have been assumed that anyone could recognize these differences as easily as if they had been uniforms which carried, as it were, corresponding badges of rank.

All this was of course inherent to a culture of 'slavocracy': of a society based on the exploitation of slave or servile labour. Its motive force, accordingly, was in truth drawn from issues of 'class' far more than from issues of 'race'. Authority and power were white, subservience and obedience were black: such was the dispensation derived from early times and carefully maintained by all who, being white or near-white, could claim authority and power. Maintenance of the 'colour line' was thus of the highest importance to its beneficiaries, even if this sharply material concern was hidden beneath a sprawling range of emotions and superstitions.

It might seem, therefore, that those in this society who could display a European or 'white' culture – even if a Portuguese culture at second hand – would impose a European or 'white' loyalty, and that this loyalty would become unquestioned. By the middle of the twentieth century, if not long before, the Portuguese of Portugal were sure that they had in fact achieved this result. Cape Verde was a part of Portugal, and Cape Verdeans, even in default of not even speaking the language, were Portuguese. Such was the official view, and to some it seemed beyond question.

For what status and civilization could there be, in Cape Verde, if these were not to be European in origin and therefore 'white'? An incident of some thirty years ago, but still well remembered in the maritime city of Mindelo on the island of São Vicente, nicely makes the point.

Nothing then was as prestigious as membership of the Gremio

club, more prized even than membership of the English golf club. Membership of the Gremio was consequently restricted to persons of guaranteed social respectability. Only the 'wealthy' could hope for admission, but 'wealthy', in Cape Verdean usage, was another way of saying white or near-white. Let in the blacks, it was easily agreed, and the club might as well shut down.

A rather wealthy baker of Mindelo applied for membership. He was certainly respectable, and could demonstrate his wealth. After the Gremio turned him down he proved this once again, to the infinite satisfaction of the lower orders, by buying in the United States the poshest car that anyone had ever seen, a vehicle more luxurious even than the Portuguese Governor's. Having shipped this monster across the Atlantic he proceeded to drive it round the town in a scandalous flaunting of cash-in-hand. So why had the Gremio turned him down? They had turned him down flat. For he was very dark in colour; he was practically black.

And yet, in spite of this anti-black prejudice, the innate culture of Cape Verde is not a borrowed European or 'white' garment; and here is a central difference which divides it from the trans-atlantic communities of Creole formation. A Cape Verdean sociologist who is also a veteran of the liberation struggle, Dulce Almada Duarte, has identified reasons for this difference. It is a difference which has much to do with the nature of Cape Verde nationalism and national consciousness. Dulce Duarte tells us,

> Save in a small way in Santiago and Fogo, and in contrast to what happened in for example the Spanish American colonies, there was no development in Cape Verde of a Creole population descended from former white colonists, such as became significant in numbers, in cultural attitudes, or in economic power: no development of a Creole people for whom the black population, above all the slave population, was only a source of profit and the object of an ever greater exploitation.

Unlike what happened in other latitudes, she continues, 'the culture of white Creoles could not serve as a model for Cape Verdean society, a model that relegated the culture of African descendants to the status of mere folklore'. There were simply not enough whites or near-whites to impose their cultural supremacy, no matter how hard they might try. That might be easy in Australia, New Zealand, Canada, where there were no or very few black slaves, and where the aboriginal peoples were wiped out or consigned to oblivion. It might be possible in Latin

America where whites and near-whites were numerous enough to weave a second-hand Spanish culture into the banner of independence, leaving Indios and Africans to perish or survive as they might.

In Cape Verde, such 'white Creoles' as there were rapidly became 'brown Creoles' – with exceptions we shall meet along the way – and these 'brown Creoles', by reason of their stiffly colonial situation as well as by their origins, were in no strength, numerically or culturally, to suffocate the identity and tradition of their black fellow-countrypeople. Dulce Duarte continues, 'And this is what has largely explained why it is that the Cape Verdean black community, in spite of much cultural mixing found in our islands since the start, was able to retain and adapt many of the features of its [African] culture.'

The descendants of African origin were 'able to retain a sense of cultural identity, and use this to oppose the degradations of slavery and colonialism: to retain an identity, that is, which they reshaped and clung to while surviving as the most oppressed class in our society'. And so it came about that in spite of colonial racism,

> a homogeneous society was forged in Cape Verde, a society whose people were neither European nor totally African, and who were proud of being Cape Verdeans.
>
> This 'Cape Verdeanness' evolved from the culture which slaves and their descendants had elaborated; and it profoundly marked the Africans of our islands, instilling a sense of pride in their own culture and of differentiation from the culture of the colonizer.

The point is worth emphasis, for it has mattered enormously in the process of anti-colonial change. In Latin American colonial societies, the Creoles or 'settler derivatives' could proclaim national independence – much like the whites in South Africa or, later still, in Rhodesia – as though they alone had rights to equality and freedom. Even in the early 1980s there were otherwise enlightened Sandinistas of Nicaragua who were still finding it difficult to accept the equality of rights and claims of Indios and blacks.

In the smaller but pregnant case of Cape Verde, nothing like that was to happen. Right down to recent times, circumstances were such that the great majority of 'browns' or Creoles were effectively excluded from 'white culture' – from the culture of their colonial masters in Portugal – and therefore came to stand, as Dulce Duarte insists, 'culturally closer to the black community'.

So the Cape Verdean 'brown', unlike his or her apparent simulacrum across the Atlantic, 'was never a person lost between two cultures, a person seeking a homeland'. Various inhibitions might assail these 'browns'. But these, she concludes, 'were inhibitions neither of identity nor of frustration for lack of an identity'. In the long process of this people's formation, 'the mestiços born of the encounter with white colonists gained a new identity, an original identity'. And with this, if not soon and not easily, they also gained 'a profound national consciousness which was to prove a powerful instrument in seeking independence'.

I believe that Dulce Duarte is in the right about all this, while the outcome of the 1980s has greatly fortified her case. But if so, what was the process of thought and action by which this people could fully realize that it *is* a people – and not a mere fragment of colonial society whose destiny must be European: not a mere assemblage of 'displaced persons' who must look elsewhere, and above all to Europe, for a homeland of their own?

The mental and other obstacles to that realization were many and various and long sustained. Few *dénouements* in the history of anti-colonial change have been as complex or as forceful in their impact. Here in these remote islands the ever destructive power of racism, however glossed and in whatever stubborn assault upon the universality of human nature, was to meet its match. But again: not easily. And not soon.

2 A system of ruin

I

The beliefs and folklore of racism were what was in everybody's head and might be argued against or, with luck, evaded. But the realities of racism were slave labour and then, after the 1850s, dirt-cheap labour for the large majority of people; and these realities could not be argued against, much less evaded. They were realities that penetrated everyone, remained always in command, were dominant and unavoidable. Even the land itself seemed to uphold them: for how except by unremitting toil could these rocks and hillsides be made to yield food?

It may be said that the years between about 1600 and 1900 brought the Cape Verdean character to maturity, and gave it a typical sense and style. If tolerance and laughter have mightily survived, and one finds that they have, underlying attitudes express the proverbial wisdom of a sombre gravity. There is an unsentimental sadness here which the music of the *morna* may best translate and history can help to explain; but the proverbs also have their say. One such familiar proverb, I think from Santiago Island, speaks of the absolute need for unremitting toil. 'Beans don't grow where monkeys are': wherever, that is, upset and confusion reign, the blunt sense being that 'whoever idles, doesn't eat'.

Yet there is more to it, for the proverb carries an underlying edge of anger and defiance. 'Monkeys' in this saying, *Fišon ka ta da na lugar di Sanču*, are represented by Sancho as we would write the name; and in Cape Verdean tradition Sancho the Monkey is the agent of upset and confusion but also, as other sayings confirm, an agent that may promise or threaten a desirable if cataclysmic 'turning of everything upside down'. Sancho is the idle mischief-maker who defeats unremitting toil. But Sancho has also been the embodiment of peasant wrath, 'the spirit of the mountain' and

A remote history of slavery, and a much more recent history of colonial neglect, have victimized a people who, in some compensation, have learned how to rely upon their own resilience and survival. Only now has a prolonged 'system of ruin' begun to give way to self-discovered strategies of transformation and development. (Photo copyright Augusta Conchiglia)

the delirious force of anarchy, the angry symbol of an impossible chance that the world may after all become different from what it is.

Or such was the Sancho of colonial times, but meanwhile there had to be acceptance of the 'system' and its demand for toil. Another two-edged proverb, also from Santiago, has spoken for that. Nicely scathing, it says: *Ta pagado é pa subi coco, dixe é si bu crê*, 'They'll pay you to climb up the coconut palm' (so as to dislodge nuts at its tall summit), 'but getting down again, that's your affair.' The 'system', in other words, would pay you to get the nuts, but not to share in the profit of your labour: the 'system' was built to exploit you, but you would have to accept it. Like most proverbs hallowed by the ironies of time, this one has acquired other meanings. Within the national liberation movement, for example, it tends to be directed against those who think the doing of one's national duty should carry automatic privilege: but no, because *dixe é si bu crê.*

The older meaning had reference to the nature of the 'system'. Until recent times, this was stratified in a few simple grades of power and status. At the apex, traditionally, were the *senhores*, the 'almost whites': the few large landowners, they numbered no more than fifty or so by the twentieth century, apart from numerous dependants. As the progeny of remote and feudal *donatórios*, or claiming to be such, they behaved as 'the lords of creation', owned most of the pockets of irrigated land, and begot quantities of children on their enslaved or supposedly free female workers. So far as legal consorts were concerned, marriage was a matter of money or alliance. Their legally begotten children were sent to school in Portugal, the boys occasionally to university, the girls invariably to convent.

Portuguese administrators could share their social standing, but other Cape Verdeans only by exception. Even so, most administrators were Cape Verdeans. But they stood on a lower rank, together with a host of small landowners whose number, by the fissuring of inheritance, steadily increased. Residing usually in the towns of the archipelago, these small landowners lived from rents paid by peasants in cash or kind; and the rents were set as high as could be squeezed from those who paid them.

As it evolved, the 'system' became one of built-in impoverishment for all concerned, but appeared to have passed beyond reach of any conceivable change. The vast majority laboured for a pittance while a small minority idled in a deepening poverty. Progressively-minded governors from Lisbon were now and then dismayed but always helpless. Governor Lacerda is found complaining in a report of 1898,

> Many owners of vast rural property which could be cultivated on a big scale to provide abundant crops for export are content to let them out in small patches for money-rent or a share in the crop. Such properties are usually let for one year at a time; and the tenants do nothing but sow their land for sufficient to provide themselves with foodstuffs for ordinary use.

For why should they produce more? There was no incentive to provide for much beyond subsistence. On the contrary:

> any tenant who improved his land and embarked on extensive cultivation could be sure, at the end of the year's lease, that the owner would renew the lease only at a higher rent. It would be the owner, in short, who gained from the improvement.

This observation of Lacerda's, comments António Carreira in 1977, 'hardly differs in sense from what could have been written at the outset of the nineteenth century', as indeed much later.

Fixed in its stagnation, the 'system' could move only into deeper misery as cyclical droughts returned and became more frequent. Everything seemed to impose poverty. Tree cover dwindled more rapidly, whether to provide firewood or feed goats, 'and as the trees vanish,' in another report of 1881, 'so do the springs dry up'. Whether or not by scientific logic, this is certainly what happened. Once a land of many trees, the archipelago was now increasingly a desert.

The ending of outright slavery, as in other Portuguese African territories, brought no real change. The 'system' merely adjusted itself to new forms of misery. When a decree of 1858 at last declared that internal slavery should end in 1878, or twenty years later, another decree of 1875 announced that ex-slaves, after 1878, were to labour for two years in continued service of their former owners. But other decrees of 1875 meanwhile saw to it that slave labour should be followed by various forms of servile or 'contracted' labour; and 'these laws', says Carreira, 'put anyone of slave origin, even freedmen, in a legal position which, in practice, deprived them of the benefits implied by the texts: freedmen and slaves both in fact remained slaves.' Has Carreira exaggerated? 'From what I have seen and observed', affirmed Governor José

Ribeiro in 1874, 'truth obliges me to say that the only change seems to be in the name of the thing.'

All this was made explicit in compendious regulations of 1899 which enshrined the victory of the former slave-owners in laws which were to remain essentially unchanged until the 1970s, the years of liberation when, at last, 'Sancho' got seriously to work. Through nearly three-quarters of a century, these and additional labour laws passed in Lisbon for the whole empire provided the legal and customary basis of forced labour although in various forms of verbal camouflage.

Detailed accounts may be found elsewhere, but with one or two differences Cape Verde shared the same fate as the mainland territories. Especially in Mozambique and Angola, peasant labour was 'recruited' by administrative force, or else it was 'supplied' to white settlers and government by subordinate chiefs and headmen. In the latter case the peasants thus 'recruited' were known, without intended irony, as 'roped volunteers': 'those', in Carreira's words, 'whom the chief summarily ordered to be tied up and sent off "on contract" '.

From Cape Verde there were, in the precise sense, few 'roped volunteers'. But drought and famine displaced the mainland rope, while for this doubtful gain there was a painful additional loss. Forced labour meant forced emigration, usually to the distant cocoa islands of São Tomé and Principe, and often for long periods. São Tomé, above all, became the *via crucis* of the archipelago's experience.

There had always been severe droughts, and therefore famines. They grew worse. That of 1864 was reported to have carried off some 30,000 Cape Verdeans by hunger or disease induced by hunger. A fairly typical governor's report of 1890 sent back a picture of 'an exhausted people who have thrown themselves on the last unripe crops'; and what the people failed to eat was devoured by locusts blown from the mainland. A three-year drought beginning in 1900 seems to have killed some 16,000 people or about 17 per cent of the population. Drought came again in 1911, and again in 1916, and again in 1921, killing in the last case another 17,000 people. Were these numbers small when compared with the victims of Ethiopian and other drought during the 1970s–80s? But 17 per cent of the Ethiopian population of 1982 would be five million people; and 17 per cent was the proportion who died in those Cape Verdean famines, not once but time and again.

By this time there was some local journalism to tell the tale and enough freedom, with the relative liberalism of the parliamentary regime in Portugal, to be able to tell it straight. 'The farming crisis continues', reported the Santiago journal *A Verdade* in an issue of early 1922.

> That of 1921 was horrific . . . yet now follows this of 1922, equally horrific but with the addition that people have spent all they possess, whether in clothes or land, livestock or trinkets, and today are in the last stage of poverty, while emigration is carrying away all whom the steamers can embark.

More than 5000 had departed for the south, *A Verdade* reported: for São Tomé and Angola, 'and still more are waiting to embark'.

II

Could nothing be done? Nothing was done. In Portugal, even during its parliamentary Republic which limped along until 1926, they were thinking of other things or else, as other Europeans tended to conclude from Portuguese official behaviour, the people who ruled Portugal were lost in dreams of 'the dear delightful Middle Ages', to borrow from the late Bishop Stubbs, and cared everything for honour but nothing for the cash.

Emotive reasons came in to support this mythology of Portugal's 'uneconomic imperialism'. There were fears of being relegated to servant status, in Africa, by the expanding mastery of stronger powers. There was the military careerism which all the empire-building countries shared. Junior officers led off expeditions into the far interior of Angola or Mozambique; and those who managed to avoid a bloody nose came back to fame. Senior officers saw to it that 'territorial gains' in unknown backlands should feed their credit. Portugal might have lost Brazil in 1822: but now, a century later, she should have her compensation in other plains and forests. And all this, certainly, was buoyed by the memory of Portugal's medieval primacy in these latitudes, rather as though the Portugal of today could best be a repeat of the Portugal of yesterday. When I first went to 'Portuguese Africa', as late as 1954, the postage stamps were still celebrating the voyage of Vasco da Gama some 470 years earlier.

Yet none of that was decisive in the imperial effort of the late nineteenth and early twentieth centuries, the period of colonial 'partition' of Africa and of 'proving effective occupation'. What was decisive was commercial gain. The relatively liberal period of the Bragança monarchy after the 1880s, and the period of the parliamentary Republic of 1910–26, saw the emergence of a middle class of entrepreneurial and financial enterprise whose leaders, along with a crush of military hangers-on and other hopeful sharers in the profit, flung themselves into colonial adventure.

No doubt this empire-building was vastly 'uneconomic' for the majority of Portuguese; and it may be easily agreed that Portugal would have fared far better if its rulers had used their resources to build a new and non-colonial economy, rather than embarking on extensions of the old. Yet any quantity of statistics can demonstrate that colonial expansion proved highly 'economic' for those groups in Portugal who were able to take the profit. For the most part this profit derived from the produce of black labour: of 'contract labour', after 1899, paid at very cheap rates or scarcely paid at all.

The 'system' in Cape Verde might be 'uneconomic' to the point of ruin for most Cape Verdeans; but it could still produce large numbers of Cape Verdean men and women to labour on plantations, whether in São Tomé and Principe or on the mainland of Angola, at dirt-cheap rates of pay. Though not 'roped volunteers' in the Angolan sense of the term, they were forced workers in all but name, driven by famine and despair as well as by administrative pressure. And they were many. In the years 1902–22, reliable but incomplete statistics show that more than 24,000 Cape Verdeans laboured on the São Tomé and Principe plantations; another 20,000 in the years 1941–9; another 34,000 in the years 1950–70.

Long-term or permanent emigration kept the 'system' otherwise afloat, and from early times. Solid communities of Cape Verdean origin were to take shape in Portugal, Senegal, and Holland. But the preferred destination, as long as that was possible, was the United States of America, and, particularly, the States of New England. Emigration there had begun in a small way by Cape Verdean crewmen on the American whaling boats, around 1800, and continued to grow in size. In the years 1902–22, for example, 18,620 Cape Verdeans are listed as having found a new home in the USA, but only 1968 in Brazil and smaller numbers elsewhere. Those who were lighter in colour, notably from the island of Brava, could try to pass as Portuguese in the USA and thus escape the sterner responses of racism. But the majority of Cape Verdeans could not do this. No doubt the social rejection they encountered may help to explain their stubborn loyalty to the land of their origins.

To families who remained in the islands these emigrants formed the habit of sending back aid in money. The Portuguese imperial economy gained from these emigrants' remittances; and by the second half of the twentieth century the size of the New England community of Cape Verdean origin had probably passed the 300,000 mark. But the 'system' had another Cape Verdean value for imperial Portugal. It produced useful intermediaries between the Portuguese colonial rulers and their black masses.

Accepted as being somehow more than 'savage Africans' though less than proper Portuguese, literate Cape Verdeans were employed in junior and sometimes even in senior administrative grades in every part of the empire as far as Timor and Macau. Regarded as Portuguese citizens although of low degree, a small but important segment of more or less urbanized Cape Verdeans could have access to primary education, and, after the First World War, even to secondary education in the archipelago's single lycée at Mindelo on São Vicente island. These and a few others, educated in Portugal, were to provide a catalytic element in crystallizing an immanent sense of Cape Verdean nationalism, and to lead, however indirectly, to the slow building of anti-colonial revolution.

III

A Sunday morning at Vila Nova Sintra, the capital town of the island of Brava, first unveiled for me an outline of this 'catalytic element' eventually decisive in modern Cape Verdean history.

The sun, as almost always in this blessed climate, is shining pleasantly, but nothing much is happening at 9 o'clock although people will soon be passing on their way to church. Up there on brown hillsides above the town the little houses stand in painted peace, while here on the *praça*, on Vila Nova's central and ceremonial 'square' in gardens lit by luminescent blue plumbago and purple bougainvillea, a gardener is sweeping leaves and rubbish cast away by dancers a few hours before.

The gardener pauses to give greetings because, Brava-like, he is moved by the *morabeza*, the comfort of hospitable welcome, which acts as counterpoint to this people's characteristic scorn of sloppy sentiment. Later there will be a fearful eruption of Protestant religion from the loudspeaker of the *praça*'s Church of the Nazarene Community, the Igreja do Nazereno, and this will continue for a long time, bawling down all civilized talk. 'It's an aggression,' says Carlos, but with forebearance. The administration has permitted this onslaught because banning it would be a discrimination against the Protestant minority. In their own time, the hugely bigger Catholic majority will think of its reply. Patience.

Otherwise all is peace, and for a while it seems we are a long way back in time, and bayed in a pleasant provincialism which makes an observer, or anyway this observer, think of the Provence of France some fifty years ago. One may object that provincialism is all very well so long as you do not have to live in it. But the effect here on Sunday morning is agreeably seductive. Besides, there are eloquent indications of local fame.

Here on the middle point of the *praça*, around where dancers jived last night, there is a neat small kiosk for a bandstand, octagonal and roofed for brass and bugles and the snore of trumpets and trombones, just as in any proper *praça* of the past, with two lean Brava hounds lifting proprietorial legs. And on this kiosk, when closely approached, a small rectangle of painted tiles is seen.

The tiles compose a memorial plaque depicting azure winds and ships with sails, an affair both exquisitely Portuguese and insistently Cape Verdean. It celebrates a Brava lion of the Press, a Cape Verdean journalist of the period of parliamentary liberalism before 1926 and the onset of generals and dictators. Before those sorrows came to pass, this writer flourished.

The visitor reads the message on the plaque:

> Lá nos confins siderais
> Brilham astros singulares
> Mas na Terra, UM brilhou
> P'ra sempre: EUGENIO TAVARES!

And translates freely for himself:

There above in planetary spheres
Shine brilliant and amazing stars:
But here on earth, ONE shines
For ever: EUGENIO TAVARES!

And turns to chat with the gardener, an ancient person of diverse memories.

With Eugenio Tavares and others such as he, one is into provincialism of a high order, into a zone where deference for Portugal with its mission to civilize the savages has mingled with a powerful local pride. But one is also into something more than this. From Tavares and company in the years after about 1910 there came a vision of the future, neither clear nor firm but all the same a vision of a world that somehow might be different, and being different, must be better. There came a thought, however hesitant and sometimes contradictory, that Cape Verde could have its own claim to civilize itself. A modern literary judgement makes the point from another angle. 'Tavares?' comments Dr Balthazar Lopes da Silva, one of Cape Verde's eminent men of letters, when I ask him for a view. 'Tavares was a very mediocre poet in Portuguese, but a very good poet in Crioulo.' In Eugenio Tavares one may surely see the faint fore-glimmerings of a national quest.

The scope for such men would arise from peculiarities of the Portuguese imperial system. The right to Portuguese citizenship had been granted to Cape Verdeans in 1914, and was afterwards maintained, so that, as we have seen, a policy of 'assimilation' gave educated Cape Verdeans a chance to make modest colonial careers. In this way a small but significant number of Cape Verdeans became – the words are those of Abilio Duarte, one of the leaders of the liberation struggle after 1956 – 'useful instruments for employment in other colonies'. Duarte continues,

In this you see the central contradiction in Portuguese policy here. On one hand they wanted to make Cape Verde into a master-product of their policy of assimilation: on the other, they abandoned this country to its poverty and despair. And this was an abandonment so profound that in 1975, when we took over, we had only two alternatives. We could accept catastrophe, or we could somehow manage to survive.

That is running ahead. What one should note is that here, as in many mainland colonies whether British or French or Portuguese, community resurgence derived in no small part from the response of persons like Tavares. An ambiguous response, as Abilio Duarte insists. For the 'elite', to use a mainland label, accepted in Cape Verde the advantages of assimilation to Portuguese culture and loyalty, 'and yet they did this in a style such as the Portuguese neither wished nor intended. They remained Cape Verdeans, so that even this literate petty-bourgeoisie played some part in the process making for national liberation'.

Another writer of the Tavares 'group' was José Lopes. Summarizing 'Journalism in Cape Verde' in an article of 1922, he defined the issue in words worth recalling. 'In our much loved but little fortunate Cape Verdean fatherland', he wrote in a local journal, *O Manduco* of Fogo, 'there have always appeared, since a certain epoch, a line of energetic champions, its sons and our brothers, to fight for the progress of our country, each according to his convictions, possibilities and ideas.'

The ideas were necessarily confused, reflecting as they did the ambiguities of assimilation. In 1912, two years after the parliamentary Republic had been installed in Lisbon with fanfares of democratic eloquence, Tavares had convoked his readers in *A Voz de Cabo Verde* to defence of this Republic of Portugal, 'which gives, to all, the rights and duties of a Portuguese citizen'; and he appeals to the Republic 'to pull the Negro race from its hateful condition of servitude' and thereby 'make a Portuguese citizen of every native'.

And the pulling, if need was, should be by any force required. One year later *A Voz de Cabo Verde*, owned by a merchant of Praia called Monteiro de Macedo, had been loud in its praise of a Portuguese conqueror of the nearby mainland of Guiné, Teixeiro Pinto, 'who has so brilliantly raised the prestige of Portuguese arms against a warlike tribe of poor and squalid character, such as that of the Guinean savage'. And in 1915 another of the same Cape Verdean group, the Juvenal Cabral who nine years later, in the mainland colony of Guiné, was to father the eventual liberator both of Guiné and Cape Verde, had again praised this same Teixeiro Pinto as 'the stern pacifier of barbarous and rebellious peoples'.

In their warm approval of the colonial mission, these 'elites' were no different from comparable groups in British and French West Africa, or indeed elsewhere in the colonial continent. At this early stage of the nation-making process they looked to an 'enlightened colonialism' as the only possible means of advance. Some of them, despairing of Portugal, hoped for salvation from elsewhere. Their most excoriating pen, as it happened, was wielded by the Angolan *assimilado*, José Fontes de Pereira (1823–90), who flayed the Portuguese in his Luanda journal, *O Arauto Africano* (*The African Herald*), for having utterly failed to civilize the 'brutish black', the *preto boçal*, or to employ men of talent such as himself as they ought to be employed. He recommended that another civilizing power be found. He proposed that Angola be handed to Britain. For 'we declare that we trust neither in the good faith nor in the sincerity of the Portuguese Colonial Party, whose members are only crocodiles crying out to lure their victims. We know them all too well. Out with them!' The advice was poorly received, and the usual mob of Portuguese settlers in Luanda marched with violent purpose on Fontes's newspaper office. But others followed where Fontes had led, and dared to write much the same thing.

Tavares and his friends never went as far as that. They were prudent reformers. Later nationalists have even tended to see all these worthy figures of the early colonial period – whether in Nigeria, the Gold Coast, Sierra Leone, The Gambia, as well as in some of the French and Portuguese territories – as feeble 'collaborators' and futile agents of Europeanization. And it is true that colonial power almost invariably jeered at them or merely ignored them as 'useless visionaries and detestable clerks', to recall the jibe of an Angolan governor-general of 1885. Of their contemporaries then and later in British West Africa, the Gambian historian Ayodele Langley has remarked that they were 'essentially co-operationists with exceedingly limited political objectives . . . Their politics was essentially the politics of survival and the politics of the *status quo*.'

It remains that these men spoke and wrote for a colonialism that should be enlightened and beneficent; and if their purpose was unreal, given that colonialism could be neither for the vast majority of Africans, these 'morning stars' of a much later nationalism were none the less respected and even loved by many for whom they wrote and spoke.

One can see why. Consider only another article in *A Voz de Cabo Verde*, this time of 1913, which quotes from a radical Portuguese governor who held the job briefly after the monarchy's fall in 1910. This governor was writing of that Cape Verdean variant of provincialism which came to be known, in those years, as *nativismo*, meaning in some sense a defence of the Cape Verdean native. '*Nativismo*', says this governor to the warm approval of *A Voz*, 'is a love of country, a love of freedom, a longing for truth and justice, a desire for moral emancipation and for a higher civilization, a hatred of racist prejudice and of oppression and extortion . . .' No wonder those who wrote for *nativismo* were admired.

As for independence, in so far as anyone wrote or spoke or even thought of that, the notion seemed absurd. 'For Cape Verde?' exclaimed Tavares in *A Voz*: 'For these poor and abandoned rocks thrown up in the sea – independence? What sense is there in that? God have pity on thoughtless men!'

What could be real and desirable – *A Voz* in 1917 – was 'a true autonomy which makes us not dependencies, but willing and valiant associates of the Metropole'. All the same, as Tavares's comment evidently indicates, there were already some for whom independence need not be a mirage.

Notable among these last was a journalist of Fogo, Pedro Cardoso, the possessor of a formidably agile and inventive talent. He called his journal *O Manduco, The Cudgel*; and his favourite signature was 'Afro', in itself a statement which questioned the culture of assimilation to European loyalties and values. The implications of 'Afro', writing around the years of the First World War, were what the nationalists of the 1950s and 1960s would affirm: that Cape Verde must look to Africa for its liberation and companionship, and not to Europe. Cardoso, in short, was a cultural nationalist in times before any such phenomenon was recognized. 'Cardoso was the first', comments *Mestre* Balthazar in 1986, 'who really tried to study Crioulo, a philologue who failed for lack of education, which was not his fault, but very courageous.'

In Cardoso's journalism one may further hear the lapping of new currents of thought from Lisbon. Among these were the ideas of the Pan-Africanist movement born at the outset of our century, and of which Lisbon saw the final sessions of its fourth congress of 1923, and heard its call for black resurgence. Other currents came on political tides set moving by Marx and his followers. Even three years before the Russian Revolution we have a poem of Cardoso's, in *A Voz de Cabo Verde*, entitled *Unido, Avante!*, 'United, Forward!' which is dedicated to 'the workers of Mindelo'. In this surprising poem Marx is mentioned as *o Mestre venerando* (venerated Master), and the poem concludes with a call to let loose 'the cry of Revolt!'

But Sancho's time, apart from peasant uproars and obscure upheavals, was still far ahead. With continued years of parliamentary liberalism there might conceivably have come a contemporary move along the road to liberation through nationalism. But soon enough, in 1926, the bars came down across that road, and the bolts were shot.

3 'But a day will come . . .'?

I

'Portuguese!' declared General Gomes da Costa, 'The nation wants a national military government, a strong government with a mission to save the Fatherland.' So said the *pronunciamento* of 28 May 1926 by which the generals overthrew the parliamentary Republic of Portugal. Nobody had consulted 'the Nation', perhaps needless to say; but the soldiers emptied the building of parliament three days later and locked the doors.

The loss was variously felt, though not severely for several years. The parliamentary Republic had been the playground and product of a largely rhetorical liberalism, and had fruitlessly run through forty-five successive governments in sixteen years. Although initially welcomed by Cape Verde's 'restless intellectuals', as the writer José Julio Gonçalves called them in a retrospective press review of 1965, the Republic's aim 'to build a modern people' was quickly seen to lie beyond its reach. Barely three years after its inception in 1910, 'there was the consciousness that freedom was not going to come to the natives of the colonies'. *A Voz de Cabo Verde* duly registered the disappointment. 'Mother!' rang its plaintive appeal, 'Send us your light! We too are sons!' But the light that came was dim, and after 1926 was snuffed out altogether.

If the parliamentary Republic had proved somewhat comic, what came after was in no way funny. Forty-eight years of stiff dictatorship followed the *pronunciamento* of 1926, but in four more or less distinct phases of authoritarian evolution. The American historian of Portugal, Douglas Wheeler, has identified the first three of these phases as 'the regime of the Young Lieutenants (1926–8); as the rise of Salazar and of civilian authoritarianism (1928–30); and as the birth of the Estado Novo, (1930–3)'. After that, this New State under António de Oliveira Salazar

Built beside a splendid sheltered harbour on the largely desert island of São Vicente, the city of Mindelo long ago became a port of call on the mid-Atlantic sea routes. Countless ships came to rely upon its safe anchorage and its bunkers of Welsh and English coal; and nowadays it remains well-known to long-haul yachtsmen and single-handed venturers. After independence in 1975 the new republic built the handsome corniche road shown here. (Photo copyright Cape Verde Photos)

(1889–1970) proceeded without delay by means of 'censorship, police terror, and more subtle devices', in Wheeler's measured words, to build 'an unprecedented centralised power'. But it was never able, being fettered within its paternalism, to resolve any of Portugal's gravest problems.

As in Mussolini's Italy, an admired model until Hitler displayed a 'stronger' one, political uproar largely ceased. As in Italy and Germany, this was to be the peace of exile or the grave for those who disagreed. 'Thousands were arrested,' in Wheeler's summation of what the generals did to Portugal, 'many were deported to the Atlantic islands or to Africa, many more chose voluntary exile.' An as yet uncounted total died in jails, whether from torture or other miseries. In the colonies, however, the generals attempted little more than to continue the policies of the parliamentary Republic. The latter had secured the colonial frontiers by negotiation with rival European powers, and had begun to prove 'effective colonial occupation'. It remained for the dictatorship to consolidate this proof and then, in the 1930s, install civilian administrations, further stiffen the laws of subjection, and organize a more penetrating exploitation.

In Cape Verde the silence deepened. A few small journals struggled on for a while, but *A Voz* had died in 1919 and others found the censorship too much for them. The Pan-African trend of thought among blacks then in Lisbon, spoken for by *O Negro* and *A Voz de Africa* during the last years of the parliamentary Republic and to which Cape Verdean writers also contributed, was faintly revived in 1930 by *Mocidade Africana* (*African Youth*), again with some Cape Verdean participation. This last included the now muted voice of Eugenio Tavares and a new name, that of Balthazar Lopes da Silva, who soon made his mark. But *Mocidade Africana* folded in November 1932, and publications of the dictatorship alone remained.

Little in any case could be written. With its underlying 'pro-Africa' note, *nativismo* was now subversive. There could be careful talk of 'regionalism', of the notion that Cape Verde should be recognized as having a regional character and culture within the Portuguese realm; but what this might really mean was never clear. In March 1933 Balthazar Lopes was writing in the first issue of a semi-official journal called *Notícias de Cabo Verde* that Cape Verdeans must become 'intransigently regionalist, and then we shall be intelligently Portuguese'; and one could interpret this as one wished.

A more effective quest for distinctive identity came with *Claridade*, a newly launched periodical with four issues between 1936 and 1941, and another six after the end of the Second World War. 'With *Claridade*', the Cape Verdean historian Carlos Lopes Pereira was going to recall in 1985, 'Cape Verdean writers turned to the problems of their own country, of their own people.' Nowadays the Claridosos, as they came to be known after the title of their journal, tend to be seen as having made a bid for the declaration of a Cape Verdean literary independence. But the reservation has to be added, I think, that they did so within the limits of a vision of Cape Verde still seen as an extension of Europe, for the Claridosos appear to have believed in no kind of 'African alternative' to the paternity of Portugal.

Perhaps they can be called 'proto-nationalist'? Literate and therefore privileged, they well saw how things stood. They resented the increasingly oppressive racism of the dictatorship which hit them too. They wished for liberalizing change. Yet most of them were very far from the 'Afro', Pedro Cardoso, who had dedicated his poem of 1913 'to the workers of Mindelo' and made his bow to the 'venerated Marx'. Any thought of anti-colonial revolution filled them with a gentlemanly horror, and would continue so to fill them until that revolution arrived and took them, much to their surprise, quite gently by the hand.

What the masses of the rural or semi-urban majority meanwhile thought about the blessings of Portuguese civilization failed to reach print or even public speech. Yet a few indications of another kind were heard to erupt. There were 'incidents' and 'troubles', some of these recalling the countless slave revolts of earlier days. One such was the 'revolution' led by 'Captain' Ambrósio in the harbour-town of Mindelo on São Vicente Island during 1934, when a carpenter urged hungry crowds to an assault on food stores in the Customs House. That locally memorable outbreak dramatized a deepening hopelessness. For at least two years before, as documents in the Mindelo municipal archives show with detail, the local business community had appealed to the Governor to find some means of relieving unemployment, and hence hunger, much worsened by a shrunken shipping use of Mindelo's great harbour during the slump of those years. Other archives suggest that this Governor, if vainly, had in fact tried to interest Lisbon in this crisis of an extreme poverty. Thus we find the British Embassy in Lisbon informing the Foreign Office in London, during July 1933, of a speech by the Cape Verdean Governor, Captain Amadeu Figueiredo, in which he complains of the neglect from which the islands suffer. The speech is worth recalling if only because it again portrays the depths of miserly indifference to which the Salazarist regime was willing to sink in the treatment even of its 'favoured' colony of Cape Verde.

The Governor is reported as saying in his speech,

> One of the most important sources of revenue for the Colony, was the transit tax on the telegrams of the [oceanic] submarine cables [linked *via* the archipelago]. Cape Verde had at first been credited with 50 per cent of this taxation in 1917–18 and was granted 75 per cent in 1929–30; since then large sums had been paid to the mother-country at times when the inhabitants of the islands were dying of hunger.

And the Governor concludes that it is high time that Cape Verde should retain 100 per cent of this cable revenue. But Lisbon remains deaf to his appeal. And the 'revolution' of Nhô Ambrósio the carpenter of Mindelo is among the consequences.

Folk memories of Ambrósio have remained vivid in São Vicente; and unthinkable years later the theatrical committee of the local Youth Organization was able to translate these memories into a street play. Their preparatory text of 1979 tells the tale.

> And so at last there came a day, the 4th of June, when crowds came into the streets under a black banner, the banner of hunger, led by Ambrósio, shouting Poverty! Hunger! . . . And they decided to start a revolt that very day if the Government in Praia should give them no good response.

A meeting with the local authorities at the Chamber of Commerce was at once demanded and agreed, and the local administrator was induced to send a telegram to Praia, the capital. Two hours passed, and the waiting crowd lost patience.

> Then their leader, Nhô Ambrósio, gave them his directive: 'People of São Vicente, [the original here is in Crioulo] did you eat today?' 'No,' they all shouted back. 'And we are hungry!' Could they find work? met the same response. At which Ambrósio raised high the black banner and shouted to them: 'We'll find food with our own hands. The big folks sit there with full bellies. We'll invade the Customs House, and there we'll find the food we need . . .'

The Customs House was looted of 'sugar, maize, beans, flour, potatoes, bananas'. The memorialist at this point was twelve at the time, 'and I can remember all that exactly, and everyone took what they could, and I got some chocolates and sugar'. Meanwhile a platoon of infantry was arriving at the double from the Fortim d'El Rei – the same little hilltop fortress where resistance militants would be imprisoned thirty years later – and the leaders of the 'revolution' were in due course deported to Angola on sentences of forced labour. 'And some of them came back years later but others, to our sorrow, died there.'

Yet none of these memories, or the folklore they have nourished, is perhaps as instructive on what the mass of people thought about Portuguese civilization as a popular song from a Santiago festival, a *batuque* of Santa Caterina, which *Claridade* dared to print in 1948, fourteen years after this 'revolution' of Ambrósio. If it passed the censorship, this was no doubt because *Claridade* printed it in Crioulo without translation. For here, if ever, was Sancho in person:

> Branco ta mora na sobrado
> Mulato ta mora na loja
> Nego ta mora na funco
> Sanču ta mora na rotcha . . .

Or somewhat freely, and from first to last:

> White lives in big house
> Mulato lives in shop
> Black lives in hut
> Sancho lives in mountain:
>
> But a day will come
> When Sancho turn all upside down:
> Horribly grimacing
> Tail curled up
> Sancho drag black from hut
> Black drag mulato from shop
> Mulato drag white from big house
> White run to mountain and there he fall.

How old was this? And what happy malice went with its singing? The answer can only be that the peasants of Santa Caterina, where the mountains of inland Santiago look down from lofty heights which sheltered the slaves of long ago, the slaves who were the peasants' forebears, somehow retained their own vision of the future.

A real despair had long accompanied that vision. 'Poverty spreads throughout the island [of Santiago] from a complete failure of the rains,' notes the *Boletim Oficial* in 1926, 'while the arrival of locusts has spread disaster.' A year later the same official source reports of the islands of Sant'Antão and São Nicolau that 'the food situation grows steadily worse'. Continuing through the 1930s, the prevailing mood was of *nhanhida*, which is Cape Verdean for despair. Exile continued. Tight US immigration controls after the First World War reduced the flow to New England, so that only 870 Cape Verdeans, according to the statistics, reached the USA in the years 1930–40 when, with the Second World War, transatlantic emigration altogether ceased for the duration. But the flow of hunger-forced workers to 'the South' countinued as before. If its scale was somewhat smaller now, its pain was no less:

> Four o'clock in the dawning
> São Vicente folk are there
> To cry their sorrow
> For sons who are sent away
> To São Tomé . . .

And then, as though the gods had forgotten pity, came the crushing drought of 1941–2. By common consent of all the sources, this killed at least 20,000 people by hunger or disease from hunger. Another, incredibly still more severe, returned in 1946–7, killing perhaps 30,000 people. In 1940 the decennial census had shown a population of 181,286, and with the birth-rate continuing very high. Yet in 1950 the census returns gave no more than 147,096 persons. 'Our cemetery at Orgãos', a peasant of Santa Cruz told me in 1986, 'had no more space for the dead, and people were buried in mass graves outside.' Many of his age recall the same grim memory.

Who else heard anything of all this? What the Portuguese governors told their masters in Lisbon remains almost completely lost in closed archives. But others on the scene now began to break the silence.

II

Hush Most Secret, the British Admiralty in London was informed by wireless message from its commander-in-chief, South Atlantic, in the U-Boat haunted year of 1942: 'Report I received of state of things in Cape Verde where there is little doubt the bulk of the population are on point of starvation.' C-in-C South Atlantic suggested that food relief should be sent. Pro-British sentiment in the archipelago could be valuable, especially if the U-Boats secured a base there.

As it was, though very secretly, the British had already made preparations to invade and seize possession of the islands. With the German victories in France during mid-1940 it was expected in London that Hitler would persuade his friend Franco in Spain to enter the war against Britain. If so, the British base at Gibraltar would almost certainly be lost. What alternative could then be found? The British Cabinet papers show that a plan was made, as early as July 1940, to use the Royal Marine brigades in an operation, code-named Accordion, to seize the Azores, and in a simultaneous operation, Sackbut, to take the Cape Verdes. For 'if Spain enters the war against us,' the British ambassador in Washington was instructed by the Foreign Office in October 1940, 'Gibraltar would probably become unusable and we should need another base in the North Atlantic.'

Seizure of the (Spanish) Canary Islands might not be practicable, the ambassador was further informed, but it would be essential for Britain to deny the Azores and Cape Verdes to the enemy. The Foreign Office continued,

> In the latter islands, we should also secure a position for ourselves. It is therefore proposed, should Spain enter the war against us, to seize and hold the Cape Verdes and the Azores as soon as possible, irrespective of the attitude of the Portuguese. The necessary forces have been assembled.

In July 1940, however, this 'Atlantic Islands Project' was conceived as a rather distant one, for an order of 24 July told the 1st and 2nd Marine Brigades' commands – the 'necessary forces' in question – to prepare to 'move overseas to a tropical climate' on or after 23 May 1941. Yet it is clear that the plan to take the islands, whether as a pre-emptive strike against a possible German plan to do the same thing, or simply as a useful action irrespective of whatever might happen in Spain, stayed very much in Churchill's mind. On 1 December, 1940, we find him telling the Chiefs of Staff in London that the necessary forces should be ready to embark at once – at 48 hours' notice after 3 or 4 December –

upon Brisk (formerly Accordion) against the Azores and upon Shrapnel (formerly Sackbut) against the Cape Verdes.

Neither operation followed, and Spanish intentions remained ambiguous. Meanwhile further Nazi German aggressions appeared certain, and the Atlantic islands might well be involved. By March 1941 Churchill reached the view that Brisk, against the Azores, should go ahead. 'I am coming to the conclusion,' he minuted to the Foreign Office on 22 March 1941, 'that this Operation must now be carried out.' He did not believe that 'the German decision to overrun the Iberian Peninsula and to occupy Spain or Portugal, or both, will be dependent upon our doing Brisk. They know what they are going to do already.'

A lively fear that the Germans might do their own Brisk against the Azores and Cape Verdes is also evident from telegrams exchanged between Churchill and the US President Franklin D. Roosevelt. Thus on 1 May we find Roosevelt explaining to Churchill, among other things, that the USA could not co-operate with Britain in preventing Germany from seizing the Azores and Cape Verde Islands. In fact none of these operations was attempted, and one is left to speculate on the interesting prospect that might have opened if British or American forces, or both, had indeed occupied these islands.

Food must surely have been sent at once. For the condition of the Cape Verdes was already tragic. So much is starkly plain from British intelligence reports of that time. These reports derived partly from concern with the U-Boat peril. This continued to increase: a rendezvous of three U-Boats 'in the Cape Verde islands' was revealed, for example, by decrypts of September 1941 of the German Admiralty's U-Boat cypher. But interest in the Cape Verdes, as in the Azores, derived as well from the continued possibility of seizing them in the British interest. And these reports had for some time spoken of famine in the Cape Verdes.

On 1 March 1941 the Director of Naval Intelligence in a general overview had told the Admiralty in London that 'by early December [1940] the situation existing in the islands had reached, to say the least, a precarious position. The people of the Northern group' – the windward islands including São Vicente with its great harbour at Mindelo – 'were approaching the starvation line as a result of drought, falling off of the coal trade, and the outcome of the Governor's policies involving price fixing', policies which had 'resulted in a deadlock causing a stoppage in the imports of the essential rice and maize on which the population exists'.

Confidential advice likewise reached London throughout the war from the British consul at Mindelo, Captain J. L. Sands. On 3 December 1941, nine months after DNI's sombre warning, Sands reports that 'the outlook for the majority of the inhabitants of these Islands for the coming year is one of extreme gravity . . . a large number are emaciated, worn out and have lost both heart and hope'. Meanwhile the Portuguese authorities in Cape Verde 'are very reticent regarding information about famine, and have checked as far as possible all references to this subject being sent outside the Islands.' He thought,

> It was evident that the Government do not wish for any outside assistance. An offer from the Caboverdeans in the United States has been turned down, and in replying to the offer a letter was written by the Administration in which it was stated that the situation had been greatly exaggerated and that no assistance was required.

Consul Sands knew otherwise. Such was the famine that 'the starving seem to accept the situation with an oriental fatalism. They do not press their claims to live, they scarcely beg, may ask you for alms once or twice, and then simply stare at you as if resigned to what is to happen.' Two months later, on 31 January 1942, he informs London that his vice-consul at Praia, on Santiago Island, has just reported more than 100 deaths a day from hunger and fever, with much worse conditions on Brava, Maio, São Nicolau and Fogo than the previous year; and in those islands 'many are reported to be dying daily of hunger'. The folk memories of all this have not lied.

If famine induced despair, other visitors at this time had different lessons to impart. The Portuguese began to garrison the islands for the first time in some strength. Exactly why they did this may be explained in the Portuguese national archives which, however, I have not found accessible. Had Lisbon got wind of British plans to seize the islands? Or of German plans to do the same? However this may have been, Salazar began sending troops. Once again in default of Portuguese archives, one turns to the conscientious Captain Sands in São Vicente. On 26 April 1941 he is reporting that Lisbon had decided to garrison the archipelago. On 30 April he notes the arrival of a first detachment of 1000 men, and 2000 more on 9 September. Two thousand of these go into garrison on São Vicente, another 1000 on the 'airport island' of Sal, and 200 on Santiago. Arrivals continue, and by November Sands estimates the total of Portuguese troops in the Cape Verdes at about 5000, half of whom are on São Vicente. By six months later, on 9 May 1942, he says that the total has risen to 6150 men with an expectation of more to come.

Sands advised London that about 10 per cent of Portuguese officers were pro-Nazi but, he thought, only one or two per cent of the other ranks, while the latter were far from happy with their lot. His report of 9 May 1942 says that there was no serious training of troops 'who don't expect to have to fight', and much friction between other ranks and officers because the latter fed well but the former got 'very poor food'. A month later, on 30 June, he informs the Foreign Office of 'troops rioting in city Sunday', meaning the port-city of Mindelo on São Vicente.

Commenced football match large number of noisy soldiers stoned referee whom officers tried to protect, accidentally officers stoned. Armed detachments called out, all soldiers in town and outposts recalled and curfew imposed at 6.30 p.m. Cause of outbreak stated to be bad food and poor feeding arrangements.

But there was more to it. The biographer of Amílcar Cabral and veteran Angolan nationalist Mario de Andrade recalls that 'this physical presence of colonial troops' was a cause of sharpened Portuguese racism: of 'violent clashes with the population and demonstrations of contempt for island society'; and Consul Sands duly bears him out. Five months after the fracas at the football match, on 25 November 1942, Sands cables that 'the atmosphere between the Portuguese troops and the Cape Verdeans is still very unfriendly, and, since the rioting, no further attempt has been made to arrange any form of sport in which both the troops and the local natives take part'.

Andrade comments that this acute racism of the early 1940s offered a constant provocation 'to people's sense of their dignity and value', while renewing old aspirations of separatist regionalism; and this indeed was a widely felt reaction throughout colonial Africa, whether in Portuguese territories or not. The war, in short, brought in Cape Verde as elsewhere a spur to the emergent nationalism of those years.

It also fathered fresh demands that something be done to alleviate the misery of the islands. In a prophetic document recovered by Andrade and dated December 1940, we find an appeal to the Governor and a list of proposals necessary to 'the economic stability of the colony'. These asked for water conservation, intensive planting of trees, reforms of land tenure and taxation, and the immediate funding of agrarian credit. Their author was the schoolmaster and man of letters Juvenal Cabral. He was ignored. Yet all these proposals of 1940 were to be put into effect thirty-five years later. And the courage and intelligence required to put them into effect were embodied in the man who made it possible more than any other: not Juvenal Cabral, but Juvenal's son Amílcar.

Though Juvenal could scarcely have foreseen it, an entirely new chapter was about to open.

Part Three

Against the Odds

No borda d'čker e kta spantod čuk:
Pluck out evil at its roots

Local advice

We for our part are sure that
the destruction of Portuguese
colonialism is what will destroy
Portuguese fascism

Amílcar Cabral in 1961,
thirteen years before the prophecy
was made true

4 Beginnings

I

When peace came to the world in 1945 this people had stumbled from an appalling drought and famine in 1941–2 but was about to suffer a still worse famine in 1947–8. Afterwards, these two grim periods of mass hunger were found, by prudent estimate, to have killed some 45,000 Cape Verdeans. Little news of those hecatombs of Cape Verdean dead reached the outside world; and the outside world, in any case, had its own wounds to nurse. Even now it may be difficult to believe the size of the catastrophe; but Carreira's carefully assembled data leave no room for doubt: 'and if they are deficient, this will be by under-estimate,' he writes, 'but not by the reverse'.

Emigration from the islands now offered the only reliable hope of survival. And as Western Europe and North America once more, if cautiously, opened their gates to the poor and starving there began periods of 'great exodus', as memories have called it, and thousands left for Europe and America every year. Those were willing emigrants who volunteered to go, but for many others the gates were too narrow. For them the only recourse was the hunger-induced but most unwilling trail to the cocoa islands of the south and to Angola. Carreira's overall figures show that some 120,000 forced workers, as he reasonably calls them, went from Cape Verde 'to the South' in the years 1940 to 1973. There thus set in the pattern of despair which, by the year of independence in 1975, was to induce a disbelief in Cape Verde's ever being able to provide a decent life for its inhabitants.

The colonial power, for its part, resolutely turned its back on that despair. Even the *Boletim Oficial* of Cape Verde in the famine years – now available for consultation in the new national archives of Praia – has nothing but vague and occasional references to the crisis of famine which had struck the islands and to the

Like other African lands, Cape Verde is a country of the young. More than half its people are under the age of fifteen. Most of school-age can at last go to school, for recent years have opened out opportunities barely dreamed of in the past. (Photo copyright Augusta Conchiglia)

corresponding need for famine relief. Little of the latter came from Portugal until 1960, and even then it came on a scale too small to meet the situation, much less to change it.

Yet the men and women who would kindle hope, and would eventually bring about that change, were already on the scene. They were very few and very young and had still to find their way through the minefields of a dictatorship stiffened by its own survival of the war. Their undoubted leader was to be Amílcar Cabral, aged seventeen when the famine of 1949 engulfed the archipelago and at that time in his second year at the lycée of Mindelo, then the only secondary school in the archipelago.

Much has been written in admiration of Cabral and by many hands; and it may be that history, as I myself believe who also knew him well through many years, will see Cabral as perhaps the most powerful mind and moral force of any produced by Africa in its long struggle for independence from colonial rule. Certainly, I think, he was the only African leader in that struggle for independence who applied himself, early in that enterprise, to the making of a serious and detailed socio-economic analysis of his country (or, rather, of his two countries, Guinea-Bissau and Cape Verde).

He won an ardent love and loyalty even from those of whom he asked the apparently impossible. The modern history of Cape Verde, I would even say the modern history of much of Africa, is unthinkable without him. Men and women of the most varied background followed him with a trust in his integrity and vision, in his practicality and good sound sense, that were not deceived. But perhaps his friend and biographer Mario de Andrade of Angola may be left to say sufficient words in this place. Seven years after Cabral's murder by agents of the Portuguese dictatorship, Andrade wrote in 1980 that Cabral even in his youth, but increasingly thereafter, possessed 'the gift of uniting an exceptional intelligence and capacity for work with an extreme sensitivity to his social environment': to the drama that gripped his people, and to the potentials and strategy of decisive change.

He won entry to the Mindelo lycée in spite of an extreme poverty and thanks to the devotion of his mother, Dona Iva Evora Pinhel, and the sewing machine by which she could make a little money. His father Juvenal encouraged him but was evidently distracted by a veritably Cape Verdean production of children. There seems to be no exact count of the number of Juvenal's offspring but they totalled, I have been told, 'at least' sixty-two. Juvenal's wife Iva Pinhel had four children, one of whom was Amílcar. She backed Amílcar in his dreams as well as in his daily work. She remained his heroine until his death.

Like others, he wrote poems when at lycée, but if he wrote them in Portuguese and not Crioulo his themes were unorthodox, his vision was his own. Andrade has rescued some of these poems of Cabral's teenage youth. Enclosing or liberating, the sea is in many of them, the sea and its fierce ambiguity:

> You live – sleeping mother,
> Naked and forgotten,
> Arid,
> Whipped by the winds
> Cradled in the music without music
> Of the waters that chain us in . . .

Another strong personality of those years, the Agostinho Neto who would lead Angola out of colonial subjection just as Cabral led Guiné and Cape Verde, would write a little later, a little further along the road to self-realization, on the same theme:

> My mother
> (black mother whose sons depart)
> You taught me to wait and hope
> As you had learnt in bitter days . . .
>
> I am not the one who waits
> But the one who is awaited
>
> And we are Hope
> Your sons . . .
> Searching for life.

Their search brought them together at university in Lisbon with a few others from the colonies. They were a handful who would make history. Meanwhile they were remarkable passers of exams, as indeed they had to be. Cabral had passed his final lycée examinations by scoring seventeen marks out of a theoretically possible twenty, an almost unheard-of achievement and had chosen, upon winning admission to university in Lisbon, the faculty of engineering. He would be an agrarian engineer specialized in tropical water resources. The poetry would remain, but the poet would become a scientist. In 1950 the university awarded him a degree after another rare score of fifteen marks out of a possible sixteen.

A 'sound colonial career' lay at his feet, well-paid, guaranteeing much prestige. He ignored its promise, not priggishly or even from romantic dreaming but because, already, he saw where his search must go.

The route had to be driven through a great deal of provincial ignorance; moreover, its passage had to be concealed. Salazar had conserved the empire through the storms of world war, and now remained immutably chained to authoritarian mind and habit. Nothing was to change save that repression, whenever required, would be more repressive. There were Portuguese individuals, even within the regime, who argued for new initiatives; they were silenced or put down. There were to be no concessions to independent thought, much less to independent action. As for the privileged students from Africa, they were to be model Portuguese of the second class; or nothing at all.

Cabral and his friends – Neto, Andrade, Tenreiro, dos Santos, and one or two others such as Mondlane who studied elsewhere – looked for the ideas and facts that could offer the keys of escape for their peoples. Even from the first, it seems, they saw clearly through the claims of the regime. Famine and forced labour might or might not be a general African plight; in any case, their own experience at home had taught them that these were certainly proof of colonialist incompetence and greed. It followed in the privacy of cloistered conversation that the colonial regimes must somehow be removed.

The clandestine Left in Portuguese society helped them, above all the banned but surviving Portuguese communist party whose members – whether in Portugal or in the colonies – were a fecund source of ideas and facts otherwise unobtainable. Ferociously persecuted, these Portuguese communists who gave their friendship to the African students – to those few African students who sought it – played a brave role in helping towards a realistic grasp of politics and policy. Other Portuguese, including socialists and liberals, likewise gave enlightening friendship.

But these were years, after 1945, when the tides of anti-colonial protest, and even of anti-colonial nationalism, were rising in a very public manner elsewhere, and from them, too, much could be learned. Contacts in Paris brought news in 1946 of a great gathering at Bamako in Mali (then Soudan) at which some 800 delegated persons from all parts of French West and Equatorial Africa, vast territories, had formed a confederal party, the

Rassemblement Democratique Africain, with aims altogether new. These, declared this RDA, were to achieve the 'union of Africans and their alliance with French democrats', a union 'of different peoples who are free and equal in their rights and duties'.

Other contacts, more slender because 'Anglo-Saxon', brought exciting news from British West African colonies: from the Gold Coast where Kwame Nkrumah launched his agitations in 1947 that would lead to the formation of an African government in 1951 (and to independence, as Ghana, in 1957), and likewise from Nigeria. But if others were beginning to win free of colonial rule, how could this be conceivable in fascist Portugal? The journey would be long and hazardous but in order to begin it, Cabral and others rapidly concluded, they must stand on the same ground as the great majority of colonized Africans. As second-class Portuguese they could achieve nothing; as 're-Africanized' Africans, they might be able to achieve much.

Patiently, they set about this difficult enterprise in 're-acculturation'. They promoted studies and discussions. They put the learning of several African languages upon their agenda. They passed round all written information they could get their hands on. They made some progress. In all this they reached a principled rejection of assimilation to Portugal, though secretly until they could see what to do next.

That is where the sources of Cabral's eventual programme of African liberation are to be found, and they had to spring from very unfavourable ground. Cape Verdeans, since 1914, were theoretically all citizens of Portugal, unlike the *indígenas*, the 'natives', of the mainland territories. With one or two rare exceptions, such as Pedro Cardoso, their educated persons had never thought of themselves as Africans, and had accepted assimilation almost without a single dissentient voice. Whatever Cape Verde's future might be it would be somewhere, they thought, within the realm of Portugal.

But Cabral, even while a student (but also, no doubt because he was a student), rejected the orthodoxies of tradition. He looked beyond the realm of Portugal. If Cape Verde were to escape from its condition – and this was while the terrible famine of 1947–8 still raged – Cape Verdeans must rejoin their African roots. With a decisive prescience whose value would be realized only later, Cabral declared for Africa.

It became the project of those years: in re-becoming Africans these young men and women would become nationalists; and in becoming nationalists they would declare war on the colonial condition. In 1948, pursuing this project, a small group of lycée students in Luanda, the Angolan capital, followed another youthful figure, Viriato da Cruz, in launching a literary journal with a masthead, *Vamos Descrobrir Angola*, 'Let's Discover Angola', which was entirely subversive in its meaning and intention. The governor-general banned it after two issues, but its message was not forgotten.

In 1949, briefly at home in Praia, Cabral attempted the same thing with a series of radio talks. Cape Verde, he broadcast, was poor but need not be. Farming was unproductive in the islands: it could be otherwise. Water was in short supply; more, much more, could be found. The governor cancelled the talks. Cabral afterwards recalled that 'a lot of people gathered on the Praia *praça* to ask for the talks to be continued, but the Portuguese held to the cancellation'. He also drew up a programme of adult education talks on the theme that 'Cape Verdeans must get to know Cape Verde'. But the governor again declined to permit them.

In 1952, at the age of twenty-eight, Cabral left a pleasant administrative job in Portugal and moved to Bissau, the little colonial capital of the very small colony of Guiné, his birthplace, where he took a position in the farming-and-forestry service, an administrative affair bereft of competent personnel. It was obscure work and poorly paid, but it was the next step in Cabral's plan. And 'the plan worked out', as he later explained, 'step by step as a contribution to rousing our people for struggle against the Portuguese. And this I did from the first day of arriving home.'

He found friends to help him, a mere handful.

II

Given the apparent hopelessness of Cabral's project, as well as its sheer difficulty and danger, the handful had to be persons of unusual courage and stubborn will. They might each deserve a book to themselves, but even a few words may be useful.

Next to Cabral, then and later as events would show, there was a twenty-nine-year-old clerk in the Bissau posts-and-telegraph office, another product of the lycée of Mindelo: Aristides Maria Pereira, twelfth child of the Catholic pastor of the island of Boa Vista. For him as for other Cape Verdean students, fearful lessons had been driven home by the famines of the 1940s. He recalls in 1986,

> They provoked a new trend of thought. There had to be a change, there had to be a different future. Many emigrated: not just for jobs but in this search for a way ahead. Some of us went to Portugal, others to Angola, several to Bissau. Yet all of us went with the same notion, the idea of finding a different way ahead.

The rare photographs of that time show the same severely handsome presence that a later world would mark and remember. And Pereira played a characteristically crucial role in those Bissau days, not least because he could listen in on official conversation telephoned from and to Lisbon (and in this way, as it would turn out, save several of the leaders from imprisonment). Later he would be Cabral's indispensable 'anchor man' throughout the liberation war, and in 1973, after Cabral's murder, he would lead the party of independence, the PAIGC, in the newly independent state of Guiné and then go on to become the first president of his native land. In all this he was both Cabral's *alter ego* and a personality who remained very much himself, 'continuing' Cabral and yet, with Cabral and after Cabral, imposing his own emphatic style of personal modesty and restraint.

Another crucial pioneer was a clerk in the Bissau bank, local branch of the Banco Ultramarino, when Cabral returned in 1952. Abilio Augusto Monteiro Duarte – so many names, in the Portuguese tradition – had met Aristides Pereira on the boat from Praia to Bissau in 1949, when Abilio, then eighteen, was emigrating for the first time and Pereira was returning from a visit. Neither remembers much of what they discussed but the politics will have been peripheral. Abilio recalls,

> Yet even when I got to Bissau for the first time, I had a vague insight into colonial realities. I had this sense of having suffered an injustice, in that everything that could speak for us as a people – a people in our own right, you understand, and not just a shadow of the Portuguese – had been repressed and driven underground.

Like Pereira, Abilio is the son of a Cape Verdean Catholic priest and could gain entry to the Mindelo lycée, in the last respect being like his future companion Dulce Almada, who, with him, was to go through the liberation struggle in a position of leadership. They and their friends joined a restless energy, positively Protestant as a northern observer may well see it, to an ebullient and optimistic love of life. And without these qualities of mind and character, no doubt, they could scarcely have survived.

In 1986 – indeed, since 1975 – Abilio Duarte is the President of the Cape Verdean National Assembly, but finds time to recall the past. Of nationalism in those Bissau days, whether in relation to Guiné or to Cape Verde, there was generally no more than a 'gut reaction' of dumb resentment. Yet even this, he explains, was side-tracked by the complex inhibitions of 'shades of colour' which set one 'level of society' against another in layers of racist mystification.

'We lived in a system of *apartheid*, though of course nobody knew the word then.' Cape Verdean officials or clerks, colonial Portugal's 'intermediaries with the natives', might have the status of second-class Portuguese: 'but not the natives, the *indígenas*, the faceless mass'. Those could claim nothing.

At nine o'clock every evening, the police sounded a siren in the city centre. That was the signal for all the 'natives' – servants, 'boys', washer-women, whatever – to be evicted from the city. Unless they had a special employer's pass, they had to walk out to their shanty slum at Chão Pepel, and walk back in again after dawn.

And out there, beyond the limits of the little colonial Bissau with its ancient fortress and its ceremonial *praça* and its governor's palace, lay the unknown forest with its crocodile-infested creeks and unreliable 'natives' among whom the Portuguese language, let alone any least literacy, was almost totally unknown. Regarding the conditions in 'Portuguese Guiné', Abilio Duarte continues,

My father was a priest, as you know, and could travel on religious duties. He used to tell us about his travels. They'd be hard for people nowadays to imagine. For instance, there were no ferries of any proper kind across those ocean creeks; there were only rafts pulled by ropes. Who pulled the ropes? Men were made to come from the nearest hamlet. They had to get into the water and wade, pulling on the ropes. Naturally, nobody paid them for doing it.

This colony of 'Portuguese Guiné' was remote in every psychological as well as physical sense. The people were somewhere out there – Fula, Mandinka, Pepel, Balante – but they lived in silence and a kind of clandestinity. How was anyone to evoke anti-colonial protest among them, let alone action? The old wars of self-defence had been finally lost in the 1930s, and no more of those seemed thinkable. And how would one communicate with these peoples, what language would one speak?

Pereira and his friends came together and talked. Among these friends was Fernando Fortes and Amílcar's younger brother Luíz who was an accountant in the Gouveia trading company, with several others. They needed to know what was going on in Africa, but who could tell them? 'Around that time we were contacted by a Portuguese pharmacist in Bissau, a woman, Sofia Pomba Guerra.' Pereira recalls her with a warm admiration. 'She greatly helped us.'

This brave woman proved to have some channels to reality outside the narrow limits of Bissau. As a more or less exiled member of the Portuguese communist party, staunchly surviving, she had managed to smuggle in pamphlets, newspapers and even books that told of political struggles up and down the world. 'She helped us to achieve an understanding of how things really were.' The liberation movements in the Portuguese colonies were to advance along paths of their own making and finding, but a handful of European radicals such as Sofia Pomba Guerra were great enlighteners at the start. Pereira continues,

> Their aim, of course, was to forward the struggle against fascism in Portugal. But then Amílcar came back, and contacted us through the help of Sofia. The conviction that he came with was for a struggle against colonialism. We must be in solidarity with anti-fascist Portuguese, but our struggle had to be our own, a struggle to free our own countries.

Countries plural: for Cabral's conviction, even then, extended to an anti-colonial struggle in and for Cape Verde as well as Guiné. Aristides Pereira

> In practice, that had seemed impossible to us, if only because the islands were surrounded by the ocean, far from the mainland, and toiling in a hopeless poverty. But Amílcar said no: there were possibilities. What we had to have was an appropriate strategy. We had to embark on a common struggle with the people of Guiné, whether or not an armed struggle might be possible in the islands. So we had to work for a struggle in Guiné while building our contacts in Cape Verde.
>
> And that was why, in 1956, we formed a party common to both countries, our African Independence Party, the PAIGC – for Guiné but equally for Cape Verde – one of Amílcar's greatest contributions to our history.

In founding this clandestine and at first very small party, 'our attitude was that everything done to liberate Guiné, there on the mainland of West Africa, would be a blow struck for the liberation of our islands. So it must be our duty to fight for Guiné as and when an armed struggle could develop there'.

The story of the liberation of the mainland, in its origins as in its development, has been told elsewhere. Early recruits were hard to find but none the less they were found. Ignacio Soares was one of them, a messenger in the Banco Ultramarino recruited by Abilio. Another Guinean was Rafael Barbosa, a central figure in those early days. Bernardo Vieira (Nino), future commander in the liberation war and then a very young man, was a third Bissau recruit. Osvaldo Vieira was a fourth: one of those, as he told me long afterwards in the bush of the 'Portuguese Guiné' which was then about to become the Republic of Guinea-Bissau, who had greatly profited from conversations with Sofia Pomba Guerra.

Looking round for legal cover, Cabral founded a 'sports club', but this was almost at once suppressed by a colonial authority which saw the club's proposed mixing of 'natives' with 'assimilated Portuguese' as a sure sign of subversion. Meanwhile Cabral and his Portuguese wife, Maria Helena Rodrigues, companion of his studies and a courageous anti-fascist, had embarked on a major venture in Cabral's career as an agrarian engineer. This was to make a first-ever analysis of the agrarian and hydraulic resources of the colony. Cabral saw the work as valuable in itself, but much more as a chance to learn the realities of rural Guiné, of that Guiné from which liberation, as he was already convinced, would have to come if it could come from anywhere.

It took them two years of incessant travel in the country, listening and asking, taking crop samples, studying village life, and learning local languages. When it was done Cabral must have known Guiné far better than anyone had ever known it. 'In the villages,' Maria Helena has recalled, 'he would hold meetings, and it was in this way that he became familiar with the whole of Guiné . . . and was amazed at what he discovered': above all, at the wisdom of the peasant cultivators with whom he talked and lived.

The inquiry and its results were much admired in Lisbon, but received by the authorities in Bissau with less enthusiasm. Cabral's political opinions, suspected or becoming known, could not possibly recommend a work of research and advice which called, in any case, for money that was not going to be spent. And now dissident talk, discussions, even leaflets were added to the count of Cape Verdean malice in the persons of Cabral and his friends. The governor, Raimundo Serrão, became alarmed. It was the moment when a youthful and somewhat shocked Abilio Duarte overheard a remark of Senhora Serrão's. 'The worst enemies of Guiné,' she opined, 'are the mosquitoes and the Cape Verdeans.'

But the time of the secret police of the dictatorship, the PIDE or Policia Internacional da Defesa do Estado, was not quite come, and no important political arrests were made in Bissau until 1962, the year before the launching of a full-scale war of liberation by the PAIGC. Meanwhile there should be prudent action. Serrão's successor, Melo e Alvim, proved to be a tolerant and patient man who may have privately deplored the dictatorship's brutality. It might be inconvenient, moreover, to act severely against a man of Cabral's glowing reputation in the scientific field.

In 1955 Melo e Alvim called him in; and Cabral's brother Luíz, then one of the leading spirits in the group that would form the PAIGC a year later, has reported the conversation that ensued:

GOVERNOR: So it's you who is the boss of the Mau Mau here?
CABRAL: To my knowledge, there is no Mau Mau here. That is in Kenya.
GOVERNOR: All right: so now you listen, Mr Engineer. Do what you must. Act as a man of your time: yes, but don't mess up my career.

The upshot was that Cabral was told to quit the colony with permission to return, now and then, to see Dona Iva who continued to live in Bissau. In September 1956, on one of these visits to his mother, he and five others formed the PAIGC in secret. Preparations for armed struggle began three years later, in 1959. The war itself was launched in January 1963, by which time Cabral had found a safe operational base in Conakry, capital of (ex-French) Guinea, across the southern frontier of 'Portuguese Guinea'. Henceforward until 1974, Conakry was to be the external centre of the activities of the PAIGC, and Cabral, when not inside 'Portuguese Guinea' or abroad elsewhere, lived here with his second wife, the admirable Ana Maria, and their children.

But all this was remotely far ahead when Cabral and Pereira, with four others, came one evening secretly together and decided to launch a party of national liberation.

III

How to begin? Hindsight must agree that it was much that they should have asked themselves the question and expected an answer. They were in great isolation and tightening danger from the police. Prudently, they began to move ahead. In Bissau they found it possible to agitate and even to recruit, and slowly to wind the springs of useful action.

But they were pledged to do as much in Cape Verde as well. Someone among them must go there and begin. Abilio Duarte would go. He would begin in Mindelo, the city-port on São Vicente; and for this choice there were convincing reasons. Mindelo had the lycée, and therefore students such as they had been. Mindelo also had the port, and therefore dockers, stevedores, the core at least of a working class. On the pretext of continuing his studies, Abilio managed to transfer himself, late in 1958, to the lycée.

This was the founding of the PAIGC in the archipelago. Abilio's gifts of tact and sensitivity allied to political courage discovered fertile ground. Soon there gathered round him a number of students among whom were several who would fight with distinction through the forest war on the mainland: to name only three among these individually very contrasting persons, Silvino da Luz, Joaquim Pedro da Silva, and Manuel dos Santos. Already in late 1958, Abilio recalls, 'I laid before them the perspective of an armed struggle, and what this must imply for each of us.'

That was done in as much secrecy as could be managed. But tremors of the coming storm were beginning to shake the routine calm, and many felt them. Among these was Luis Fonseca, later to be a leader of the clandestine struggle, and after independence a militant activist with many duties.

Aged fourteen 'when Abilio came from Bissau' – a phrase that many use when recounting these obscure beginnings – Luis Fonseca was too young a lycée student to know Abilio in person. 'But I'd taken my first political steps': propelled initially, he says, by childhood experience of the famine of 1947, 'when I saw the dead people carried away on bamboo stretchers' from his native village of Ponto do Sol on Sant'Antão.

> And by a chance it happened that my stepfather was a brother of Aristides Pereira, and, like him, a senior official in the post office – in his case, at

Mindelo. So they were in touch, and my stepfather received Party literature from Aristides Pereira in Bissau.

This was towards the end of 1958, and the Gold Coast Colony had just become independent Ghana,

a development which had a big influence on a lot of our people. The Party (PAIGC) literature wrote of this, and although my stepfather had hidden these papers I knew where they were. I used to go and read them at night. I began to think about Africa. I even wrote a school essay on the ancient empire of Ghana, an essay greeted at the lycée as an exciting discovery! In short, I began to think as an African.

Night-time visits to hidden PAIGC writings quickened the experience of those years. Part of that was the spectacle of the *contratados*, the so-called 'contract' workers who were forced workers in all but name, being shipped away to the cocoa islands.

Those peasants from our villages were given 500 escudos [perhaps £5 or 15 dollars, or thereabouts] before being put on board, and when they took the money and fled they were chased by the police and terribly beaten up. And then I saw them coming back from completed 'contracts' in the islands, and they were in worse shape than when they'd gone.

Colonial experience could offer its own enlightenments. 'The President of Portugal, Craveiro Lopes, came on official visit and we kids were given bits of uniform and lined up to applaud him.' Luis Fonseca laughs drily at the memory. 'And the child that I was saw that he was very white while most of us were very black, and I wondered how he could be the chief and leader of all us black people in "Portuguese Africa".' In that, too, there surfaced the awareness of racism and its discriminations against Cape Verdean blacks. 'For my stepfather was very black, and suffered discrimination from some of the less-black Cape Verdeans as much as from the Portuguese.'

In 1959 his father sent him away from Mindelo to a newly-created lycée in Praia on Santiago Island, some 300 kilometres by inter-island boat. The night-time readings had been discovered, and his stepfather feared a schoolboy's indiscretion, especially as they were discovered during a visit by Aristides Pereira, greeted with enthusiasm, while the latter was on his way from Bissau to Lisbon: the visit, ostensibly for a holiday, which was to prelude Pereira's onward journey to France and the beginnings of the liberation struggle.

The lycée in Praia proved another focus of political debate and agitation. Already the students there had garnered rumours of a coming fight for independence for Cape Verde while the year of 1960, of course, was to bring independence to many of the mainland colonies. It was not long before Praia students, a handful but with the wind in their sails, formed a 'commando' to paint up slogans on public walls: *Fora os Portugueses* (Out with the Portuguese), *Viva a Independência*, and so on. 'We even wrote them on the Governor's palace walls.'

Another result of Abilio's return to the islands in 1958 was to prove valuable to the future. He came with 'new ideas and new initiatives' at a time when 'nothing else was clear to us'. The words are those of the governor of the Bank of Cape Verde after independence, Amaro da Luz, talking in 1986 of the long struggle that was to be required of these young nationalists.

The few who had reached an anti-colonial position joined the PAIGC at this time, though of course clandestinely. Amaro da Luz recalls,

> But we still had no idea of how to start useful work. None of us had any political experience, let alone experience of clandestine work, and this made our situation very precarious. I even thought that if *I* could see that colonialism was wrong, then everyone else must see it too.

Scared of indiscretions, persons who had appeared sympathetic sheered away from the handful of nationalists. By now, too, the political police (PIDE) had begun to make its first arrests in Praia. Though transferred from his clerkship in Praia to the branch of the Banco Ultramarino in Mindelo, Amaro waited to be arrested in his turn. 'But in the event they didn't arrest me. Maybe they thought that it would better serve them to have me out of prison, so as to see where I might lead them.'

With the PIDE at his heels, Amaro had the duty of promoting the PAIGC in the archipelago. Looking around, he came to the conclusion that any real political development would have to start outside the islands. 'For although we'd begun to build the Party in Cape Verde the arrests spread fear, and we remained without any clear view of how we should act.' His first intention was somehow to get to Conakry, where Cabral and the Party leadership were now installed under the still doubtful and doubting protection of the president of independent (ex-French) Guinea, Sékou Touré. But while on holiday in Lisbon Amaro managed to find work in the bank there, 'and I saw that useful work would be possible'. Amaro became the secret Party link in the Portuguese capital after the armed struggle had begun in 1963, and this, too, was to have a crucial importance.

And then there were the stevedores of Mindelo, a small but notably self-reliant group of wage-workers whose political isolation was less than that of other urban groups, and much less than that of the peasants, because they worked in a port with maritime links to the mainland and to Europe. Coming from Bissau, Abilio thought that the stevedores would play their part. In fact they had already begun, secretly, to talk the politics of resistance. Here is one of them, José Zacarias Soares, remembering those days:

I came out of army service in 1951. I was twenty-one and I couldn't find a job that paid better than 50 escudos, a wage of hunger. So I went to Angola as *contratado*, and I was there at the time of the São Tomista rising.

Little known and less admitted, this remote rising of 1953 was made not by 'contract'-workers but by local men of the island of São Tomé who had become convinced that the Portuguese governor, by name Gorgulho, intended to break with tradition and force them into 'contract'-labour from which they were legally exempt. Gorgulho shot them down in scores, and called for more troops.

The Portuguese tried to induce those of us in Angola who'd been in the army to go as soldiers to São Tomé, offering higher pay than what we were getting as 'contract'-workers. But I refused. And I still refused when the *administrador* said I'd be sent anyway. In fact they sent me to Dundo [far away in the Angolan interior] and there I finished my three-year 'contract' and returned to Praia. I found no work there and went once more as *contratado*, this time to São Tomé. That was in 1955. And in São Tomé I met Dul. And through Dul I met Onésimo Silveira. And there was talk of finding some way to free our country . ..

A sturdily handsome brown man in his fifties, Dul's real name is Adriano da Cruz Brito but everyone still calls him Dul, the name he took when beginning in the late 1950s to act as the Party's clandestine liaison link among the stevedores. Thinking back, he comments that 'I had only the smallest beginnings of a political consciousness' when returning from the plantations in 1956, the year of the Party's foundation on the mainland: 'Just a vague idea of nationalism forming in my head.' Onésimo Silveira had helped him in that, for Onésimo was already thinking of the possible routes to liberation, even if, later on, Onésimo was going to shy away from them. Onésimo Silveira's real importance, as many have told me, lay in his poetry. He had made the admirable if astonishing gesture of volunteering for 'contract' labour to see exactly what it meant, and, having seen, to write about its realities. Circulated in manuscript in the 1960s, Onésimo's poems were read and loved:

> O povo des ilhas quer um poema diferente
> Para o povo das ilhas . . .

> The people of the isles want a different poem
> For the people of the isles:
> A poem without the pain of men deported
> From the savour of their lives
> A poem without children whose food
> Is the black milk of hungry lands
> A poem without mothers who know the nightmare
> Of their children without mothers . . .

Such poems, obscurely pushed around and listened to, are remembered as a spur to hope and courage in those years.

A group of stevedores, still working or retired, join in telling me how they found their way to one another's trust along paths of chance or conversation, stumbling, seeing not much ahead, following an instinct which literature calls the longing for freedom but which may be in truth a mingling of emotions, with anger not least among them. 'When I was twenty', says Amancio Manuel dos Santos, 'it was 1957, and I went as *contratado* to São Tomé and worked a seven-day week there for next to nothing. So I was still there in 1959 at the time of Pidgiguiti.' He is referring to the dockers' strike, at the Pidgiguiti harbour in Bissau on the mainland, when at least fifty strikers were shot down by the police, a massacre which was to launch the PAIGC, active behind the strike, upon the road to insurrection. 'And in São Tomé I met some of the Bissau dockers who'd been deported there, they'd been sentenced to fifteen years hard labour. And I learned their story.'

Death by shooting or fifteen years' hard labour for a wages strike: such was the colonial reality, however hard to believe it now. The story is sombre, and Amancio tells it that way. He could meet the deported Bissau dockers only on 'church occasions'. Even then talk was difficult, but talk was possible.

So when I came back to Cape Verde in 1960 we began to think about the situation, my friends and me. But I'd been sent home from São Tomé as a 'trouble maker', and there wasn't any work for me. So I did another 'contract' on São Tomé, a short one of six months. And for that they paid me exactly 18½ escudos for the six months [much less than one pound sterling]. I threw down the coins in front of them and they threatened to arrest me, shouting 'How dare you throw down the Flag?' [the sacred flag on the Portuguese escudo].

But I had a secret contact with Dul, and Dul was the electrician on Crisanto's yacht. So I got to hear about the movements, about all the movements [the PAIGC in Guiné, the MPLA in Angola, and other anti-colonial movements which were to lead to FRELIMO in Mozambique].

Amancio nods to Crisanto, who speaks next. Now aged fifty-three, Crisanto Rufino Lopes is a Cape Verdean of the sea, a mariner with a sailor's loose-limbed strength and self-reliance. He speaks well, carefully remembering distant years. He had gone to sea while still a boy and then at eighteen done his term of military conscription. 'After that – well, back to sea on the Dakar run. Dakar was the big continental port for us. Our window on the world you could say.' There in the capital of Senegal one could learn many things, and the PAIGC had contacts there. 'I got in touch with the Party even before the end of 1956, and then in 1961 there came the big risings in Angola, and I became devoted to the PAIGC and its aims.' The Angolan insurrections of that year, put down by the Portuguese with a huge ferocity, are remembered by Cape Verdean activists as a decisive influence.

Crisanto acquired his own small ship, and began to act as Party messenger between São Vicente and Senegal. This provided a link of rare value, but Crisanto is modest about it. Well aware that it might exist, the Portuguese authorities watched for it and tried hard to destroy it. By this time, moreover, the political police (PIDE) and its agents were active in checking on possibly dissident sailors.

But Crisanto persisted. By early in the 1960s, when the Party was taking shape in the archipelago, he was its 'regular bridge' between the islands and Dakar. Crisanto smuggled persons as well as letters, first on his small boat and then on a large yacht, the *Novas de Alegria*: 'British-built she was, and with her I went on serving as the Party's bridge with Dakar.' This he did for seven years.

They were the years in which the liberation war on the mainland of Guiné developed with success; when Amílcar Cabral carried his message and appeal for aid across the world from East to West; and when, in Cape Verde, Abilio's recruits sowed their own difficult harvest.

IV

Abilio himself had to run for it as early as November 1960. The fault was none of his. In Accra, since 1957 the capital of an independent Ghana, a congress of the 'World Association of Youth' was being prepared, and its organizers, having Abilio's name as an active nationalist, blithely sent him an invitation through the open post together with an air ticket to Accra, just as though no Portuguese dictatorship and political police so much as existed. 'That ruined my chance of any further work in Cape Verde', for the PIDE, having stopped the ticket in the Mindelo post office, redoubled their surveillance. Abilio got away to Dakar, and thence to Paris.

He was lucky to get away. The police were already confiscating travel documents. Only three days after his departure, the PIDE inspector Correia arrived from Dakar with a warrant for Abilio's arrest. Although installed in the islands, the political police had still to take the measure of their adversaries. Amaro da Luz comments on this point:

> Their central failure was that the Portuguese in control had no understanding of what we were about in this process of national liberation. They still believed that Portuguese prestige and power would dominate student attitudes. And it was true that any student ready to serve them was promised the earth. A few were bought like that . . .

He is here referring chiefly to African students in the universities of Portugal.

Blandly sure of their superiority of intelligence and will, as well as of the means of corruption, the Salazarist generals and politicians seem to have had no least idea of the storms that were about to engulf them. But the leaders of the liberation movements, moving around the world in 1959 and 1960, began to see the possibilities of which Cabral had spoken. The Algerians were winning their war of liberation against France after six years of ferocious warfare, and promised to become valiant allies. Up and down the world, not least in Vietnam, there were reasons for encouragement.

Even before Abilio reached Paris at the end of 1960, Cabral in London had pinned his colours to the mast when addressing a press conference called for him at the House of Commons, and had published a written indictment of Portuguese colonialism in an English-language pamphlet which achieved wide circulation. In June 1962, again widening their appeal, Dulce Duarte was able to address the UN special committee on decolonization in Rabat. She told the committee,

> Like other peoples of the Portuguese colonies, the Cape Verdeans have never had the opportunity of deciding for or against Portuguese nationality. That has been imposed on them. Their struggle is thus for the right of self-determination, to wrest the sovereignty of their country from Portuguese hands, and to end the sufferings which Portuguese domination – from slavery through fascism – has imposed on them.

They had wanted peaceful change, and repeatedly appealed for it. One must emphasize that this was more than a propagandist ploy. Even after they had accepted that an armed struggle for independence could not be avoided, Cabral and those closest to him, notably Aristides Pereira, continued to distrust the implications of violence. They harboured no romantic illusions on the 'cleansing virtues' of war. They saw that liberation war could risk the degradations of terrorism, and that these would be fatal to their cause. It stands on the record that they resisted these temptations. In all the harsh years of warfare that followed after 1962, the PAIGC and its army opposed attacks on civilian targets, killed no prisoners and tortured no traitors. Such was their claim, then and later, and the present writer was among foreign observers who were well placed to confirm that this struggle for liberation was indeed conducted with a minimal necessary violence.

Yet the necessary violence had to be considerable. 'And as our struggle continued,' comments Pereira in 1986, 'we tried to measure its consequences for this materially very backward peasant society of Guiné.' Fighting spread rapidly across that colony after its inception in January 1963.

> But what did it mean in the minds of these peasants now using modern and even sophisticated weapons? We looked for answers and did not find

them. We had to follow this route of armed struggle. There was no other way. And yet it was an act of violence upon our peasants too, a violent changing of village mentality. A dangerous route! So we said to ourselves: All right, we must persevere, and we'll see . . .

But if armed struggle on the Guiné mainland proved as possible as it was necessary, no such conclusion was at all obvious for the islands in the ocean. While the best of the Cape Verdean students and other volunteers made their way to Conakry and thence to the ranks of the army of the PAIGC, there were others, especially in the numerous Cape Verdean community of Dakar in Senegal, who voiced doubts and discontent. As Cabral was to explain in the wake of a secret party meeting during July 1963, held in Dakar, there were many in this Cape Verdean community who were in no way drawn to the challenges of nationalism, but who, none the less, 'have been watching with attention the good work done by our organization in Guiné. Yet some are asking why our Party does so much for Guiné and so little for Cape Verde?'

It was an awkward question, and remained awkward. Cabral met it by enlarging on the Party's work in publicizing its appeals for change and in mobilizing support within the islands. Their appeals to the UN, for example, had established the true condition of the islands against every Portuguese effort to depict the islands as an 'overseas province' of equal rights and opportunities. And anyone, he claimed, who took account of all the work the PAIGC had achieved, 'in mobilizing the people, in secretly circulating the Party's documents, in isolating the Portuguese troops and PIDE', or in other ways, 'can only agree that the struggle in Cape Verde is not dragging behind the struggle in Guiné'.

It was an optimistic gloss upon events, and the same statement of 21 July 1963 continued on a still less realistic note. 'Our Party knows that the struggle in Cape Verde is about to enter a new phase, an urgent development . . . as soon as certain problems are resolved.' These were, though secretly, the problems of infiltrating arms and fighters to the archipelago, and of initiating liberation war there. But no such problems were resolved in 1963, nor even seriously considered.

Yet the personnel to tackle these problems, however improbably, were on the way. The statement of 21 July noted that among Cape Verdean nationalists present at the Dakar conference of a few days earlier was one who had 'recently arrived from Angola'.

An escapee from the Portuguese army then fighting the great insurrections in Angola, this was a lieutenant in rank aged twenty-four, by name Silvino da Luz.

Silvino's arrival marked in fact another phase and portent: the entry on the scene of action of the Mindelo lycée students whom Abilio had mobilized in 1959–60. Some came from Portuguese universities and a handful, like Silvino, from the Portuguese armed forces. They were to be Cape Verdean commanders of liberation war. But considering their stories in retrospect, it must seem remarkable that they could arrive at all.

V

Abilio came down to the harbour to bid me goodbye. His last words to me, I remember them as if it was yesterday. He said: 'So you'll accept your call-up, you'll join the Portuguese army. And you'll learn all you can. When we're ready the Party will tell you to desert. Then you'll find your way to us.'

That was said in the autumn of 1960; and in 1980, with Silvino da Luz digging into his memory and his archives, it is twenty-six years later. But the search is fruitful, for Silvino has vivid memories and papers to support them. Besides, he is Cape Verde's Minister of Foreign Affairs, and nothing if not methodical. A strong personality with a fortunate sense of fun, he also shares his comrades' respect for the rights and virtues of history. He and I have known each other for many years and in many situations, some enjoyable and others not, but I have never before heard the details of his escape from the Portuguese army. It has its place in this history.

He had joined the clandestine party of liberation, PAIGC, with a dozen or so other lycée students, after Abilio's arrival from Bissau in 1958. Having finished his lycée studies a year later, when he was twenty, he aimed at higher education in Ghana, then entering its third year of independence. That proving impossible, he applied to study medicine in Portugal and sat his entrance exams to the University of Coimbra with success.

But the authorities delayed accepting me until 1960 – until, that is, I was liable for conscription, whereupon they ordered me to Lisbon on an officers' training course. The party's instructions were to accept this and use the experience for the armed struggle which, we already thought, must lie ahead of us.

Three others in his group followed this line of action: José Brito, Honorio Chantre, and Joaquim Pedro da Silva.

Events now moved fast. No sooner had Silvino completed a six months' training course in Portugal than the capital of Angola, the city of Luanda, erupted with the insurrection of the MPLA, Angola's nascent liberation movement. That was in February 1961.

The Portuguese began at once to gather troops for Angola, and at this point a letter came from Abilio [then based in Paris as a member of the PAIGC executive committee] telling us to get out of Portugal by way of going to Angola, and, once in Angola, to desert as soon as possible after making contact with the MPLA. Or, if that contact couldn't be made, to desert at all costs.

Now a lieutenant, Silvino arrived in Luanda with Portuguese reinforcements in May 1961: 'indeed a terrible moment, for there were mass killings of Africans in Luanda and outside the city'. One may recall here that the February rising in Luanda was followed by another in the northern districts of Angola, the work of a local movement then called UPA and afterwards FNLA. This northern revolt was conducted on a wild and murderous method which led to the wanton killing of some two hundred Portuguese settlers. But the Portuguese reprisals which followed these killings were far more terrible. Some 20,000 Angolan African civilians, above all those with some literacy and therefore as was believed a sympathy with Angolan nationalism, were hunted down and slain without mercy; and the figure of 20,000, by all the evidence, must be regarded as conservative. Nothing else that the Portuguese had done or would ever do in Africa was as bad as this, and not until the last months of 1962 did the killings come to an end. Much of this a deeply worried Silvino had to witness.

In these circumstances, any contact with the scattered and crushed MPLA proved extremely difficult, while the mere prospect of escape from the army could be little better. Silvino continues,

Honorio Chantre did manage to get across the frontier into Zaire. But he and I were the only ones who got away from the army in Angola. Baro [Joaquim da Silva] managed to escape while still in Portugal. But José Brito was taken while trying to escape from Angola and put before a firing squad. As for me, I was able to make a fragile contact with the MPLA as well as with two dissident Portuguese in the army, one a socialist and the other a communist. We exchanged ideas and papers, secretly of course, but I saw that the PIDE were on my track.

They proposed that I should go to Lisbon on a course. I smelt a rat and stalled. They repeated the offer early in 1963 and this time I agreed. But I left Angola a week before they expected, and on a plane which made a stop in Kano, in northern Nigeria. That was going to be my only chance to escape. And luckily, there, I was helped by a Nigerian immigration officer. To this day I haven't discovered who he was.

This was great good fortune, for it came out that the Portuguese police on the plane already suspected that Silvino was going to make a run for it.

They kept asking the airport police for me, and, worse still, their onward take-off was delayed by a passenger's having died on the flight from Luanda. They had to disembark the corpse and go through formalities, all time-demanding.

But the Nigerian immigration officer hid me in his office, and then smuggled me out of the passenger building. 'Jump from that window,' he said, 'and you'll find a bicycle. Take it and I'll go with you.' So he took me to a sentry-post at the gates and shoved me in there till the plane at last took off.

This was Nigeria's third year of independence, and Nigerian sympathies with the still colonized could be strong.

After that, back at the passenger building on Kano Airport, Silvino was questioned by a British police officer, but with less sympathy.

Who was I, and why had I fled the plane? I told him that I'd done it as a patriotic duty. He didn't much enjoy that, and the police locked me into a hotel room somewhere in Kano. There they kept me for four and a half months. With a sentry on the door, and the window barred.

But his luck held, if not easily.

You'll remember, just then there was the foundation of the OAU [the Organization of African Unity] in Addis Ababa. And the new member-states, including of course Nigeria, decided to sever relations with Portugal and its colonial governments. That was a big help. Because I'd managed to send out letters through the boy who brought my food: I gave him what little cash I had. I wrote to Amílcar who was then at our PAIGC base in Conakry [ex-French Guinea, next door to 'Portuguese Guinea']. But I also sent a letter to Lagos newspapers. One of them printed it under a big headline. *SOS from a Portuguese Officer Detained*, or something a bit muddled like that. But it did its job. The British police officer brought me the clipping and wanted to know how I'd sent my letter. I said I'd put it in the post.

After those months locked up in Kano, he was eventually set free in June 1963.

They just put me out into the street, penniless, and left me. I'd asked them, when they set me free, to send me to Léopoldville [Kinshasa, capital of the ex-Belgian Congo]. That was where, I knew, the MPLA had an external office and I meant to join the MPLA and fight for Angola. Maybe, I don't know, from a certain sense of guilt at having served in Angola with the Portuguese army, a kind of paying of a debt of conscience. But the police did nothing for me.

Still penniless, Silvino managed to get himself to Lagos. 'Luckily again, someone in the social services found me a bed in an Old Persons' Home, and I stayed there for two months.' He laughs at the memory of himself, a lean but sturdy man of rising twenty-four in an old persons' home.

Then a letter reached me from Amílcar in Conakry. Amílcar said I should go to Léopoldville and join the MPLA if that was what I really wanted. But the PAIGC needed me, and so he needed me to go to Conakry. I went as soon as I was able, and I reached Amílcar at last in July 1963.

The records of African nationalism in those years are repeatedly the records of last-ditch chances narrowly lost or won. Nationalism in retrospect may well seem to have been an easy option and an irresistible force. It was seldom how it seemed at the time. By a long shot, Amílcar's letter had got through to Silvino, and Silvino entered the scene of action at something of a turning point.

VI

The war to liberate 'Portuguese Guinea' from colonial rule, and found a free country whose name had yet to be chosen – Kinara, after an area of its southern region, was to become a favourite, but Guinea-Bissau would prevail in the end – seemed to be going well. After six months of forest fighting, several zones had been cleared of Portuguese officials, troops and traders; and colonial counter-offensives with reinforcements from Portugal had entirely failed to dominate the rising. Neighbouring African countries were proving variously helpful. The government of (ex-French) Guinea to the south had withdrawn an initial hostility, and now appeared to be a friend. To the north, the government of Senegal was troubled by fears of 'communism' in the PAIGC but was willing to turn a blind eye on prudent frontier crossings. While the PAIGC kept its chief external base in the relative safety of Conakry, the (ex-French) Guinea capital, Cabral and his closest comrades could meet in Dakar provided that they were discreet. All this might be much worse.

At and soon after the time of the secret Dakar meeting of July 1963, Cabral's grasp of a winning strategy was already well advanced. That could be squarely seen, if not by the Portuguese commanders whose racism continued to blind them, some three or four years later. In 1964, at an emergency congess in the southern forest of Guiné, the party leadership was able to terminate several desperate outbreaks of indiscipline and local tyranny, and, building on this, lay foundations for a mobile army on guerilla lines. 'Three thousand volunteered', Cabral told me in 1967, 'and for a start we chose nine hundred.' In 1965 the military strategy emerged more clearly. It was to draw the Portuguese commanders into dispersal of their numerically far stronger forces to many fortified camps and strongpoints. By 1966–67 these commanders had in fact dispersed their forces into several hundred fortified positions, and were beginning to be barricaded into these by small besieging units of the growing PAIGC army. Although outnumbered by at least eight to one, the guerrilla army possessed an increasing mobility and power of rapid concentration, and was now able to defend large zones from which the enemy was excluded save in big offensives. These 'liberated zones' – as distinct from 'contested zones' where neither side had superiority – were to be the social and political laboratories of 'people's power', of grass-roots democracy, whereby the new state would be given its foundations.

Another new stage opened in 1966 with the use of mortars, small portable cannon (recoilless 75 mm weapons), and bazookas against the enemy's fortified camps and strongpoints. At the end of 1966 Cabral could report that 'having delivered more than 100 attacks on fortified positions', during the year, 'we have succeeded in ravaging twenty-five enemy camps, several of them being very important . . . as well as damaging twenty-five others'.

With better training, chiefly inside the liberated zones, and better weapons that now came mostly from the USSR, the growing scale of attacks on barricaded camps, isolated posts, roads, harbours and fixed installations produced a situation in which – looking ahead a little – the year of 1968 was going to confirm the PAIGC in possession of a strategic initiative which they would not lose. It could thus be said at the end of 1968, if privately, that the liberation war was won even while much hard fighting still lay ahead. Neither the Portuguese commanders nor their many and powerful friends and suppliers were able to perceive this; but they learned better in the end.

Cabral had evolved this winning strategy from his years of 'study on the ground', whether of the mentality of Portuguese fascism or of the realities of Guiné. The first had taught him that the Portuguese commanders would respond on conventional military lines while invariably under-estimating the skill and courage of 'natives'. The second had led him to believe, and the belief proved sound, that old forms of peasant resistance – ended in Guiné only during the 1930s – could be successfully transformed into new forms, provided always that the defence of peasant interests was put first. And although nothing proved easy or simple or free from setbacks, blunders, and the fragilities of human nature, the war did more or less proceed along the lines that Cabral had planned and usually foreseen.

This success arose from his realistic analysis of the social structure and culture of the peoples of the colony. And in making and elucidating this analysis he displayed his capacity of judgement both in penetrating to essentials and, at the same time, evading the pitfalls of dogma and doctrine. People followed him through every challenge and hazard because he said what he thought, but also because they recognized that what he thought went to the heart of their living reality. At the Dakar meeting of July 1963, rising to the need to answer basic questions at a moment of enormous importance for the whole movement, Cabral turned to the living reality of Cape Verde. What were its structure and culture? How should these be understood in terms of a struggle for liberation?

Cabral's superiority of thought over the pioneers of the old *nativismo*, 'regionalism', and the writers of *Claridade* emerges from the records of this Dakar meeting. Hitherto, no Cape Verdean analysis had gone beyond the 'colour categories' of Portuguese and colonial racism, and even the few who had gone as far as that had thought that 'class and colour' must be synonymous concepts. In one of the last issues of *Claridade*, that of July 1948, the Fogo writer Teixeira da Sousa had summarized this attitude. He wrote,

> We may say that Fogo has four classes: the class of *Whites*; the class of *Mulatos*, offspring of a white father and a mulato or black mother, those we commonly call *Mestiços*; *Mulatos* properly speaking, meaning offspring of mulato fathers and mothers; and finally the class which is that of the *People* (*o Povo*).

Cabral cast all such attitudes aside. While in no way denying the cultural pressures of 'colour category' – he had lived with them, after all, since a child – he looked to the realities which underlay them. One should distinguish, to begin with, the society of the Cape Verdean towns from that of the rural areas. In the latter, essentially, there was a small number of large landowners. By 1963 this number was very small, since their lavish taking of mortgages had cost many of them their titles of ownership through foreclosure by the Banco Ultramarino. These few relatively rich people, sons of the old *senhores*, would be invariably against any idea of anti-colonial liberation, since colonial rule was their sole remaining guarantee of privilege.

Then there were small landowners, comparatively very numerous, who lived mainly off their rents in cash or in kind. Many owned no more than three hectares (less than seven acres), and might yield some support for liberation but would be hesitant and unreliable in the manner of a petty-bourgeoisie. Rural wage-earners were so few as to count, politically, for no significant force. But the vast majority of rural people could certainly be won for the ideas of liberation. This was true of *parceiros* (share croppers usually working for a half or a third of their annual produce, the rest going to their respective landowner), but still more true of the many *rendeiros* who paid rent in cash. As Cabral wrote,

> For the rent-payer [*rendeiro*] lives under the constant threat of sanctions if he should fail to pay. If he fails in time of economic crisis they will take his stock, his tools, even the doors of his house, or his windows or his roof. So he vividly dreams of owning a piece of land. He and his kind are those who are best aware of the reasons for a liberation struggle.

Cabral went on to analyse the society of the towns. At the base of the urban 'pyramid' were wage-workers and unemployed, but they could not be counted as a conscious working class. Above them, low-paid employees of the public and private sectors formed a sort of petty-bourgeoisie, including lycée students (with a lycée now in Praia as well as in Mindelo), lawyers, a few doctors and the like. Above these, again, was a small group of Cape Verdean employers of uncertain consciousness: for 'although they have a bourgeois life-style they cannot be said to be a "national bourgeoisie" but rather an intrusion of the bourgeoisie of Portugal under a Cape Verdean cover'. The dominant class in Cape Verde, Cabral concluded, was the *colonial class*: 'The bourgeoisie which exploits the colony lives in Portugal, exercising its power through the regime's apparatus of repression. And this is why the social struggle in Cape Verde coincides with the national struggle.'

It further followed – and events would again confirm him – that the social categories at the summit of the 'pyramid', whether they were Cape Verdean officials or Portuguese officials, white or brown or whatever, would show nothing but hostility. 'And yet we cannot ignore the nationalist feelings of some of these persons . . . for the barriers imposed on them by colonial reality can cause senior Cape Verdean officials to perceive national liberation as a possible gain for themselves.' Such persons would hold back and meanwhile serve the enemy, but some of them might also belong to the 'possibilities'.

If insurrection on the mainland could be launched with success, and this was the case by July 1963 even if its consolidation had still to be made secure, why should insurrection be beyond their reach in the archipelago? The question at Dakar, as we have seen, was posed cautiously, 'certain problems still needing to be resolved'. Yet preparations could still be made. These called for volunteers with soldierly experience, and, secondly, facilities for specialized military training.

Based now in a newly independent Algeria, Abilio Duarte was able to report that Algerian aid would provide the facilities. And the volunteers, for their part, were also at hand: not many but enough, including Honorio Chantre, Silvino da Luz and Joaquim da Silva who had done a period of conscription in the Portuguese army, Julio de Carvalho and other students 'channeled out' of Portugal along the links formed in Lisbon by Amaro da Luz. The future commander and Prime Minister Pedro Pires, a crucial figure in years ahead, would join them later.

But discreet and adequate facilities for specialized training still proved hard to find. The Algerians were very willing to help but at grips with the myriad problems of a newly-won independence. A small opening was discovered in China, and Honorio Chantre did a little training there. Others, like Silvino da Luz, filled in time by moving to Senegal on Algerian passports. There they registered for study in the medical faculty of the University of Dakar. 'In this way,' da Luz recalls, 'we could at least eat, and besides, we were serious students.'

But their minds were still on the landings plan, and at last a serviceable training ground was found. Early in 1966 Pedro Pires and part of the group were welcomed in Cuba, and the rest quickly followed them there. Now they numbered thirty in all, and here in Cuba they could train as they wished. They settled into their chosen formation: two groups for penetration of the archipelago, one under Honorio Chantre for Sant'Antão and the other under Pedro Pires for Santiago. They trained in the use of portable artillery, mortars, and the like. Early in 1967 they practised landing from the sea against simulated enemy opposition; penetration inland; techniques of survival and the tactics of assault that were foreseen. 'Not all of us were going to come through, we knew that very well,' recalls Olivio Pires, one of the group for Sant'Antão. 'But we were ready for that. In those years we were ready for anything.'

But first they had to find a ship to carry them from Cuba directly to Cape Verde so that they should arrive with complete surprise. And another ship to follow with food and fresh supplies of ammunition . . .

5 The struggle in the islands

I

From the distant islands, meanwhile, little came save silence or harrowing news of setback. What now happened there was to prove its value in the climax of 1974, but at the time could seem nothing or insignificant. With the PIDE ever more active and balefully better at its work, the only reliable line of communication, in or out, remained by way of Amaro da Luz in Lisbon. This route was difficult, and was to become insecure as well as slow.

Indiscretions and betrayals were thinning ranks never more than slender; and yet small groups held on, chiefly in Santiago and São Vicente. Crisanto Lopes had passed on his 'bridge' in 1963, and come ashore to reinforce morale among the stevedores of Mindelo. 'By 1970 we had built a strong Party cell, perhaps twenty of us', he recalls. 'We met on Sundays after dark, taking precautions.' Adriano da Cruz Brito, who was 'Dul', had the responsibility for conserving their numbers. When, for example, José de Rosario decided in 1966 to go to sea for want of work ashore, 'Dul said no, I should stay in the port, for if everyone goes, who'll be left?' Another stevedore who followed the same advice was José Soares who had worked as *contratado* on São Tomé. He formed a plan of getting to Conakry and then joining the armed struggle in Guiné. 'I saved up money for three months and then asked Dul for a contact there. But Dul refused. He said I shouldn't leave.' By this time, too, Dul was regularly 'circulating party literature, and talks he'd taped from Radio Libertação', the PAIGC broadcasting unit then established with Swedish technical aid at Conakry.

Additional advice and writings came from Amaro da Luz in Lisbon. He had other problems of his own, and wryly reflects on them. His orders from Amílcar 'by a letter which I could and did

A son of the island of Boa Vista, Aristides Pereira is President of the Republic and Secretary-General of its liberation movement, the Partido Africano de Independência de Cabo Verde. He joined the struggle for independence at its very inception, and was for many years the closest fellow-worker of Cape Verde's national hero, Amílcar Cabral, whom agents of the Portuguese dictatorship murdered in 1973, little more than a year before that dictatorship was overthrown. (Photo copyright Augusta Conchiglia)

use, when necessary, as my personal legitimation for remaining in Lisbon', were to stay in Lisbon and not attempt to join the armed struggle. He was to enlarge Party contacts and membership, and smuggle out of Portugal volunteers for the war. Everything proved difficult.

I was one of the few of us who had a job, so I could support others as well as myself. But we had to learn underground work, and it's a mystery how the PIDE failed to catch up with us. Perhaps they thought that arresting us would simply lead to the flight of others. And some students who were threatened by conscription, Julio de Carvalho and others, did in fact take refuge in France before getting to the armed struggle.

He turns to another problem of those years, presented by the anti-fascist movement inside Portugal itself. 'Of course we needed to be part and parcel of that movement. Yet just as much we had to hold firm to our Party and its anti-colonial priority.' He confirms, talking in 1986, that the Portuguese communist party which formed the core of the anti-fascist movement in Lisbon had agreed in 1957 to cease attempting to form overseas branches in the colonies, and instruct its members there to throw in their lot with the anti-colonial movements. But what was agreed 'at the top' did not always register further down.

We came to feel that they tended to see us as instruments for their own party purposes which, however justified in Portugal, were not necessarily the same as our purposes. So we had to defend our struggle within the Portuguese movement.

There was no presence of any communist party in Cape Verde save for an elderly German refugee living in Fogo. But our students going on holiday to Cape Verde came out of the Portuguese anti-fascist movement. They thought of themselves as marxists, and expected to find that our militants in the islands were also marxists, and when they found this wasn't so they'd return to Lisbon discontented. And there'd be useless talk and intrigue.

He speaks of the student upsurge of 1968 that saw its climax in Paris. This led to

illusions about revolution, especially among our students at the University of Coimbra. There I met with doubts about our Party. Perhaps this arose from a half-felt fear on their part that our nationalism might turn into a kind of reaction. Or perhaps it came from the feeling that 'youth must lead', for example in defending our Party against petty-bourgeois tendencies and so on.

There were going to be other distractions of that order, for there was much confusion of ideas and aims. 'But we ourselves', says Amaro,

were working our way through it. We had begun to receive our Party's directives and explanations without trouble, at first by way of Paris, and then from Holland after Olívio Pires went there late in 1968. We saw where we were, and what we had to do. Marxism might be an indispensable tool, but we had to learn how to apply it to our colonial circumstances, following Cabral's lead. And the problem really was an old one – of how to be part of the revolutionary movement in Europe and yet conduct an independent struggle for liberation of the colonies. A problem all the more difficult, for us, because the movement in Portugal gave us great and continuing aid.

The core of this always touchy problem was that the movement in Portugal naturally believed that the downfall of fascism had to come before the downfall of colonialism. But Cabral's teaching was just the reverse; and it was to be Cabral's teaching which proved right. Yet these were remote issues for the militants in Cape Verde. They knew nothing of doctrinal differences, or even of revolutionary history. With the older lycée leavers gone to join the war, or else prudently quiescent in government jobs, the lead had passed among the students of the next generation six or seven years younger. Very few of these, as yet, had been admitted to the Party's increasingly clandestine membership.

'We lived in a cultural blackout', remembers Luis Fonseca, the secret reader of his stepfather's secret Party papers and, today in 1986, secretary of the big Praia Party section. 'There were no books that could explain our colonial condition, let alone question it. The first radical book I ever saw was one of my stepfather's about the trial of a Cuban revolutionary. Of course I wanted more.' He has kept his sense of humour from the years of persecution.

I found it in the regime's books. They attacked Marxism with long quotes from Lenin and so on. Then around 1962 we students got our first PAIGC documents by way of Dul in the port. Some of us were thrown out of the lycée, but we didn't give in.

They were expelled for protests against the lycée's rector,

truly a fascist type who tried to enforce fascist loyalty. We called him Semente de Mango [Mango-Nuthead] and scrawled up slogans against him on the inside walls. When they closed the lycée because of this we got together the first-ever political demonstration against the regime. We marched down the mainstreet from the lycée *praça* [*Praça de Zimbabwe* today] shouting slogans against Semente de Mango, until the police grabbed us. And you could say that this little action was the fruit of nationalism, of a certain nationalist awakening, still vague but pushed along by a longing for real change.

Expelled from the lycée, the activists survived as they could. Luis Fonseca talked his way into a job in the São Vicente broadcasting station, Radio Barlavento, but soon was sacked for sarcastic commentaries at the expense of the authorities and even of the Governor, the strictly Salazarist General Silvério Marques. Then he worked as an English translator in the Mindelo fish-refrigerating plant: 'not translating very well, I'm afraid'.

Luis was among the handful who now became targets for a regular persecution by the PIDE, frequently arrested and hauled in for questioning but not yet beaten or tortured.

We went on trying to learn. We had Onésimo Silveira's poems, and we loved those poems. And Onésimo himself, back from São Tomé, had brought books with him, wonderful quantities of books. Lenin's *State and Revolution*, others of that quality. And now there were more poems to spur us on. Those of Alda de Espirito Santo [of São Tomé] and of Noémie de Sousa in Mozambique. *This land is ours, not yours* . . . It became our theme too.

Onésimo fled in 1965 to escape arrest, though in fact he wasn't really in agreement with the PAIGC, but he'd got us a contact with Silvino da Luz [then in Dakar before going to Cuba for the landings project]. With Silvino's encouragement we formed a Party cell with Carlos Reis [afterwards Cape Verdean minister of education and in 1986 ambassador in Lisbon] and we worked with the stevedores as well.

Their cell was betrayed to the PIDE in 1964 by a messenger on the Dakar route; but the PIDE, now comfortably established in a villa near the harbour of Mindelo, was still in no hurry to make arrests.

I think they couldn't believe that we students, on our own, would have done the slogan-painting and so on. They thought there must be a 'big man' hidden behind us. Who is your leader? was their invariable question when they took us in. Of course our leader was Cabral, far away in Guiné or travelling the world. But they suspected it might be Balthazar Lopes, the venerable one-time editor of *Claridade*.

They were wide of the mark.

Taken in by the PIDE in 1966, this time Fonseca was beaten up after a search of his room proved vain. 'They went through my shelves but stopped before the gramophone records, and so they missed the Party literature I'd concealed in the sleeves.' But the PIDE inspectors found a book of Bertrand Russell's in which the philosopher explained why he was not a Christian; and this they judged undoubtedly subversive.

'Are you a Christian or a Protestant?' one of the inspectors asked Fonseca, and, concluding the worst, took him to the *fortinho*, their prison on the headland above the magnificent harbour of Mindelo. Two years later, locked in there again, he was going to contract rheumatic fever. In 1966 they held him only for a few days, but re-arrested him in January 1967. This time, in the PIDE basement, he found a companion, 'a Portuguese communist who happened to have become a Maoist'. A Maoist, whatever was that? More private sessions on the history of revolution followed.

Released again in 1967, he had grown tired of this cat-and-mouse game of the PIDE's. He went into hiding and arranged to escape by sea. He was once more betrayed, 'and the PIDE took me out of the ship for Dakar that I'd got myself smuggled into by the stevedores. The PIDE took me out at gunpoint and kept me until 1973, at first in the *fortinho* and then at Tarrafal.' Tarrafal had long become the principal jail for Portuguese Africa's 'politicals', and many passed through its cells. Their grim and hopeless isolation at the northern tip of Santiago island is another part of this struggle that is not forgotten.

II

What happened to Luis Fonseca happened to others as well; some of them, for example Carlos Tavares, we have already met along the way. Their merit was to hold firm when their links with the PAIGC were remote or broken, when they could know nothing of the Party's plans, and finally through long years of imprisonment. But one or two, older and closer to the Party leadership, had some notion by 1967 of the landings project.

One of these was Lineo Miranda of Sant'Antão. For long a senior inspector of schools – 'in so far as there were any schools to inspect' – Lineo in 1986 is an elder in this land of abundant youth. Retired to a pleasant little stone house in the canyon of

Ribeira Grande, he unites Cape Verdean *morabeza*, which is better even than hospitality, with a sound memory and a capacious experience.

We sit on Lineo's verandah shaded by banana fronds, and sample the throaty *grog* of Sant'Antão from a neighbour's *trapiche*, the local version of the transatlantic *engenho* or open-air distillery; and we discuss the landings plan which had to be abandoned, very wisely as it proved. Lineo is a man of gentle courtesy and speaks of this, I think, with the reluctance of unhappy memories. 'They would have got ashore all right, and they'd have had no hard job in ambushing Portuguese patrols.' From Lineo's verandah it is easy to see why.

Nothing in nature can be much more astonishing than Lineo's mighty canyon. From its narrow floor, where his house is placed, sheer granite walls climb out of sight above you. Down from the tangled inland mountains there arrive small roads that spin and circle in countless hairpin turns, while little irrigation channels run impossibly across these walls. Here, too, the peasants have niched and excavated six-foot terraces for sugar cane and maize, bringing soil from wherever they can find any. Guerrillas here would have had people to back them, and even water. For there is water here, the only 'river' in all Cape Verde so far as I have seen, a trickle of good water snaking down the canyon from springs far above: a trickle, yet unfailing.

'But it is easy in retrospect,' consents Lineo, 'to realize that it was a doomed enterprise. They'd have got ashore, they'd have survived, some of them at least. But then they would have starved. For in 1968 the drought came again, and famine.' Yet people to back them?

Yes, because by 1968 we here had worked with success at gathering support for the idea of independence and what this might entail. We were sorely lacking in experience of any sort of underground activity, and our precautions, my precautions, were quite inadequate. Yet we'd gathered effective support for independence from as many as a thousand persons on this island. Not Party members, you understand, not regular militants, but people simmering with anger against the Portuguese. And I'd even say that there was a sense of shame at being considered to belong to that Portugal [he means the Portugal of the Salazarist dictatorship, the so-called New State], a feeling shared above all among our seamen who travelled and knew what Fascist Portugal's standing really was.

Lineo Miranda was at the centre of this work of gathering

support because he was known to the Party leadership and a leading figure in the family networks of the island. 'And we did this political work of preparation at meetings with friends and families. Then we talked of what was wrong, but everything was wrong, and how we could hope to set it right.' Yet late in 1967 Lineo tired of his isolation and decided that he would be more useful in the armed struggle on the mainland.

Being a schools inspector, an important position in this colonial country, I managed to get a seat to Lisbon on a military plane. Once in Lisbon I was helped by young Portuguese captains, the kind of men who afterwards brought down the dictatorship in 1974. They got me a passport for Paris, and there I hoped to find Cabral.

Cabral turned up in Paris a few weeks later and decided to take Lineo back to Conakry, chief external base of the PAIGC. The journey went well, but might have been disastrous, for the plane flew by way of the Canary Islands, part of hostile Spain.

The Franco officials refused to let Cabral go further, no doubt they'd been tipped off by their Portuguese friends. But luckily our fellow-passengers included an ambassador of [ex French] Guinea, and Cabral was travelling on a Guinean diplomatic passport, though under a false name. Cabral persuaded this ambassador to intervene, and we went safely on to Conakry.

There it was decided that Lineo should return home.

And Cabral was right, for he needed me as a kind of 'visiting card' of local respectability, given that I stood high in our family networks here. I could undermine the horror stories put around by the Portuguese – that we were terrorists, knives-between-the-teeth communists, devourers of women and such.

But enthusiasm, back in Sant'Antão, now got the better of precaution.

This was in October 1967. An inspector of the PIDE sent from Lisbon with two others arrested me for subversion, as they said. They put me on public trial in Praia, and that was their big mistake. It gave our Party's cause a wide publicity for the first time.

But Lineo, duly sentenced, joined the others in the jail at Tarrafal.

Drought and the PIDE had now gone far to wreck the landings project. Failure to find the necessary shipping for the run from Cuba, as well as second thoughts in Havana on the wisdom of the plan itself, finally sank it. Given that the thirty volunteers included most of the Cape Verdean leadership, as well as most of the post-independence government from the Prime Minister down, this was undoubtedly a great mercy, though not so admitted at the time.

But perhaps a lesser project might still be possible, a landing of arms rather than of armed men? There were those in Praia who were sure of it. Pedro Martins and other students in the senior class of the new Praia lycée were among them. 'Late in the 1960s,' Pedro Martins explains, 'we were active in gathering support for the Party, mainly at Santa Caterina', Santiago's second town in a zone of fairly dense population. Here they found strong peasant support, and it helped that the name of Amílcar Cabral was well known, for his father Juvenal had lived here and so had Amílcar, as a schoolboy, during holidays from the Mindelo lycée. Around Santa Caterina, moreover, there lingered the ancient traditions of slave revolt, and it was a *batuque* song of Santa Caterina which had promised that:

> A day will come
> When Sancho turn all upside down . . .

Recruiting support there and elsewhere, Martins and his comrades became convinced by 1969 that 'we could take and hold Praia by an armed struggle, provided that arms were brought in and the struggle could be brief'. By now, accordingly, 'we were expecting arms from the mainland, and I myself was in contact with those through whom the arms would be landed'.

Here one may note that Portuguese fears were also rising. Official statistics show that the regime spent 19.7 billion escudos in 1967 on military purposes in Cape Verde, but 25.2 billion in 1968; and the figure was to rise annually until reaching a summit of 41.1 billion assigned to 1973. Partly there were fears of insurrection in the islands. Partly the dictatorship hoped to persuade the Powers of the North Atlantic Treaty Organization to use Cape Verde as a permanent base, and thereby strengthen Portugal's hold on its Cape Verdean 'province'.

Martins and his friends could know nothing of that intention, but what they did know was that

> the regime was becoming increasingly anxious about its security here. Meanwhile our own security against the PIDE grew weaker as our

mobilization grew stronger, and the PIDE became aware of our widening influence in the countryside.

Finally, having learned that arms were expected, the PIDE laid its trap. They fitted out an inter-island boat, the *Perola do Oceano* ostensibly for a trip to Dakar, and arranged by infiltration that this boat should be believed to be going to Dakar for a consignment of arms.

The captain of the *Perola* even got himself presented to us as a colonel in the army of the PAIGC. I saw that the whole thing must be a fake, for I knew there was no such rank in our PAIGC army in Guiné. In any case I knew about anyone of ours who came from the mainland, but I didn't know this man.

Yet in spite of Martins's warning, fourteen of their group put to sea in the *Perola* on 12 August 1970.

She simply put back to a beach near Praia and delivered the fourteen to the waiting PIDE. I'd refused to go and stayed in Praia, but I saw that I was bound to be arrested too. They came for me after seven days. Altogether they arrested thirty of us.

Incarcerated at Tarrafal and beaten for several months, the political prisoners were to stay there until 1 May 1974, another day of drama which we shall reach in due course. Yet it seems clear that their agitations had not been for nothing. Popular sympathy widened, and among the peasants of Santiago the name of Cabral appears to have acquired an almost mystical force: Cabral would come, and Cabral would give them a new life. A strong and even messianic expectation now flowed beneath the surface, awaiting the time when 'Sancho turn all upside-down' and the poor would inherit the earth.

In the city of Praia, too, 1971 brought renewed clashes between the poorest folk there, who were many, and police or troops in garrison. One of the Party's most effective young militants then in Praia was Alexandre da Pina. In 1986 he recalls a growing atmosphere of revolt as the 1970s began. Using wall graffiti and illegal pamphlets these young militants in Praia – da Pina thinks they numbered about fifty-six – campaigned against the regime's drive for Cape Verdean army recruits who would be sent, as was thought, to the colonial wars on the mainland. All this climaxed in a big demonstration of 21 September 1972, when da Pina was among those arrested. Taken to Tarrafal he was almost at once flown to Lisbon and then to the São Nicolau concentration camp in southern Angola where many politicals from the Portuguese African territories were held.

The happy events of 1974 were going to prove that these efforts had not been in vain. To the Cape Verdean leaders on the mainland, meanwhile, the outlook in the archipelago now appeared extremely bleak. With the news of continued arrests in the islands, they saw that the landings project must be abandoned. 'It became clear to us', comments Aristides Pereira who, with Cabral, stood at the centre of the PAIGC's network of information based at Conakry,

> that repression had reached a point where our movement in the islands was practically cut down to nothing. All our effective militants were now in prison. Meantime the Portuguese, and above all their military and naval commanders, were entirely determined to hang on to the islands.

But abandonment of the landings project revealed itself as an immediate blessing. The thirty volunteers, well trained in the use of small artillery, and in any case the most educationally advanced group of men in all the PAIGC, became available for the war in Guiné. Though in a mood of impatience and frustration, they were flown back across the Atlantic from Cuba. Pedro Pires acceded to command of the crucial frontier sector on the boundaries with independent Guinea. Most of the others completed their artillery training in the USSR, and returned in 1970 to take over newly-formed strike units using large mortars and the Soviet 122 mm *grad* or 'rocket'.

This development was to combine with another turning point.

III

Triumph and tragedy now moved jaggedly together. In 1972 the army of the PAIGC confirmed its tactical domination of the war on the mainland. At least half of Guiné was firmly under the protection of its fighting units, while nothing now in the power of the Portuguese governor and commanding general, António Spinola, was capable of reversing the tide of his defeat. Other large areas were removed from any sure Portuguese control. Little remained to Spínola but his fortress zone of Bissau, the city capital, and some small areas of the eastern savannah. His army, save for newly-raised 'commandos' using helicopters, was pinned down in a wide scatter of besieged garrisons. Only in the air did he retain an uncontested supremacy; and this I also saw myself.

Yet traitors could still be found, and used. At ten o'clock at night on 20 January 1973, Cabral was shot down and killed by traitors within the army organization at Conakry, the party's chief external base. The same men, having murdered Cabral, at once seized Aristides Pereira and put him on a fast launch for Bissau, distant several hours up the West African coast. Towards midnight a group of these conspirators went to the presidential palace in Conakry, some fifteen minutes by car from the office of the PAIGC, and presented themselves to President Sékou Touré, evidently expecting his approval. But Touré ordered one of his naval craft to chase the traitors' launch. They overhauled it not far from the point at which it would have entered the territorial waters of 'Portuguese Guiné'. Severely handled but rescued at the last moment, Pereira was brought back to safety.

The complexities of all this have been set forth in my book of 1981, *No Fist is Big Enough to Hide the Sky*. Briefly told, the loss of Cabral was a traumatic nightmare for those who had loved and followed him, and would in due course prove disastrous for the country that was to become Guinea-Bissau. But it made no difference to the final winning of the war of independence: rather did it hasten that victory by shaking the army of the PAIGC out of a certain routine and military stagnation. Burning anger at losing Cabral, and also a sense of shame that they should have lost him by betrayal in their own ranks, took shape in powerful new offensives. And this was the moment, too, when they at last acquired some ground-to-air missiles, portable SAM-7s, from the USSR. In March 1973 they began knocking Spínola's hitherto invulnerable air force out of the skies. Mortar units commanded by Julio de Carvalho went on to smash some of Spínola's strongest garrisons such as the one at Guileje. The end was plainly near.

In September of that same year of 1973 the People's National Assembly of Guiné (now Guinea-Bissau), elected by universal adult suffrage and secret ballot throughout the liberated zones a year earlier, met at Boé in the eastern grasslands and proclaimed the independence of the country. Its capital of Bissau and several other zones were still under Portuguese control and occupation, but some seventy-five countries up and down the world unhesitatingly recognized this new Republic, and were quickly followed by others. On 2 November an overwhelming majority of the General

Assembly of the United Nations demanded that Portugal should cease all acts of aggression in Guinea-Bissau; and on 19 November this former colony became the forty-second member-state of the Organization of African Unity.

If the loss of Cabral remained an anguish, this was also a moment of elation, and not least for the hundred or so Cape Verdean men and women who had joined their fate to that of their comrades in Guinea-Bissau, and had fought through to the end. Pedro Pires comments,

> For us, you must bear in mind that the take-off point for any independence in Cape Verde had to be the winning of the struggle in Guinea-Bissau. We knew that one Portuguese colony, at least one Portuguese colony, had to be set free in order to release the process whereby the others could be set free. We had to win in Guinea-Bissau. We had to begin the process.

The process now moved rapidly on this mainland of Africa. Formed primarily by young officers in the Portuguese army in Guiné (in Guinea-Bissau), an Armed Forces Movement carried through a *coup d'état* in Lisbon, on 25 April 1974, and overthrew the dictatorship. These young officers had behind them the bulk of the rank-and-file of the armed forces. Their spokesmen in Bissau were to say a little later that they and their colleagues 'have learned in Africa the horrors of a war without prospect, and have therefore understood the roots of the evils which afflict the society of Portugal'.

But the process was far from smooth. The Armed Forces Movement had overthrown the dictatorship and opened the floodgates to Portuguese democratic resurgence; but it had also taken General Spínola as its leader, and Spínola, as President of Portugal, was far from sharing in the general happiness. His idea was to lead the 'revolution' in Portugal back to familiar ground and retain the substance of Portuguese control of the African territories. Spínola hedged and havered, and budged in the end only because his armies had decided that the wars should terminate. They had fought long and hard, often very courageously, but they could now see no sense or gain in fighting further.

In Guinea-Bissau, by August 1974, all Portuguese garrisons began withdrawing on Bissau, as a prelude to evacuation by sea, through local agreement with the PAIGC and in despite of

Spínola's intentions. On 15 October the last of these approximately 30,000 troops quit Bissau on their transports, and the country was free, with Amílcar's younger brother, Luíz Cabral, as its first President. In this rare case of peaceful change, not a single man lost his life.

After that it was evident that Mozambique and Angola, if by a far more complex process in the case of the latter, would also accede to independence. But it remained by no means evident that the distant and much forgotten islands of Cape Verde would follow. Some of the PAIGC's best foreign friends, when their attention was drawn to this, took the view that Cape Verdean independence must now be automatic: the PAIGC should simply ask for it. But the Cape Verdean leadership in the PAIGC had no such confidence. 'We knew', recalls Aristides Pereira, who had become secretary-general of the PAIGC after the loss of Cabral, 'that the Portuguese, and above all Spínola, would do their utmost to keep the archipelago, even if they might talk of some form of federal status.'

Little of what was going forward in Guinea-Bissau was understood as yet in the outside world, and even less about what should or could happen in Cape Verde. Aristides Pereira in 1986:

> For instance, I sent a delegation to the USA to explain to members of the Congress just what was Spínola's intention, and what was our own which, of course, was non-aligned independence. They said to him: 'You want us to support you? When you're going to transform Cape Verde into a Soviet base?' But a strange thing occurred. Pires was able to convince them that no such thing was going to happen.

A dilemma had surfaced before the Portuguese recognition of an independent Guinea-Bissau in August 1974. 'Lisbon was saying then', comments Pedro Pires who led the PAIGC in all these various negotiations,

> yes to independence for Guinea-Bissau, but no to independence for Cape Verde. Yet we still had to be careful to keep the two separate. For if we insisted on independence for both at the same time, we should obstruct the whole process.

So they accepted the first without the second. But they took their precautions. Untrammelled independence for Guinea-Bissau was conceded by Lisbon at negotiations in July and August, at first in London and then in Algiers. And in this agreement of 1974 the PAIGC delegation under Pires managed to secure Portuguese consent, however reluctantly or insincerely, to the principle of Cape Verde's right to its own self-determination and independence. With this the nature of the problem changed. Now the problem was to put the principle into practice.

That was still not much. For how was the principle to be made good when all leading militants in the archipelago were under close arrest, and all the executive command outside the archipelago? How was this principle to get itself heard above the happy roar of the dictatorship's collapse, and with Cape Verde's future about the last of the world's worries?

Here it may be useful, at this distance in time, to insist upon their complete conviction that nothing but a full independence could save their forgotten islands. Theirs had long ceased to be a romantic nationalism nourished by remote aspirations or resentments: they knew that any kind of partial independence or 'regional autonomy' must fail to break through the misery and despair of decades. All their experience drove them from the thought that a compromise with Portugal, with any Portugal or its equivalent supposing one were offered, could save their people from continued disaster: only the bracing shock of independence, with its challenge to self-salvation, could hope to do that. It was the cause that they had fought for; they were not going to let it go.

Fortunately, another useful step had been taken a year earlier in July 1973, during the PAIGC's negotiations with Lisbon's emissaries in London and Algiers. The executive command of the PAIGC accepted an internal proposal, though not without argument and even dissent by some of the non-Cape Verdean leaders, which was now to make a large difference. Put forward by Abilio Duarte and backed by Aristides Pereira, this provided for the establishment of a National Council of Cape Verde. One or two in the executive demurred, saying that it was unnecessary; others held that it would act as a distraction from what was then the main issue, Portugal's recognition of the independence of Guinea-Bissau. That debate of 1973 was lively, as the minutes show, but Duarte won his case:

> And this forming of our National Council really went far to save our situation. Without it, we Cape Verdeans would have been left to start again, in the islands, practically from zero. As it was, our National Council's existence committed the whole PAIGC to continued struggle

for the islands. It reinforced our bid, a year later in 1974, to secure Portuguese agreement to the principle of our independence.

For the moment, in 1973, this National Council could be only a name and a commitment. Some of its members, like Abilio Duarte and Silvino da Luz, were on diplomatic or military missions. Others, like Julio de Carvalho and Osvaldo da Silva, were smashing into Spínola's fortified garrisons. But in April 1974, with the dictatorship overturned in Lisbon, extraordinary things began to happen. And then, with local truce in Guinea-Bissau transformed after June 1974 into local peace and Portuguese evacuation, some of the National Council could be despatched to the islands.

These included Silvino da Luz, Osvaldo da Silva and Corsino Tolentino. With Guinea-Bissauans of the PAIGC they reached Bissau with Portuguese military assistance, flying from the southern forest to the capital and there being welcomed by the territorial leaders of the Armed Forces Movement which had brought down the dictatorship. From Bissau the Cape Verdeans among them flew onward to the archipelago in one of Lisbon's civilian airliners.

The present writer, still marvelling at these turns of fortune, was able to be present with the PAIGC on that memorable scene, and to accompany the Cape Verdeans on their journey home.

6 The challenge of 1974

I

The handful of veterans returning from victory on the mainland were greeted at the airport on Sal island with rapturous welcome. I saw them walk from the plane into the arms of many supporters who had somehow managed to get here from Santiago and other islands. They were hoisted on triumphant shoulders. The day was 25 August, only four months since the fall of the dictatorship, but so much had happened since then that it might have been a lifetime.

They flew on from Sal by inter-island plane to the smaller airport of Praia, the capital city on Santiago Island. The rapturous welcome continued, but in Praia they began to catch up with reality. They had found euphoria. Now they also found confusion.

Much had happened, but much had not. As the local branch of the Portuguese Armed Forces Movement was to note in the following November, when looking back on those months since the *coup d'état* in Lisbon, 'the sole novelty in the process of decolonization [in Cape Verde] has so far been the extinction of the PIDE/DGS', DGS being the lately renamed secret police. Otherwise, Portuguese authority had remained intact and working hard, urged on by Spínola in Lisbon, to ensure continued colonial rule. Decolonization might be high on the new regime's agenda, but not for Cape Verde, considered as a 'special case' which, with Madeira and the Azores, was to stay in the category of 'adjacent islands of the Motherland'.

Yet politics had begun. For the first time in history, a political contest had been opened. Gingerly at first, PAIGC militants not in prison had surfaced after the overthrow of the dictatorship in April, and, though the PAIGC was still a banned organization, begun open agitation throughout the islands. On 1 May the political prisoners in the Tarrafal jail were released after huge

The prospects for 1975, when independence was won, were not just those of building a state and political system, neither of which then existed, but also of trying to tackle the backwardness inherited from the colonial past. Reducing a very high rate of illiteracy, especially among women, has been among those challenges. (Photo copyright Cape Verde Photos)

demonstrations of public pressure. Suddenly it was seen that the long clandestine struggle of the years before had not been fruitless, and that the cause of the PAIGC had become this people's cause.

The orthodox and respectable suffered understandable forebodings. For them, as they made clear at the time, there was the dreadful prospect of Sancho's coming down his mountain, 'horribly grimacing, tail curled up', even if, for the moment, the Portuguese army and administration were still in place and, apparently, little affected by the democratic elation of the Armed Forces Movement which had made the Lisbon *coup d'état*. Duly exhorted by Spínola's people, the orthodox and respectable now hastened to enter the contest on the side of continuity and 'safe government'. With administrative aid and stimulus, as the Lisbon records were to show in due course, they began by forming a 'movement' – in fact, a letter-head, an office and a few spokesmen – called the UDC (Democratic Union of Cape Verde). Speaking for a few dozen or so 'middle-class' persons who were lawyers, senior civil servants, and the like, they called meetings and printed leaflets, some of which have fortunately survived for inspection. Few outside their own group possessed the literacy to understand these writings, and perhaps this was as well for those who wrote them. They pitched the issue of independence and all that it might mean, now erupting irrepressibly throughout the islands, in the light of an irresponsible adventure.

The UDC's inherent absurdity was illustrated in a fairly characteristic leaflet of June in this climactic year of 1974. Handed round only weeks after great numbers of Praia people, with reinforcements from other towns and islands, had journeyed to the Tarrafal jail to insist on the release of the PAIGC prisoners, as well as other 'politicals' from Angola, Mozambique and Portugal itself, this UDC leaflet condemned the PAIGC as a tyranny. The Party of independence, it said, meant to 'prepare the basis for a Neo-Fascism copied from the odious methods of Salazar'. Coming from men who had always sheltered within the Fascism of Salazar, this kind of thing understandably failed to take. All too clearly, the UDC was a colonialist facade.

Something more effective was therefore desirable. It should be better camouflaged, and claim even to speak for Sancho himself. Already in shadow existence, this alternative was the UPICV (Union of the People of the Cape Verde Islands). The founder and spokesman of this practically memberless body was a certain

José Leitão da Graça, who stood now for a markedly Leftist programme of 'separate and sovereign independence'. But wasn't this what the PAIGC was calling for? Not at all: in letters to the General Assembly of the United Nations, da Graça explained that the policy of the Party of Cabral was not for Cape Verdean independence, 'but to annex Cape Verde to Guinea-Bissau'. PAIGC policy 'could only assist the penetration into Cape Verde,' wrote da Graça to the UN Secretary-General, 'of a Power which calls itself socialist, but is in reality as imperialist as the USA. That Power is the Soviet Union which stands behind the leadership of the PAIGC.'

This improbable line corresponded with an afflux of Leftism, often called 'Trotskyism' at the time, that was then coming in from Portugal by way of a number of Cape Verdean students from the university of Coimbra. As an attempt to undermine the Party of Cabral it added to the confusions of 1974, but evidently not much. There might be plenty of Cape Verdeans to suspect, however groundlessly, that the PAIGC was communist and therefore Soviet-inspired, and plenty who had no love for Guinea-Bissau, a 'savage land' better kept at arm's length. But PAIGC militants and the politicals from Tarrafal jail had suffered for a cause that was most plainly Cape Verdean, one which the large majority of Cape Verdeans vividly respected, even if the politics of it went beyond their experience or understanding. The PAIGC fighters from the war on the mainland, moreover, came back or were about to come back with a powerfully patriotic prestige. And then, apart from all this, the arguments adopted by da Graça and his like were a lot too 'clever'. The USSR might be the very devil to the orthodox and respectable, as to the emigrant community in New England. But none of these would possibly see the USA as an equivalent of the USSR.

Generally, da Graça's UPICV fared no better than its companion the UDC. What did much to kill each of them from the start, in any case, was that their spokesmen were given ready access to the colonial regime's broadcasting station on São Vicente, *Radio Barlavento* (owned incidentally by the 'upper-class' club called the Gremio), while the spokesmen of the PAIGC were barred from any broadcasting access. These little 'movements' against the PAIGC were manifestly in collusion with the colonial regime.

Meanwhile, amid all this claim and counterclaim, the surviving ancients of *Claridade*, the Claridosos as they were known, were in no way ready to support the militant nationalism of the PAIGC. They had spoken valiantly in the 1940s for a 'Cape Verdean consciousness' and even nationhood, but now the project of independence seemed an impossible extremism. It would be hard to hold this against them, for they were elderly and anxious as well as politically naive. Perhaps, like the venerable *Mestre* Balthazar, they could not find it in themselves to forgive their former students for knowing better. Perhaps, like the admirable Teixeira de Sousa, they had too long stood on provincial sidelines.

As late as the end of July in this year of challenge, Teixeira de Sousa put out a pamphlet entitled 'Cape Verde and Its Political Destiny'. While the PAIGC had the imminent reality of independence in its sights, de Sousa remained in the realm of fantasy. He argued that Cape Verde could not aspire to sovereignty, essentially for economic reasons; and that the archipelago, instead, could achieve an internal self-determination by free association with Portugal. But this would be 'a solution of last resource'. The 'ideal solution for us' would be an 'independence protected and financed by the United Nations, so as to be neutral in relation to the Atlantic ambitions of the super-Powers'.

The Cape Verdeans, on this view, were helpless to protect themselves. Nor should they think of 'unification with Guinea-Bissau', since there could be 'no advantage for us or for the Guineans'. The whole history of liberation had simply passed by this otherwise thoughtful Cape Verdean intellectual. That Cabral and the PAIGC had already won independence for Guinea-Bissau was already clear and known. That this independence was then proving itself the indispensable condition for Cape Verdean independence – of any kind – was very obvious. But salvation, for these Claridosos, must still come from Europe or from the United Nations, or else there could be none. When it reached them from Africa, they could neither accept nor believe it.

Yet PAIGC militants were finding that the peasants in their majority had no such hang-up. It seems clear that the peasants had absorbed Cabral into their own traditions; and the PAIGC for them was Cabral. This absorption had evidently gone quite far by the middle of 1974. A photo of that time, for example, shows a church interior with the Pope's head and features painted on one wall and Cabral's on another. The peasants listened to the men and women of the PAIGC, and wondered what was going to be done for peasant needs.

Many situations in nationalist Africa had revealed and would continue to reveal this ambiguity. The rural majorities ardently wanted radical change, but repeatedly proved unable to produce the necessary leadership. An academic view has therefore argued that no State power can be constructed, in African practice, which can realize 'the programme of the peasantry'. If the rural majorities do in fact receive benefits, they will not be the makers thereof. The nationalist leadership produced by the 'petty-bourgeois' strata will be the makers, or, as may be much more likely to prove the case, the non-makers of peasant advancement.

Here in Cape Verde the PAIGC leadership, often 'petty-bourgeois' in its origins, remained well aware of this prognostic on their fate, and Cabral himself had long before examined its perils. Their answer to those perils, as they firmly believed, had proved its worth. It lay in the practice of mass participation, rural participation, which they had installed within the liberated zones of wartime Guinea-Bissau. There were and could be no such zones in colonial Cape Verde, but the same answer could still be made valid. The drama would lie in the ways in which that answer *was* made good. Meanwhile, somehow or other, independence had to be wrested from an unwilling or unheeding Portugal.

II

What was being argued in the islands was that independence need no longer appear as an unthinkable or even distant destination. The extraordinary overturn of the dictatorship on 25 April seemed to legitimate hopes that had barely dared to say their name in public. Here was a people which, however confusedly, now began to perceive a different future.

On 1 May, six days after Lisbon's 'revolution of the carnations', the 'politicals' were released from the jail at Tarrafal. Some of them, from Angola and Portugal, had been rotting there for years; none had expected merciful release. As it was, they were thrust out into the arms of a jubilant multitude. Great numbers of people now managed to get to Tarrafal from Praia, about 80 kilometres away at the other end of Santiago Island, and crowded at the gates.

'Thousands came,' recalls the Cape Verdean writer Oswaldo

Osório, one of the 'surfaced militants' who succeeded in organizing this mass demand for freedom. 'Truly a multitude – by cars, trucks, on bicycles, any way they could.'

Arriving down the cliffside road, on that first of May, the leading trucks were halted by soldiers under arms.

Oswaldo Osório:

But we had telegraphed to Lisbon, to the Ministry of Justice, and we'd received an answer. This was a telegram. It said that the prisoners were to be let out. So we passed in that telegram, and the prison governor, a Cape Verdean, acted on it.

The 'politicals' came out one by one and then in little clusters, utterly astonished, some of them crying for the joy of it; and the multitude cheered them and embraced them and carried them to Praia.

From Praia the Cape Verdean 'politicals' spread about their islands, while the Angolans and other non-Cape Verdeans awaited transport home. With this release, the movement for independence gathered speed.

Yet nearly four months would have to pass before the veterans from the war in Guinea-Bissau were able to get here. Meanwhile much could be attempted, but it would have to be attempted with tact and discretion, even if the general mood of vivid expectation allowed for neither. To see why this was so one can usefully turn to the Portuguese side of the picture.

Though official Portuguese archives are largely unavailable, much evidence survives from documents of the Armed Forces Movement (AFM) which overthrew the dictatorship. I am especially grateful to General Vasco Gonçalves, Prime Minister of Portugal after July 1974, for a valuable memoir written to assist this narrative. A man of austere and courageously patriotic principles, General Gonçalves was at the centre of events in Lisbon. He points out that

the process of decolonization in the minds of the Armed Forces Movement was neither a linear development nor a smooth one. On the contrary, it was the target after 25 April [the day of the young officers' coup in Lisbon] of an acute conflict between two basic political lines.

One of these was the libertarian, anti-neocolonialist and anti-imperialist trend of the progressive sectors of the AFM. The other trend was neocolonialist, representing Rightist sectors of the AFM and most of the officers and sergeants, with their leader being the President of the Republic, General Spínola.

This sharp dichotomy within the AFM was natural to the situation, but also painful. For while

> the struggle of the liberation movements in the Portuguese colonies [PAIGC, MPLA, FRELIMO] had decisively influenced the rise of the Armed Forces Movement, and contributed much to the advancement of ideas of political justice among young Portuguese officers, notably the captains, on the need to end the fascist-colonialist dictatorship and the colonial wars, thus giving way to the rights of the colonized to self-determination and independence,

none of this could be easy. 'On the contrary, in many cases it was painful and imposed by the very conditions we were in.'

General Gonçalves is too modest to say it himself, but history will judge that the progressive sectors of the AFM deserve great admiration. They worked for a Portuguese salvation that was extremely difficult for most Portuguese to accept. The whole political culture of official Portugal stood against them, while none of Portugal's Western partners, least of all Washington and London, showed them anything but discouragement. Against them, moreover, they had an agile as well as arrogant opponent in the man whom the AFM had chosen as leader and made President of Portugal, General António Spínola, as well as a majority of the officers in the AFM itself. This majority changed sides, as it were, only late in 1974. Even then the progressive trends still had much against them, and Spínola's aggressively Right-wing influence continued to obstruct them until the failed Spínolist *coup d'état* of 11 May 1975.

AFM documents amply trace the same division within the armed forces in Cape Verde where, apart from this, no armed struggle for independence had been able to teach its lessons as these had been taught on the mainland. While the local Cape Verdean AFM 'was formed after 25 April by young officers, patriots and progressives, with the aim of promoting the AFM programme of democratization and decolonization', its statutes could be approved only in the following November after, among other things, the removal of Spínola from supreme executive authority. In these months the progressives in the Cape Verdean AFM set about launching political initiatives of one kind or another, and gradually won over the Cape Verdean garrisons, at least in their majority, to the aims of democratization and decolonization; and there was created a situation – the words are again those of General Gonçalves – 'a situation very helpful to the action of the Cape Verdean PAIGC and its corresponding work of politicizing and mobilizing the people there.'

But Spínola and his people were likewise energetic in those months, as they would continue to be even after Spínola's fall from power at the end of September. A newly formed association of officers of the army in Cape Verde sent a warning note to the AFM on 25 September that clashes with the population, provoked by reactionary trends, had occurred and might reoccur. A plenary session of the same association, held at naval headquarters on São Vicente Island on 11 October, spelt out the same warning in a long and detailed motion; declared that relations between the armed forces and the people were continuing to deteriorate; repeated that 'the PAIGC, without any margin of doubt, is the only party which mobilizes the masses'; and called for an 'urgent and concrete programme of decolonization, and, parallel with this, the urgent constitution of organs of [Cape Verdean] sovereignty'. Another motion, this time of the officers of the AFM on São Vicente meeting on 1 November in plenâry session, denounced the Spínolist Governor of Cape Verde (Sergio Fonseca, as we shall see) as lacking moral authority, and called for his replacement.

These matters belong properly to a history of the Armed Forces Movement but may be useful here as revealing the difficult and uncertain situation faced by the nationalists during these months. They had much to contend with. As late as 7 November, for example, a lengthy analysis by five officers of the AFM is found deploring the official backing given to 'opportunists and false democrats' who were being encouraged – specifically, the analysis refers to the UDC and UPICV groups – to 'develop their divisive activities and lies' in such a way that the armed forces could seem responsible for what might become a new era of colonial domination'. Against these intrigues and manoeuvres the AFM could 'see no other solution than recognition of the PAIGC as the legitimate representative of the Cape Verdean population'. Only the PAIGC, this analysis concluded, was capable of carrying through a genuine decolonization.

This was proved to be the case after Spínola's fall at the end of September, at which we will arrive in a moment. Here it may be well to emphasize that the whole process of Portuguese withdrawal, whether on the mainland or in the islands, passed through two phases: *before* the removal of Spínola at the end of September 1974 (by which time peace was achieved only in Guinea-Bissau), and *after* that removal. Neither phase proved simple for the Cape Verdean PAIGC, but the first was far more hazardous than the second.

So it had to come about that the Cape Verdean 'politicals', emerging from Tarrafal on 1 May, found much to worry and bewilder them. All established authority was against them, while the progressive wing of the Cape Verdean AFM was still weak. Their party remained illegal. They themselves were by no means guaranteed their freedom. How best to act in the unavoidable absence of their veteran leaders?

Answers were found. All the history of large political upheavals seems to show that people learn fast at such times. And for these harassed militants of the PAIGC the means of learning could be drawn from many sources: from what was known of their prestigious and successful leadership in the liberation war on the mainland, from their activists in the islands as well as in the little towns of the mainland such as Bissau and Bolama, and from others in Portugal. One could say – as of a number of countries in Europe under Nazi occupation during the Second World War – that a *culture of resistance* had come into being; and this proved powerfully instructive.

In the archipelago, at this point, the lead was taken by activists in the capital of Praia. Distrusting Spínola's intentions, facing an AFM still in Spínolist hands, these activists looked sensibly for a political cover which could somewhat shield their party if bad times returned but which, meanwhile, could act as a kind of umbrella for PAIGC agitation and mobilization. They formed what was called a *frente amplo de resistência nacional*, 'a broad front of national resistance'. And just how tricky the situation remained was seen in Praia on 19 May, when exasperated troops shot into a demonstration called by this *frente amplo*, killing one man and wounding others.

The same political device spread to São Vicente, where a *frente amplo* was declared in Mindelo on 6 May and at once proved useful. One of those who formed it, Jorge Alberto Brito, recalls that 'only a day after we formed it an officer of the local AFM got into touch with us. Through him we met other Portuguese officers who were sympathetic, although they were still in a minority in the Cape Verdean AFM as a whole.' Even so it remained far from sure which way things would go, and the local PIDE had still not been sent back to Portugal.

The activists thus organized were sparse in number, some sixteen in Mindelo and perhaps twice as many in Praia, but they could count on an ebullient mass support. Addressing this, their immediate target was Lisbon's cherished plan for a referendum in the archipelago. Cape Verdeans would be asked to declare for a form of federal status with Portugal, and thus for continued acceptance of Portuguese citizenship. For the PAIGC, however, this meant acceptance of some form of 'neo-colonial' status by which Lisbon's indirect control would be assured; and, successfully, they rejected the proposed referendum as a trap. A cyclostyled leaflet of this phase, put out by the Praia *frente amplo*, denounced this project of referendum as

> false democracy which asks our people to say if they want to be Portuguese or not: as if our people had not learned in their sufferings that being 'overseas Portuguese' means exploitation, contempt, racism . . . . What cynical hypocrisy to ask our people, buried in hundreds in the mass graves of 1947, paid 30 escudos a month with whips and kicks in São Tomé, daily humiliated in this country, if it wants to continue under the boot of colonialism! Do they really think they can fool our people?

Therefore *No* to any referendum, and *Yes* to 'immediate and total independence'.

Confidence grew as the weeks of May went by. On 6 June, 'the living, authentic and representative political forces of São Vicente' – another label for the *frente amplo* – 'met in assembly at the Eden Park cinema of Mindelo', and approved a motion that was cabled to the Portuguese President Spínola in Lisbon, demanding independence and asserting the PAIGC as 'the sole legitimate representative of Cape Verde'.

The pace quickened. On 3 July Cape Verdean recruits called to the Portuguese colours refused to take the oath, declaring that 'from now on our flag is the flag of the PAIGC'; and the example was followed by Cape Verdeans already in the army's ranks. In August the first veterans from the mainland war came triumphantly home, as we have seen, and hopes began to run high. Then on 14 September came the news that Portugal had recognized the untrammelled independence of Guinea-Bissau; and a delegation of Cape Verdean militants at once set off for Boé, in eastern Guinea-Bissau, where Aristides Pereira and the now functioning Cape Verdean National Council were in session on the mainland.

The latter had lost no time in sending arms secretly to the archipelago, by shipping from the coast of Mauretania in agreement with the government of that country, and then storing these arms at *caches* in various islands. But a peaceful outcome now seemed possible. Briefly in Lisbon to visit the AFM, on the occasion of Lisbon's recognition of the independence of Guinea-Bissau, Pedro Pires and several colleagues reached the conclusion that

> while there were many hesitations on the Portuguese side – Spínola, after all, was still the President of Portugal – we could achieve cordial relations with at least part of the AFM.

Pedro Pires in 1986:

> There was mutual respect between us, and, besides, the Portuguese needed an honourable outcome from a humiliating situation. For our part we had no wish or need to trumpet the victory we had won in Guinea-Bissau. On the contrary, we wanted to find a solution good for us but also good for democratic trends in Portugal.

Pires accordingly told the PAIGC delegates from Cape Verde that they must call off aggressive attitudes towards the Portuguese, and 'seek the road of good will. For we must avoid war, we must negotiate our way to independence. A political outcome is essential.'

With this in mind, it was decided that Pires should go to Cape Verde and argue the case for all possible unity behind a peaceful route to a full independence. Alerted to this, Spínola in Lisbon ordered that Pires' flight from Bissau to Sal should be prevented. Spínola was strong enough, still, to make this order stick but then, almost at once, progressive trends within the AFM in Portugal got the upper hand. At the end of September they thrust Spínola from power. In doing so, they changed the prospects.

III

Spínola appears to have been the only general of the Salazarist dictatorship with the wit to perceive, even if too late in the day, that what was being lost on the field of battle in the African colonies might yet be saved by political manoeuvre. After the April coup of 1974 and his accession to the presidency of Portugal, he counted on drawing the liberation movements into an unconditional ceasefire. This should be the means of entrapping them within the bounds of a territorial autonomy which should leave Lisbon in supreme control. But the liberation movements would have none of it. Spínola was left with the ground slipping from beneath him.

By early September, however, he evidently thought that he might be able to recover this ground in the case of Angola. To that end – and the case of Angola was far from simple – he needed to ensure the continued hostility of the dictator of Zaire, Mobutu Ssese-Seko, to the MPLA, Angola's liberation movement. He accordingly arranged with Mobutu that they meet privately on the island of Sal. This was now the only major airport left to Spínola in West Africa, because the newly-independent government of Guinea-Bissau, where there was another major airport, had just refused him permission to land. As for Cape Verde's future, Spínola appears to have taken it for granted that the islands would remain Portuguese.

In Praia, meanwhile, the now strongly reinforced PAIGC leadership got wind of Spínola's intention to land on Sal, and decided to make use of this for their own purposes. Silvino da Luz:

> By now we had sound information on whatever was going forward in the top administration here. Learning of Spínola's forthcoming conference with Mobutu on Sal, we got ready to stage a mass demonstration there. We hired such small aircraft as we could, as well as boats, and managed to convey a host of people to Sal. I myself went there secretly.

And so it came about that when Spínola disembarked from his Lisbon plane on 14 September he was confronted by several hundred people waving banners, calling for Cape Verdean independence, and so on. 'There was nothing he could do to stop us.' Mobutu arrived from Zaire shortly after to the same reception. Silvino continues:

> We knew they were going to have their talk at the *pousada* at Santa Maria [then the only and modest hostel on this desert island, though nowadays there are two comfortable hotels] and the night before we'd painted independence slogans on the tarmac road to the *pousada*, you couldn't but see them. We'd hired trucks for our people to follow to the *pousada*. They went there and we sent in messages.

Spínola wouldn't receive anything, and ordered an officer to tell us to disperse within twenty minutes or the troops would open fire. But we stood our ground, and I sent in letters by two of our people, a civilian man and a crippled young woman – for I thought they'd scarcely shoot at a cripple – and this time our messages were delivered.

One letter was to Spínola, the other to Mobutu. Happily they survive in the archives, for they have an historical interest in portraying the diplomacy of the PAIGC at this critical moment.

The President of Portugal was told

The people of Cape Verde, like their brother Africans of Guinea-Bissau, Angola, Mozambique, and São Tomé/Principe, have for centuries suffered humiliating and obscurantist domination by Portuguese colonialism . . . and have proved by their struggles under the lead of the PAIGC that they are firmly determined to be free and independent.

Not only was the programme of the Armed Forces Movement one of decolonization, but 'Portugal has already recognized the right of the Cape Verdeans to self-determination and to independence': a reference to the London/Algiers agreements of the previous July and August. This being so, 'all idea of a referendum on the future of Cape Verde must be abandoned . . . [and] a People's National Assembly must be elected within an acceptable limit of time . . . so that our people may become the masters of their own destiny'.

The letter to Mobutu was in French, and 'signed by the people of the island of Sal'. It appealed to their 'dear brother' of Zaire that he should support them, and in words which must have brought a smile to that potentate's otherwise no doubt puzzled face, went on to 'wish you, Elder Brother, a long life in the service of Africa; and with your help we shall celebrate the anthem of our freedom'. Mobutu must have savoured the moment. Here he was on a supposedly desert island, bidden to meet the military leader of Portugal, only to find himself engulfed in the kind of demonstration that he had silenced in Zaire and that could least please his brother president of Portugal, a personage of well-known European presumption.

Silvino da Luz: 'The letters delivered, I told our people to disperse and disappear, just in case Spínola or some of his people should decide upon reprisals.' But Spínola refrained from shooting into the crowd or attempting arrests: the time, it seems, was too late for either. Instead he fell upon his hapless governor of Cape Verde, the Portuguese Admiral Silva Horta, sacked him on the spot and ordered him to Lisbon in the same plane as himself, claiming that Horta was an incompetent who had misled him on the Cape Verdean situation and, to boot, a coward. A firmer hand was needed.

In place of Horta, there came at once a new governor of tried colonial quality, the Cape Verdean Serge Fonseca. He arrived with orders to apply the strong hand, and forthwith did so. Pedro Pires was to be stopped from reaching Cape Verde. Others, already in Cape Verde, were to be arrested.

Silvino da Luz learned of this from a senior customs officer who asked to see him.

This officer told me he was against us, but all the same he was a good Cape Verdean. These, he said, were the orders given to the new governor. So I and others took our revolvers and went into hiding in Santa Caterina. But within a fortnight Spínola was out of office.

Effectively, Spínola fell on 28 September but put in his formal resignation two days later. This followed an attempt to stage a Spínolist coup within the Armed Forces leadership that should hamstring the progressive officers. On 28 September, according to the British press a little later, it became evident in Lisbon during the afternoon that

an attempted Right-wing coup, under cover of a peaceful demonstration, had been thwarted and prisoners had been taken. . . . This demonstration had been planned by the 'Liberal Party' supposedly on behalf of the 'silent majority', and was to have been a rally of Right-wingers in honour of Spínola. . . . Approval was given for the mass meeting but following protests from the Left it was cancelled. The prohibition did not deter extreme Right-wing elements from endeavouring to enter Lisbon.

But the Left was now in the ascendant, no matter what might happen later. The British press report continued,

First-hand information coming from the barricades [in streets entering the centre of Lisbon] told of carloads of insurgents trapped and captured with their weapons and the greatest prize of all: Barbieri Cardoso, formerly Number 2 in the hated PIDE/DGS organization, caught in the dragnet after being at liberty since the April 25 coup [which had brought down the dictatorship].

With Spínola ousted, Pedro Pires was able to come at once to Cape Verde and then Aristides Pereira with others in the leadership. The process of negotiating the country's independence could begin. This was assisted by the local Armed Forces Movement (AFM), now of the view in its own words of 7 November that 'we see no other solution than the recognition of the PAIGC as the legitimate representative of the population of Cape Verde, and capable of taking those measures necessary to a true decolonization . . .'

I am quoting here from an internal AFM statement, of early November 1974, which has also survived. It goes on to explain why the local AFM had reached this conclusion.

> The mass mobilization launched by the PAIGC since 25 April is truly impressive: its meetings and demonstrations culminated, between 27 and 30 September, in a paralysing strike which seriously hit the administrative services and cut the islands from each other.

The strike had been a notable success, exceeding even what had been expected. 'This demonstration of the control of political power cannot be ignored by anyone, no matter whom, and proves the powerful implantation of the PAIGC . . .' The AFM, the statement ended, must accordingly co-operate 'in the effort to obtain a political solution'. It was the conclusion for which Pires in the name of the PAIGC had tirelessly preached in Cape Verde since his arrival on 13 October.

At this juncture, looking for a wider support, Pires went on a tour of African leaders. 'Among others I went to see President Siad Barre of Somalia, then chairman of the Organization of African Unity. I found him an altogether admirable man, and very understanding of our needs . . .' Then with Spínola again defeated in another coup attempt of November, the way was clear. Together with the unflinching Vasco Gonçalves, now Portugal's Prime Minister, and the progressive members of the AFM in Lisbon, the Cape Verdean leadership was able to move from one planned stage of negotiation to the next.

A less mature leadership might have gone for immediate Portuguese evacuation. 'But our aim, then or later', Pedro Pires comments, 'was to keep solidarity with democrats in Portugal, and give away no ground for possible action by *revanchists* in Lisbon.' So Pires, for the Cape Verdean PAIGC, proposed a six-months' government of transition, with each side having three ministers of its respective choice. This government would prepare for a general election to be supervised by the Portuguese as well as by the PAIGC, thereby killing any possible claim, by spokesmen of the UDC or UPICV who were still vocal in Praia and Mindelo, that an electoral victory for the PAIGC would be faked.

Six months after final agreement on 19 December 1974, a general election at the end of June 1975 gave the PAIGC an overwhelming landslide. Of votes cast by 85 per cent of the entire adult population, female and male, 92 per cent were given to candidates of the PAIGC. The resultant National Assembly, with Abilio Duarte in the chair, proclaimed the independence of Cape Verde on 5 July 1975. On the same day Aristides Pereira told a mass meeting in Praia that they were entering 'a new time, a time of freedom and dignity for our people'.

A day later, to another mass meeting in Praia, the Prime Minister of Portugal, General Vasco Gonçalves, spoke in the name of the Republic of Portugal. 'And above all in the name of the people of Portugal, I say to you from the bottom of our hearts: Long live the independence of Cape Verde!'

It was a moment to remember those Portuguese who had courageously led the way out of the dictatorship, and accepted that democracy without decolonization could be no democracy worth having. They had not done it easily. They had done it by throwing off the mental habits of their childhood and overcoming the fury of their opponents at home, the ridicule of their elders and the malice of a whole world of yesterday. When Vasco Gonçalves spoke in Cape Verde he found an audience who loved him for what he said, and who rejoiced to find in Portugal a people that wished to be friends and not masters.

These were dramatic moments. They were felt as such. Nothing symbolized this better, perhaps, than the moment in Praia when a boisterous crowd burst into government offices and pitched the files they found there into the street: great quantities of official paper, at least two centuries of colonial dictatorship, stacks of correspondence dating from the 1960s, and much else besides. They threw it all into the street, for how better signal and proclaim the end of all that?

But the last word on the months before independence may perhaps be left with men and women who had struggled for so long inside the islands. Right through 1974, after the April coup in Lisbon, the official broadcasting station *Radio Barlavento* had transmitted the propaganda of the little groupings called UDC and UPICV: of those whom the officers of the local Armed Forces

Movement of Portugal denounced, in November, as 'betrayers of the Cape Verdean people'. With the cause of the PAIGC sweeping the islands, this anti-PAIGC propaganda gave bitter offence. At last, on 9 December, Silvino da Luz sent out the leadership's order to militants in Mindelo, where the station was situated, to seize and use the station for patriotic purposes.

Jorge Alberto Brito:

For months our people were clamouring against the station, but we'd been told to wait till the time was ripe. So we were ready when the order came.

People were called to assemble quietly,

and at 20.00 hours we went in. They were about to broadcast the news, heavily anti-PAIGC and pro-UDCV. We came in with our own cassettes and seized the microphones. Luis Fonseca arrived at once and took control.

Luis Fonseca:

We read out declarations – the Rights of Man, the Geneva Convention – and we played revolutionary music we'd recorded weeks earlier. Then we went to the Portuguese military command and told them what we had done. People at once dispersed, but we made sure we didn't lose the station. Dozens of local people, hundreds even, kept watch on it for us through many weeks.

It was to be Sancho's last fearsome 'flailing of his tail'. Nobody got hurt, as it happened, but the spectacle was alarming to the orthodox and respectable. A dozen venerable gentlemen of Mindelo, whose names it will be kinder to forget, felt it wise to cable the government in Lisbon with an appeal for troops to control the mob and rescue civilization. But other and altogether different saviours were on the scene.

Part Four

Continuing Cabral

The people aren't fighting for ideas, for the things in anyone's head. They're fighting to win material benefits, to live better and in peace, to see their lives go forward and guard the future of their children.

Amílcar Cabral in 1965

7 From the bare ground

I

Much should be said in praise of the democrats of Portugal who overthrew the dictatorship and accepted with relief the end of Lusitanian empire. But what was left in the African territories when that end came was little better than a wasteland, and nowhere was this legacy more painful than here in Cape Verde. Of all the newly independent countries, this was the most fragile and enfeebled: resourceless, cashless, deprived of everything from any useful goods for sale abroad to the merest structures of a state.

Worse still, by 1974 this was a country of despair. One who speaks of this with the authority of long and harsh experience was now the President of the new Republic. Aristides Pereira had come through all these years of struggle, and seen beside him so many lost and so much destroyed by a ruthless enemy or by the sheer attrition of the Salazarist system, and yet retained his stern optimism and unbending modesty of style. If this people has been singularly fortunate in the genius and character of Cabral, it can thank its stars for then being able to rely upon the courage and shrewd judgement of Pereira. For those who have known them well, it is impossible to think of the one man without thinking of the other. The poorest country, it seems, can produce the best of human beings.

Pereira looks back in 1986 on the legacy to which he and his comrades returned.

> Our islands were sunk in hopelessness. Severe drought had continued without a break for six years, and it still continued. Emigration once again was the only escape. There was almost no work for wages save as charity handouts for labour on roads or the like, mere pittances, often denied to many.

Through all the events and dangers of the quarter of a century

Building 'from the bare ground' in 1975 wasn't just a turn of phrase. This was a country with almost no public facilities. Photographed in 1983, these people are giving their unpaid labour to the construction of one of the new *polivalenti*, multi-purpose social centres, which are designed to house various organizations of 'people's participation' by means of which Cape Verdeans are beginning to exercise 'democracy at the base'. (Photo copyright Augusta Conchiglia)

that I have known him, he has not been given to exaggerate. He is not exaggerating now. All the archival materials, for their part, bear him out. Exports in 1975 were practically nil; exports in 1976 could cover less than 6 per cent of the value of imports, and 55 per cent of those imports were food without which famine was a certainty. In September 1974 the last reserves of administrative cash had vanished.

This was a dying society. 'By 1974, on the brink of the independence we had won, our people had lost the belief that their country could be of use to them. We came back to a society which had simply fallen apart. We came back to disaster.' The old records show that emigration had been usually conceived as a more or less temporary exile, even though many stayed with the life they found abroad. But emigration now was seen increasingly, even overwhelmingly, as an escape from which there would be no return.

Cape Verde being independent, factual research soon became possible. It has repeatedly confirmed Pereira's recollection. Olivier Le Brun, for example, found that dominant trends threatened 'a veritable collapse of rural communities that compose nearly two-thirds of the population'. Abandoning a countryside where antique rules of tenure allowed cultivation only at swingeing rates of rent or share-cropping, peasants were crowding into the few urban centres. A census of 1980 showed nearly 90 per cent of all Cape Verdeans living in four islands, but almost half the total in Santiago, where Praia city was expanding far beyond its means of self-support.

Movement to the cities also had to be movement to emigrate. From copious evidence, Le Brun found that 'a great proportion of the young intend to emigrate, probably a majority'. Already in these years immediately after independence, more than half of all emigrants were between the ages of fifteen and twenty-nine. Almost half the young men in this age-group on Santiago and São Nicolau had gone by the early 1980s, and more than a third of the young women, most of the latter for work as domestics in Italy. 'And this route opened by the Church is now self-perpetuating: young women who have gone to Italy obtain the necessary papers, work-permits above all, for their friends who want to join them.'

A galloping birth-rate seems always in the past to have been an instinctive response to periods of famine and disease. Now in the unbroken drought of the 1970s 'natural growth' appears to have risen from a guessed 1.8 per cent in 1970 towards 3 per cent in 1980; and the growth after 1975 was tending more steeply upward because of a falling death-rate thanks to health services and more food. Yet the 1980 census still showed that three islands – Brava, Sant'Antão and São Nicolau – had smaller populations than ten years earlier.

To grasp the despair that lay behind this emigration may call for an effort of the imagination about the life that many emigrants could expect. Writing of the young women who have gone away to domestic service in Italy and Portugal and Spain, Le Brun notes that a few could gain good situations and a chance to learn about the world, even though the onset of European recession was closing in on jobs abroad for young women as well as men. But most of these young women

> remain shut away for years, thousands of kilometres from home, within a narrow universe and an individual work-process which is particularly alienating. The photos they send back, showing them with the families they must serve, are eloquent witness of the kind of dependence they undergo.

He calls it 'flunkey-ization', and the word seems not too strong. They had fled from despair, but despair must all too often have stayed with them.

Hope was lit by the coming of independence with its grand feeling that life might after all be capable of becoming better; but fuel to keep the hope burning was hard to find. Olivio Pires, aged 31 in 1974, was among the veterans who returned from the victory on the mainland. 'Certainly,' he recalls,

> there was a dynamic of political development in train, an existing PAIGC in Santiago and to some extent in São Vicente and Sant'Antão. And this dynamic spurred an upsurge of support for us, enlarging our Party from a few dozens to hundreds and later to thousands.
>
> That was very positive. But still you have to see that we were a very youthful party, young in years but younger still in political experience. And apart from the little that we ourselves had set going here in terms of organization, we found a void, a complete political void. We found no structures of political action or experience outside our own initiatives: none at all. As for the economic position, that was catastrophic. Effectively, there existed no national economy.

They had the crucial and decisive advantage of a real political and moral independence. Without that, there could be no prospect of change, no hope of relieving despair, no chance of bringing these islands to life again. But with independence it still remained that everything from daily subsistence to any form of statehood would have to be built from the bare ground.

II

After independence at mid-1975 the first three years were given to surviving as well as possible while clearing space, mentally and otherwise, for this building from the bare ground. The second would be difficult, but the first was still more so. With no rain, the maize and bean harvests of 1975 and 1976 were negligible; those of 1977 were nil.

Help was found. It came generously from a wide range of countries, just as it also went to Guinea-Bissau, for the struggle of the PAIGC and Cabral himself had become known and admired since the mid-1960s. UN officials arrived even before independence, and recorded the seriousness and realism of the prospective Republic's leaders. In October 1975 the World Food Programme financed the despatch of 19,000 tons of maize and other foodstuffs. Relieved to find that the new regime meant what it had said about non-alignment, and that no Soviet base was in question, the US administration came up with an initial gift of $7 million. Sweden, Holland and some other middle-rank countries gave with an open hand, while aid also came from the USSR.

And so they survived, a little by way of miracle as it seemed at the time and a good deal by way of foresight. The latter induced various decisions not always understood by donors at the outset. The World Food Programme had taken it for granted that its officials would not only bring in food but also supervise distribution; this, after all, was what its statutes ordered. Pereira and his colleagues rejected this. They were grateful for the food, but the World Food Programme's intention to distribute smacked unacceptably of the Portuguese system of *apoio*, by which food had been handed round as charity. Insisting that they do the distribution themselves, the Cape Verdean government set up a wages fund and sold the food to 30,000 otherwise jobless workers in exchange for wage-paid construction work on water-retention and anti-erosion dykes and barrages. With intensive planting of trees after 1977, the cumulative results were to become impressive.

UN personnel could report in July 1978 that development aid, whether in finance or other means, would enable the government's public investment for that year to reach $36,900,000, 'which is twice that of 1977 and about three times the amount spent in 1976'. At this point, moreover, rural hamlets and homesteads began to show signs of regaining a little confidence in the future. Sancho had not turned out a monstrous 'communist devil' after all; no women were being devoured, no homes laid waste, no churches burned or ravaged. On the contrary, Sancho had been useful and then gone back up his mountain. There might be more to life, it seemed, than waiting to depart. The countryside began to come alive again, and 7000 Cape Verdeans actually returned from Angola.

If the legacy was 'bare ground', this could also be turned to advantage. Here there were none of the internal rivalries and conflicts which history elsewhere in Africa had implanted through ethnic multiplicity, and which colonial rule had deepened by its administrative promotion of the rigidities of 'tribalism'. Cape Verdean patriotism might still be largely the sum of various 'island patriotisms', but this was no real obstacle to creating a national unity. The ocean might surround them, but this was no confinement imposed by human agency. The colonial partition had driven no frontiers through the Cape Verdean people, nor crippled any pre-colonial trading zone.

Non-alignment between the world's power-blocs could bring other advantages. This had always been Cabral's conviction, and the conviction was maintained: no other course would allow an open choice of social system or give reality to independence. But as recently as 1974 there had been fears that Portugal meant to reinforce its hold on Cape Verde by implanting there a base for the naval forces of the North Atlantic Treaty Alliance. The archives have yet to reveal how far these fears were justified. They seemed dangerously so at the time. In June 1974, with Spínola still the powerful President of Portugal, an assembly of PAIGC militants in São Vicente had been moved to send a telegram to Spínola, then at a meeting with President Richard Nixon in the Azores, 'affirming our opposition to any kind of military base for NATO in the Islands of Cape Verde, having in view the possibility of agreements to that end between you and President

Nixon'. And they had followed this with a corresponding telegram to the NATO Secretary-General.

Happily for the PAIGC, no such base materialized. The independent government was further delighted to find that the Portuguese had installed valuable equipment, chiefly at an observatory on the highest peak of Santiago, for purposes of weather reconnaissance in the mid-Atlantic region and for communications by satellite. This would shortly enable the independent government to play its part in Atlantic weather reconnaissance, and benefit from satellite telephony. The visitor a few years later was astonished to find that he could dial his home in England from, for example, Lineo Miranda's sitting-room in the canyons of Sant'Antão.

Useful agreements could soon be made with a friendly Portugal, notably in the spheres of trade and aid; while democratic Portuguese, for their part, were comforted to know that in place of a despised and hostile servant their country had gained a respected friend. The much-loved Portuguese writer José Saramago put this sentiment memorably well after a visit in 1986. The old Discoverers of the fifteenth century, he wrote, had discovered a handful of abandoned islands: 'but in those islands I have discovered a world'.

Beyond all this, there was no problem of being left with social or economic structures which many other Africans, by this time, were deploring as 'neo-colonial'. The little 'bourgeois' groupings known as UDC and UPICV had vanished from the scene, leaving no focus of loyalty except the PAIGC. So the 'bare ground' possessed a clear value, provided always that the liberators knew what to build and how to build it. But these were prepared precisely in this respect. They brought with them the political lessons of their struggle on the mainland. Their programme of political construction was tried and clear, and it had a name. They called it *participação popular*, 'mass participation', and were convinced that its realization must be the central test of their success.

In Cape Verde, as on the mainland in Guinea-Bissau, an effective mass participation was conceived as 'the key element in the construction of our State'; while in Guinea-Bissau 'it had not been necessary to await independence before beginning to transfer, into the hands of the people, the instruments of their self-determination'. Onwards from 1964, the establishment in Guinea-Bissau of the first liberated regions made possible, in practice, the teaching of the philosophy of power which the founders of the Party, Amílcar Cabral above all, defined for the two countries during the struggle for emancipation.

This philosophy had taken shape in liberated zones that were regarded as laboratories of political experiment in the practice of grass-roots democracy. Any real progress, it was argued, must turn on the launching and enlargement of participation – mental, moral and therefore political – by which communities and individuals within these communities would take a real control over their lives.

Only those who thereby free themselves, it was held, can achieve a consciousness of freedom; but only those who win a consciousness of freedom have understood that freedom is also a struggle against oneself, against one's own failings, as much as against the enemy who denies freedom. Liberation on this view had to mean an active and personal commitment to a process – perhaps above all, in Cabral's concept, a cultural process – for the advancement of which a mere sympathy or 'support' could never be enough. With whatever shortcomings, this commitment which Cabral asked of those who followed him was the central project of his discourse, the measure of his originality.

On the longer view of history, one may add, this was the culture-changing process which defined the typological difference between revolutionary nationalism and the reformist or populist nationalism of the movements of 'primary decolonization' in the Africa of the 1950s and 1960s. The latter often won a wide mass support for their aims; none of them achieved, or even saw the need to achieve (the UPC in Cameroun possibly excepted) a mass participation in the modes and structures of the decolonizing effort.

Much has been written about the participation achieved in liberated zones of Guinea-Bissau. In its mature form, it demonstrated 'a new society taking shape in such a way that practically no aspect of community life lay outside its influence and action'. This was done through patient work in the creation of a dense network of village committees, derived from village assemblies and increasingly elective in nature, concerned with the administration of local affairs, the provision of justice through village tribunals, the servicing of schools and health clinics, and other tasks including (since this was wartime) the raising and feeding of local self-defence militias.

There was one missing element, as Lars Rudebeck has remarked in a shrewdly sympathetic commentary, that was to be sorely felt after independence. Whether for lack of time or personnel or possibility, and certainly because the war pressed hard, nothing was done to evoke a change in economic patterns within these zones: to advance, for example, at least towards early forms of collective or co-operative cultivation. Within some two years after independence, the Guinea-Bissau leadership had moved to the towns and left the peasants, for the most part, with a sense of abandonment. That was to be one large reason behind the military coup, in Bissau, of November 1980.

It remains that the mass participation achieved in the wartime liberated zones was none the less 'the beginning of a true self-determination', to quote a retrospective of 1984,

> and of a people's acceptance of responsibility for itself: a conquest of an importance without precedent if one considers that Portuguese colonialism, for centuries, was pledged to deprive its colonized peoples of any kind of responsibility for themselves, and to root out from their collective memory any thought of need to assume the defence of their own interests.

It is a point that could be made widely, I think, to those in later years who have questioned the value of these anti-colonial struggles. For the Portuguese, in this respect, were by no means unique; and in the matter of depriving 'their Africans' of all initiative, of any self-belief that they were capable of such initiative, were probably outdone by the Belgians in the Congo and by the semi-settler regimes of British East and Central Africa. The peoples who were sometimes said to be being 'prepared for nationhood' were in fact 'prepared' for a continued subservience. It is a disagreeable point to have to make, but it is certainly a real one.

To prepare themselves for nationhood, a people 'must do it for themselves': in the Guiné-Criole saying popular during the liberation war, *ke povo na manda na si cabeça*. And it was in *this* development of grass-roots political and social initiative that Cabral and those closest to him saw the central justification of their own leadership. At the outset they had been obliged to substitute themselves for their people. They had been 'nationalists without a nation' in Cabral's own words. But they had led the peasants of the liberated zones in such a way that these peasants, during that struggle, came increasingly to identify the PAIGC with the embodiment of their own interests, of their 'programme', of their 'living better and seeing their lives go forward'. Many in the outside world failed to see this truth, or mocked it as utopian propaganda. They were left, like Salazar's generals, with no valid explanation of the reasons why six men in 1956 could raise an unbeatable army of peasants.

III

But if the veterans of the victory in Guinea-Bissau came back with clear ideas about what ought to be done, they can have had few illusions about the difficulty of doing it. They had gone through instructive years and were acutely aware, as Olívio Pires was to write in 1984, that the project of mass participation

> has to meet the most varied types of resistance. Old habits, old ideas, the remnants or distortions of old evils and colonial miseries such as authoritarianism, *caciquismo* [local tyranny], corruption, and the trade in influence, bureaucratism, etc., which always tend to take root and reproduce themselves.

Back in 1963, at the outset of war in Guiné, those kinds of resistance had all but wrecked the PAIGC and were stopped only in the nick of time. As late as January 1973 the murder of Cabral by traitors had flared another warning of terrible perversions. The ninety or so Cape Verdean veterans who came home in 1974 had no ground for nourishing illusions.

Their project emerged from the tough reality of the liberated zones. It evolved in clarity of definition even when, after 1977, continued democratic progress within an independent Guinea-Bissau would soon come into question. Providing a succinct statement of method to the Party congress of 1977 – a congress held in Bissau for a still united party – Secretary-General Pereira had laid it down that:

> The model which our Party builds is one in which participation at the base is guaranteed in all decisions, and at every level, by democratic organization and method . . . [These] presume the existence, alongside every executive committe, of an assembly of delegates elected from the level of that committee, an assembly which elects and controls the committee in question.

That degree of purity of democratic structure would take long to achieve, even if it were not in any case expecting too much of human nature. Meanwhile, that was the goal to work towards. For 'there would not be, nor ever was, any national liberation without mass participation', in words spoken by the vice-chairman of the newly-elected Cape Verdean National Assembly in 1980.

> None of the aims of the PAIGC that relate to National Reconstruction, none of our government's objectives in the years ahead, can be realized without mass participation. Without this participation, no future can be built, no material foundations that will guarantee the well-being of our people.

By 1980 the years of mere survival after independence were beginning to pass into the years of new construction and development. And the system they had chosen to construct, continued the same speaker, could be called 'national revolutionary democracy': national because its source lay in the interests and action of all the country's social forces; revolutionary because it destroyed colonial domination and because its principal strength arose from 'the wide masses of our people, chief actors and beneficiaries of the transformations which our society has to undergo'; and democratic 'because there can be no liberation not identified in the people or by substitution for the people'.

No such system could be conceived as a thing complete: life would bring its own enlightenments and correctives. 'National revolutionary democracy', this speaker concluded, 'is therefore a means and process of apprenticeship in which persons and institutions are called on to evolve, day by day, in search for better solutions, for better forms of action.'

Sure of this perspective from experience of peasant participation through the war years between 1968 and 1974, they were otherwise little concerned with wider issues of theory. They knew from their own lives how much they had to learn about peasant realities, how little anyone in Europe had understood these realities. If they had absorbed much from Marx in terms of an indispensable socio-economic analysis, they became sure that the analytical tools derived from Marx needed here a new cutting-edge, a different application. Though mostly of peasant origin themselves, social self-knowledge in colonial times had been practically beyond reach. Acquiring it now, they followed Cabral in thinking that 'the people aren't fighting for the things in anyone's head, but to live better and see their lives go forward'. They proceeded from this axiom.

Clearly there could be no acceptance of the Western orthodoxies of capitalism. What would befall with that acceptance must be what they had widely seen in many ex-colonies: there being no indigenous capitalist system in those colonies, Western orthodoxies after independence had confirmed the colonial subordination to capitalist systems elsewhere, above all to those of the former colonial powers as well as the USA. This had meant strongly centralized governments, therefore élitist governments and therefore – soon or late – minority control and in due course military dictatorship. Along with this would go the deepening contradiction between an ever-stronger State-capitalist initiative and an ever-weaker State apparatus and stability. Rhetoric apart, the project of a 'programme for the peasants', a reconstruction for the benefit of the majority, would go by the board. Ditched in a sea of confusion and corruption, the programme of the peasants would surely drown.

But their own experience had likewise led them to believe that an import of Eastern orthodoxies, however socialism might be construed, would be no more serviceable. There, it seemed, the State was embodied in an all-powerful party, and the party in an all-pervasive bureaucracy; and the project of mass participation – the soviets or local councils which once had promised so much – was again ditched in another if different sea of frustration. They owed a lot to Soviet wartime aid and friendship. I think myself that most of the Cape Verdean veterans would have agreed that some form of socialism, yet to be defined and practised, must probably be the hope of the world, if nuclear disaster could meanwhile be averted. But I also think that socialism as a present aim could have no meaning for them. What had meaning was their concept of participation as a grass-roots apprenticeship in democratic practice, attitude and aim, along with initiatives to solve or begin to solve the overbearing problems of a social and economic wilderness. What had meaning was the ending of *systemic* exploitation.

IV

Conclusions followed. The influence and leadership of the Party must remain paramount: of the Cape Verdean PAIGC, which became PAICV (Partido Africano de Independência de Cabo Verde) after the rupture which occurred with Guinea-Bissau because of the November 1980 coup there. If the practice and theory of mass participation were vital to progress, there could be no plurality of parties. Plurality would bring the disunities of personal or group ambition, useless rivalries, external intrigues: inducing a waste of effort and resources when there was none to spare of either, and eventually frustration and defeat. The warnings they had heard were legion, and not only African.

For the measurable future there must be a one-party State. Party power would have to be separate from State power, if with an ambiguity at the top which we shall see. But there must be a one-party State. Then how protect the rights and duties of democracy in this absence of a plurality of parties? It was a question with which their experience was painfully familiar. They had been obliged to watch the steady petrification of political life in a number of one-party African States, and in my opinion most disturbingly in the (ex-French) Guinea of Sékou Touré where, descending from one outrage to a worse, bloodstained tyranny had eventually swallowed no few of the children of that 'revolution'. They had seen much else. They had travelled widely. They had sojourned in many countries; and the spectacle of what could happen to the one-party State was a chilling one.

Discussing this in 1986 the executive secretary of this single party, the PAICV, could reasonably claim that 'we have been able to measure the bad as well as the good. Yet I have to say,' continued Olivio Pires, 'that none of this experience of ours, however varied and vivid and discussed among ourselves, has been able to persuade us that the European model of the multi-party State can be workable in Africa.' Equally, the one-party State without a real mass participation was also not workable. 'We remain convinced that a living grass-roots democracy is indispensable to progress. But we are just as much convinced that this democracy can be promoted and protected only by the force of mass participation.'

This was the political baggage they came home with in 1974; and the remainder of my book will attempt to show, at least in outline, how they unpacked and have used it, and what has followed from this. I am aware that any confident words on such a subject must expect, in the wake of the 1980s, to face a pile of doubts and disbelief. The one-party State in Africa or anywhere else has precious few credits but many debits. Why should it be otherwise in Cape Verde? Is it otherwise? Can mass participation become real, or must this nation-state's capacity to realize 'the programme of the peasants' remain in any case chimerical?

Legitimate questions; and there are others. How does a small people 'on the margins of the world' find its own way ahead? How can this people, so critically dependent on external aid, none the less intend to keep its freedom of choice and action? What follows in answer here is written with a bias of sympathy. Readers will be aware of this. But they will also allow, I hope, for the habit of criticism, and of self-criticism of personal errors of judgement along the way, which has accompanied the history I have shared with Cape Verdeans, in small but real degree, since the outset of the 1960s.

It would be pleasant to say that the political baggage, containing many hard-earned lessons, was used with quick success. But to say this would be to rob the story of its drama as well as of its truth.

The unpacking, for its part, proved easy enough. The veterans found no problem in gaining an audience: on the contrary, they were greeted as heroes who were expected to be heroes, if much to their own surprise. Remote peasants climbed down from crags and corniches to question and listen to these men and women who had brought Sancho with them, but shown as well that they could master Sancho's extravagance. Villagers from roadless hamlets tramped for hours to reach the little *praças* of Santa Caterina, São Filipe, Ribeira Grande and the like, and hear the news of what was going to happen next. In this extraordinary upheaval, where hope was jostled by the deepest scepticism, what was going to be asked of them? What did it all mean?

8 Launching participation

I

The answers arrived slowly and sometimes partially, little by little, hard to hear at first and still harder to believe when heard. Yet they were answers of the kind that Africa in these times of continental famine and betrayal was waiting for, I think, and would come increasingly to accept in this form or in that as other and familiar answers have failed and fail again.

Yet this is a small people, modest in its claims, very weak in every material sense, only now emerging from despair at its legacies of ruin. Is it right and reasonable to place them in a continental scenario, above all when most of the people in that picture barely so much as know of Cape Verde's existence? Subject always to the fearful temptations of wish and hope, one can only say what one has seen and heard: here and elsewhere, and over many years.

I returned in 1980, four years after another visit of 1976. Amid various researches and inquiries I travelled in the island of Sant'Antão with a friend of the war years, Corsino Tolentino, one of the veterans with whom I had come from Guinea-Bissau in 1974. Corsino is a good companion for such seeings and listenings. Though likewise subject to the temptations of wish and hope – and who amongst us would have come through without those beacons? – Corsino was a long-time soldier of the liberation war and is therefore given to finding out what is, strictly and on the ground, before going on to say what ought to be. Taut and handsome in the Cape Verdean style, he shares a proper scepticism with a sense of humour and, like most of these veterans, believes that laughter is likely to be useful to good judgement. It was one of Cabral's beliefs as well. In 1980, I suppose, Corsino was rising thirty-five.

We looked, mainly, into the personnel and condition of the

A woman's voluntary collective transporting water for the reservoir of one of the new *polivalenti*, multi-purpose social centres: in this case on the island of Santiago. (Photo copyright Augusta Conchiglia)

Party. Little more than a handful of harried militants in 1974, joined then by the ninety or so veterans from the liberation war as well as by the political prisoners from Tarrafal and other jails, the Party (the PAIGC) had grown since then. This growth was indispensable to any stability or progress, since it was what could form sure ground, whether institutional or political, in the otherwise all-pervasive void. And the Party in Sant'Antão, as in most of the islands, had grown rapidly: perhaps a little too rapidly, for some had joined who were mere 'tailers-along behind the victors'. There had been, or there would have to be, due weedings-out.

The Cape Verdean PAIGC of mid-1980 – soon to become PAICV after the disruptive coup of November 1980 in Guinea-Bissau – numbered a little more than 4000 members, or about 1 in 75 of the population. Analysed by social status, about 16 per cent of this membership were wage-workers and 38 per cent 'small peasants' or sharecroppers – these two latter having usually an acre or less, though seldom in their possession – while 30 per cent were state employees. The remaining 15 per cent or so were students of the two lycées, a few traders, some artisans and professional men and women, doctors and the like. Rather more than 46 per cent of the total membership were under thirty; another 36 per cent between thirty and fifty.

The basic organization was likewise in existence. The approximately 4000 members – women as well as men, but we will come to that – were organized in *grupos de base*, 'base groups', of which in 1980 there were about 400, or about one for every 750 souls but with some islands more developed in this respect than others. These 400-odd 'base groups' of Party members elected delegates to seventy-three section committees which, in turn, elected or would elect to fifteen sector committees designed to embody the scattered nature of the people – scattered in nine islands but, in the bigger islands, scattered again in many homesteads and hamlets and little towns. The elective process was as yet far from smooth or complete, from lack of any such habit or experience; but nomination from above was subject to the test of public assemblies for approval or disapproval of nominated persons.

What did this Party do? In principle its members possessed (and possess) no executive authority outside its ranks. It could lead, exhort, explain and work by example. But it could (and can) order or command nobody not a member. In practice, at this early stage, the best of its members had to fulfil several different functions in or out of the Party, for people looked to them in default of anyone else to show the way things should be done. The inherited void of democratic structures saw to that. Reducing this 'polyvalence' of duties would be a task for the future.

Corsino, as a leading militant of his native Sant'Antão, was invited on this occasion to the first Party conference of the sector of Paúl, a conference to review work done and work projected. Paúl is a village on the coast a little way from Ribeira Grande along beetling cliffs which face out to the Atlantic, while its district is a branched canyon that is scoured into steep mountains characteristic of the island. We went there by car along a stretch of cobbled road built since independence by wage-workers paid from UN funds, a nice piece of 'impossible' engineering which steers and burrows along and below the seaward cliffs.

The area is rather prosperous. Paúl canyon has a 'river' formed by water-seepage from the crater bowl of Caldeira de Covo on the 'top' of the island, some 1500 metres above the floor of Paúl canyon. Paúl farmers grow market-produce in their canyon as well as scaling their cliffs to do the same in the crater bowl. Now, with the good hard road to Ribeira Grande, they were already getting their produce out by truck.

Paúl is also a remote place; but while the rest of the world knows nothing of Paúl, the same is not true in reverse. Emigration has long sent the sons and daughters of Paúl up and down the world, while a substantial number of the veterans of the liberation war in Guinea-Bissau were from Paúl and neighbouring localities. This is one of Cape Verde's contradictions: remoteness from the world but acute awareness of the world.

We found the Party conference ready to begin proceedings in the open air of a warm July evening. The party secretary of Paúl, José Lima, gets things under way. He is a large man in his thirties who speaks with confidence but without bravado. After welcoming his seventy-five members and various guests and persons from the public who have cared to attend, he recalls the sacrifices that had to be made 'before we could realize this conference, comrades: the sacrifices of those who have nourished our land with their blood and are immortal heroes'. Heroes with the ancestors, heroes who therefore cannot die: and the visitor understands again how close he is to Africa and its conceptions. 'Among them Amílcar Cabral the Founder of our Nationality, Domingos Ramos, Titina Sila . . .', men and women who gave their lives in the liberation war. Domingos Ramos and Titina Sila were among the Guinea-Bissauans who were killed in action; and the secretary dwells on this, dwells on the importance of the programmed union of Cape Verde with Guinea-Bissau 'if we wish to be the true continuers of the task those heroes undertook for us'.

The conference of Party delegates has before it a sixteen-page cyclostyled report by its sector secretary, and will discuss this for the next two days. The report runs through recent history. At first after independence there were 'administrative commissions' of local government, set up as foundations of a State structure which had yet to exist. These were then displaced by 'deliberative councils' of local government, a first small stage on the road to mass participation. 'And much else happened, comrades: much else became possible. . . . Our festivals, forbidden by colonial law to the point that even drumming was forbidden, have come back to us . . .'

Much else, he continues, is well known not to have been achieved, or not as it should have been. Literacy classes, informative lectures, political meetings, seminars of explanation . . . 'have not been achieved by some of our militants who've failed to appear or failed to understand'; and so 'we have called other meetings to examine these failures, and these other meetings have aroused interest and better participation . . .' He thinks the overall outcome is positive, 'and the situation of the Party in our Sector is fairly acceptable'.

This speech and its occasion, I think, were reasonably typical of the Party's drive to become a democratic instrument of pressure and supervision. And the results were promising. Paúl's slender population had produced seventy-five unpaid volunteers for Party work in the public interest, work that entailed some hours every week and much effort in walking from place to place, often up cliffs and down mountains, aside from the moral commitment required.

The Party of independence, in short, was under way by 1980 as the flywheel of self-government. But it was not self-government itself. That would have to be built on non-Party structures, on forms of grass-roots democracy through which, and within which, the active participation of citizens could take shape in the self-government of their society. And although there would certainly be Party members in these non-Party structures of self-government, they would not command or control it. They would be there as citizens of equal but not superior rights to non-Party citizens.

A tentative start had been made soon after independence in the launching of forms of local government, notably with an effort to establish village or town-quarter tribunals to fill the legal void. A national elective system had likewise been installed, early in 1975, so as to enable the creation of a People's National Assembly with a five-year mandate, the constitutional fount of all power and law on the basis of universal adult suffrage; and this had proved effective and was working smoothly. But the chief arena of participation had to be in local government. It was in this that mass participation would or would not take real shape and presence. It was in this that a people never before able to govern itself in any degree at all would or would not be drawn into the daily administration of its public life. It was here, in short, that a real process of democracy would or would not displace the mental habits and political constrictions of colonial dictatorship. Effective local self-government was going to be the acid test of anti-colonial liberation.

This has been, I think, a general truth in Africa. No political failure of African independence has been as pregnant with disaster as failure in this test: failure, that is, to balance effective forms of local self-government against increasingly centralized and bureaucratic national government. With this failure, national government has ceased to be, or even seem to be, any real form of self-government for the mass of the people, above all of rural people, in a long list of newly-independent countries. The peasants in their multitude have turned away from those who claim to govern in their name, convinced that 'they' are pursuing interests and gains which 'we' do not and even cannot share. The peasants have retreated from the 'national' scene, withdrawn from the 'national' economy, preferred all too often to smuggle their saleable excess of produce across 'national' frontiers rather than deliver it to a 'national' market at prices they consider a form of theft.

This kind of disaster must infallibly hit Cape Verde as well if its leaders remained content to govern by their own executive power at the centre. The peasants here might have no handy frontiers across which to smuggle any excess of produce they might have; but they would certainly continue to extract themselves in ever increasing numbers by the route of emigration. Much more than effective local self-government would be required. But effective local self-government would remain the essential starting point.

The Portuguese had ruled through orders passed down from Lisbon, by way of their governor in Cape Verde to a network of *administradores*, usually Cape Verdeans who were the instruments of Portuguese power. There had been no local representation nor even any means of consultation. Against that difficult background, the leadership of the PAICV moved towards the creation of local self-government as early as 1978.

Village or locality meetings of as many inhabitants as could be persuaded to attend were asked, in each place of settlement, to produce *comissões de moradores*, 'residents' commissions' or what we in Britain might call parish or district councils: local councils. In principle, each locality was to elect its council. In practice, the local Party had to begin by nominating volunteers thought likely to be effective, and presenting these nominees to the approval or disapproval of local assemblies. This process proved popular. Assembly meetings became an occasion for airing a flood of often passionate commentary.

Local councils began to take shape in a multitude of places. Powers were devolved to them in a widening field of local affairs. There were innumerable hiccups and misunderstandings. But this was an 'apprenticeship' in self-government that continued. By 1980 it had begun to have real presence and effect.

On a very local testing of this presence and effectiveness in 1980, I went with Corsino Tolentino on a tour of inland hamlets of Sant'Antão tucked away behind the coastal mountains, and reached by some of Cape Verde's most improbable roads. Santa Igreja was one of them, a cluster of huts and small houses in a rolling landscape of cliffs and corniches linked by narrow tracks known here as *caminhos vicinais*.

We found that no local council, *comissõe de moradores*, had yet been formed at Santa Igreja. But the village tribunal was in session. Three elderly judges sat on a raised bench with plaintiff and defender in front of them and, beyond these, a dozen or so villagers who had come to listen, with others leaning on the sills of opened windows outside the 'court house'. The case seemed rather a tense one, and there was no public chatter. Afterwards, translating from the local dialect of Crioulo, Corsino explained that they had been considering an allegation of witchcraft. Africa, I thought again, is not so far away.

The local Party was also in session in its one-roomed hut not far from the tribunal. Half a dozen serious young peasants, but all male as I remember, welcomed Corsino and unfolded their problem. Their local militia was in function but not well; its commander needed replacing . . . 'Important for them', Corsino comments, 'for the militia is their power, their people's power.' The claim could sound mere rhetoric, which is what it has usually been in Africa. But not here.

> In this island, there are about 45,000 people. There are exactly eleven State police and there are no troops. Whenever a tribunal needs executive power of arrest, incarceration, whatever, it calls on the volunteers of the local militia it has raised. There's no one else to call on.

II

I returned to the islands in 1986, after a brief intervening visit in 1983, and found the process of mass participation a long way advanced from the launching stage, even if, in a comment of Aristides Pereira's, 'we still have a long way to go'.

On Sant'Antão in 1980 there had been twenty-two local councils of which some were still in take-off troubles; while the Party had 430 members organized in fifty-five *grupos de base*. Now in 1986 there were forty-four local councils, or about one local council for every 1000 of the island's inhabitants. Party membership had increased from the 430 of 1980 to 1307; rather more than a desirable maximum, I gathered, and likely to be somewhat reduced by removal of idlers or incompetents.

In terms of direct people's power, Sant'Antão now disposed of twenty-six local tribunals with an available total of 183 judges (or, as the British term would be, magistrates) who would call at need on an executive force of 1670 young men in voluntary militias. State police on this hugely mountainous island still numbered only sixteen, while the army consisted of precisely one officer, a major and veteran of the liberation war whom I had known in the struggle on the mainland. His job here was to give elementary weapons' training and drill to the militiamen.

Women's participation was still fragile and admitted to be such: of the 183 magistrates on Sant'Antão in 1986 only nineteen were women, while a populous village and district like Paúl had no more than 4 per cent of women among its party members. Even this poor total had been clearly hard to achieve, given the male chauvinism of Cape Verdean attitudes in which, as the proverb holds, *Onde o galo canta, a galinha não pia*: 'where the cock crows, women stay away'. Yet the institutions of participation, here as in the other islands, appeared by 1986 to be a solid system-in-place, functioning on the daily scene, penetrating everywhere in rural areas as well as towns. Cape Verdean politics, no matter how fallible, was now unthinkable without this 'power emanating from the people'.

All the same, a deep colonial suspicion that all real power to do or to get things done is a 'government matter', a power which 'they' alone possess, remains in 1986 a widespread thought. To accept that power has now become primarily a 'people's matter', a matter for 'us', means assuming what you have never assumed before or thought conceivable to assume before. It has to be a gradual conquest; not everybody makes it. Today there is to be a peasant gathering at Janela which will prove instructive on this point; and I am able to attend it with Olívio Pires, executive secretary of the PAICV as well as a native of Paúl next-door to Janela.

It is not yet the simplest thing to reach Janela, for in 1986 the new coast road from Paúl has still to get there. After the present ending of the road, a little along the coast from Paúl, one takes to a corniche path carved in the seaward precipice of high cliffs or trickled, here and there, across pebble beaches or built in steeps to wayside homesteads. It is about an hour's walk to Janela, going fast, and all Cape Verdean peasants, not least Olívio Pires, go at a pace which leaves the visitor in wry regret for a distant youth. But the scenery soon lifts the heart. Panting, the visitor admires it.

Here on the outer face of Sant'Antão, looking aslant towards the Caribbean several thousand miles away, the northerly trades bowl glittering rollers that burst and shower against the cliffside. This is a cloud-free spectacle of sea and sky where ocean birds, gannet and albatross and greater black-backed gulls, cruise and glide while little petrels, whenever you can see them, skid and paddle on the nimbus of the waves. Poor in many things, Cape Verde is splendidly rich in scenic power.

The meeting at Janela begins at ten o'clock in the single large room of the primary school, a stone building clustered with others on the spit of sea-girt rock where Janela stands. The room is soon crowded with some sixty men and women, many of whom, Olívio tells me while we are waiting for everyone to settle down, have walked here from homesteads on the ridges far above. Olívio takes a chair behind the table at one end of the room, together with Party colleagues from Paúl and Ribeira Grande who have also come for the discussion. Two 'rich peasants' have come, since most of the discussion is going to be about land tenure and land reform; they are 'the two light-skinned ones over on the right of the door', owners of 5 or 10 hectares farmed partly by cultivators on share-cropping 'contracts'. Otherwise this is a meeting of peasants who own no land but pay rent in cash or kind.

I reflect that it is not surprising that the atmosphere is businesslike and expectant: nobody, after all, is going to walk for hours to hear nothing useful said. With the school benches packed and the overflow leaning on the wall at the back, Olivio opens the proceedings, not standing or orating but sitting easily and talking in the high-pitched voice that is common here, a highlander's voice that reminds me of the voices of Wales. He speaks briefly, a person from Paúl talking to his neighbours of Janela. Then the peasants take over. They also speak in Crioulo. Olívio gives me the gist.

Later, as the discussion flows back and forth, this ease of relationship between the mountain people of Janela and the important Party official from the capital city, several hundred miles away, occurs to me as a thing that will scarcely be believed when I am home again. It will read like one of those hopeful novels in which the good cadre from the capital is received like a long-lost brother. But the directness and force of what people are saying here, their manner of saying it as well as what they say, are clear enough: they are saying what they think to someone they respect.

A proverb from Ghana, surfacing for me from years past, offers a comment, *Wobefora dua a, wofi n'ase na womfi soro*: 'If you want to climb a tree, you had better start at the bottom.' It used to be said in deprecation of those who start 'at the top', lifted there by privilege or greed and not by honest effort, and who thereby incur the distrust of their neighbours and, worse still, the contempt of the gods. If Olívio is undoubtedly at the top of the Cape Verdean tree, he climbed there from the pit of exile and through the perils of the liberation struggle; and everyone knows it. Privilege and greed have nothing to do with Olívio's being where he is; and a proven indifference to personal gain is what may win surprise among a peasant people, but certainly wins respect. When the person in question is a local man, it wins pride and affection as well.

The injustice of long-established laws and customs of colonial land tenure is these peasants' target. New laws of land reform are in fact several years old, but their application by argument and persuasion has not been easy and is still far from complete. The reasons are various and complex, as we shall see, but lie chiefly in the weight of habit and tradition. Immediate aims have been to abolish share-cropping in favour of tenure by money-rent, and to transform tenure by rent into titles to outright ownership.

But this is a country of infinite division of land into small or tiny lots, and therefore into a micro-network of customary rights, claims, and expectations, often shared by emigrants in America, Holland and a dozen other distant places. The resultant peasant economy has been, and still is, painfully bad for productivity, a source of deepening poverty, and a plague on the future. Then why not abolish all rent? Why not decree the amalgamation of tiny properties into viable collectives?

The thinkers of the PAICV are aware of what the books have said on these and other matters. They have conned their texts in the midnight oil of years of waiting. But their idea of progress is precisely that people must achieve it for themselves. The government of the PAICV has the executive power to abolish overnight all rent and decree collectives: but that would have to be by force not by argument and persuasion; and using force, in their judgement, would deserve a sure disaster.

Here is another tree that has to be climbed from the bottom. Which does not mean, of course, that the poor or landless peasants of Cape Verde have lost sight of the 'class issue'. The meeting at Janela demonstrates that they have not.

The first peasant to take the floor, which he does with great assurance and vigour, goes straight to it. He says that he is a former share-cropper, *parceiro*, who now pays rent and thinks the change is good. But the land reform, *reforma agraria* in the term they all use, doesn't go far enough. The 'landowners', by whom he means the relatively few with several hectares and some irrigation, possess all the *grog* distilleries; and now they are revenging themselves on their former share-croppers by keeping the use of distilleries to themselves. The speaker describes this as a blackmail, and goes into lengthy detail. What he wants is that there should be a new distillery open to everyone, 'a *trapiche* for all of us', so that everyone may make his own rum. The Party should see to this. The Party should provide it.

The next speaker is another peasant in middle-age, again dressed for the occasion in ceremonial suit and tie. He has a grievance, and clearly has seated himself in the front row with every intention of airing it. He too speaks against 'landowners', and, while himself a rent-payer, *rendeiro*, goes into the evils of share-cropping. The landowners are greedy. They evade the land reform. They want to keep their share-croppers. They sabotage the drawing up of rent-paying contracts on the terms agreed by the land reform commissions. This peasant doesn't say what needs to be done, except that the Party should act against greedy landowners.

Olívio takes notes, and waits. While this peasant enlarges by repetition. I myself recall a meeting a little while back with one of these 'greedy landowners'. Resting on another breathless chase through *caminhos vicinais* along the wall of a canyon, we had come to a pleasant house niched into the cliffside amid a garden of maize and sugar cane.

The hospitable owner invites us into his sitting-room. It is comfortably furnished and decorated with framed photos of a daughter in Lisbon, as we learn, and a son in Holland. There is talk of family affairs and of the virtues of Portugal, and our host brings us glasses of excellent *grog* he has distilled himself.

This is a farmer with many hectares, perhaps as many as 20, which makes him a big landowner in these parts. Yet he is not the personal owner of all this land, as he explains, but the manager of a family estate of which the income is shared among emigrant brothers as well as himself. They have accumulated it little by little over the years; and this is the custom of the country. Then again, the hectares are divided into forty-five small parcels worked by share-croppers, each by an individual 'agreement' or 'contract' that represents a bargain in which the owner has of course the upper hand. He can kick his share-croppers off his land, cut down their shares, lean on them for extra services. So it has 'always' been; and nothing in the colonial dispensation, under which this 'system' took shape, could stop him except some violent uproar that was ended, usually, by the share-croppers being sent on forced labour to São Tomé or Angola.

Or such had been the case until three weeks earlier. But three weeks earlier the land reform, no overnight transaction but a process, had at last arrived on this property. Now there are no more share-croppers here, but as many tenants with rents fixed by the local land reform commission, and with security of tenure. A big change, and not without hard feelings. Our host admits to none while we are sipping his *grog*, but afterwards, back on the cliffside trail, Olivio reviews what had happened. One of the new tenants had come to ask the landowner to sell him some harvested maize, another customary transaction; but the landowner, much hurt in his feelings as well as in his pocket, had refused. 'Go and buy it from the Land Reform – as for me, I'll take your house away.' To which the peasant, as was widely and happily reported, had answered: 'You won't. It's my house now. I'm not your donkey any more.'

So the 'class issue' is centrally there. A third speaker has a taste for pleasing generalities, but goes to the same point. He says that he is satisfied with the progress of the land reform: 'the big landowners still oppose it, but we'll go ahead and complete it'. Until the land reform came the landowners 'practised slavery on us, but now it's different'. But the Party should see to it that the landowners stopped monopolizing irrigation water. The Party should provide more credit.

Another speaker says that he agrees with what has been said, but 'there are still some of us who are afraid to speak out'. The Party should stop wrong things being done. His family's landowner, a woman, has refused to sign a contract of tenancy according to the law of the land reform, but can it be an accident that her daughter is married to a policeman? The speaker evidently thinks not. Others speak; the details multiply. Only one speaker reads out what he wants to say. This is a young man of the JAAC – Juventude Africano Amílcar Cabral, the youth organization – and he concludes with slogans. Nobody minds, so far as I can tell, but nobody takes much notice either.

Olivío waits in his tactful way for a longish pause late in the discussion, and then replies at length. The history of the Party shows that the land reform is an organic part of 'the whole process of winning our independence'. Some might have doubted its value, even its bare possibility, but Party history has shown that the few who begin can become the many who continue: 'for the Party began with six persons, but now the Party is many thousands'.

Then he gets to the issues raised. The distillery-for-all: 'That's for you to solve yourselves. If you want a distillery, then organize and work for one. Don't wait for the Party to solve everything, for the Party can't do it and won't try. The Party can show you the way, but it's you who have to make the journey . . .' Another speaker had asked for better sea transport, and gets the same reply. 'Well, but don't wait for leaders to come here. Insist to your member of the National Assembly. Draw up your case. Send it to him . . .'

A woman had asked that young women be given more educational opportunities, and gone on to speak against discrimination. 'In the times before' – she means before independence, but there is no need for her to say it – 'we were slaves to men, we didn't come to meetings, we stayed in the kitchen and the men ate at table . . .' Not any more, she affirms with a challenging look around an audience, predominantly male, which responds with no enthusiasm on this point: 'but we're still not far enough, not nearly'. Olívio agrees. He speaks of the new laws on gender equality and the defence of women's rights. But the Party won't enforce what the people haven't accepted. 'It's for every element of our society to bring these matters into the open, and use the new laws. To discuss them and act on them, women as much as men . . .'

We return to Paúl, pleased with the feelings left by this long meeting. But its message, like the stony trail along the way, remains hard and unavoidable. The problem with mass participation as a transfer of authority and responsibility from 'top' to 'bottom' is not that the receivers do not like it or accept it. The problem has not been to launch this transfer. The problem now is to ensure that mass participation moves of itself, out of its own needs and dynamism, and makes use of the power transferred.

This is where the local councils have their central role.

III

Roughly circular in shape, the island of Brava rises inland to a tall hump; and here at its summit the hamlet of Campo Baixo sits narrowly on a ridge some 670 metres above the sea. So does its neighbour, Nossa Senhora do Mont, where houses crouch against the rockside as though expecting that the ocean wind will any moment snatch them skyward. Roofs of thatch and tile nestle just below, and these are Covo de Joana. Dizzily down again, far beneath, there lies the winking mirror of the sea. Its curling waves are mere ripples in the distance.

If you lean far out on this ridge of Campo Baixo, you can glimpse the roofs of another hamlet along a band of silver beach, immensely far down there; and this is the fishing village of Fajã d'Agua. That is where the airport of Brava is being thrust by clever engineering along the last low cliffs; and its tail will be on stilts above the sea itself. Good citizens of Rhode Island and New Bedford, returning to ancestral homes or new ones they have lately built on Brava, need no longer take the ocean ferry from Santiago. This remote Cape Verdean outpost to the south will be linked next year by airways to the world.

We have been looking at the work of local councils. How is mass participation doing here? Brava in 1986 was at an early stage in the development of *poder local*, local power, compared with advanced places such as Santa Caterina or Santa Cruz on the big island of Santiago. The people here none the less supply some interesting answers to how *poder local* works for them.

Six of Brava's local councils, formed three years ago, are officially 'paralysed', out of action for lack of personnel or facilities. For people here still emigrate as soon as their relatives 'at the other end' can arrange for entrance and work permits. But fourteen councils on this island of fewer than 6000 souls are in existence and at work, and one of these is the local council of Campo Baixo and its neighbourhood. A lengthy meeting with five of its members – their total is eight – has just explained this council's work and its difficulties. Four of these five are wage-workers and the fifth is the schoolmaster of Campo Baixo; their average age may be about twenty-five. Their council also has two women, who are not present.

They meet in the schoolroom 'because we have no place of our own', which they regret. The problem is common: very few councils have a place of their own. In more advanced communities like those of Santa Caterina on Santiago island, *polivalenti* have been built to remedy this lack, stone-built multi-use centres with rooms for the various organizations of local participation. I found them sensibly designed and much employed buildings, and more are under construction.

The Campo Baixo secretary, a wage-worker, explains their duties. The council is a new one, re-elected in November 1985 from a founding predecessor elected in July 1983. Only one member of the first council is a member of this new one, for this is voluntary work calling for a lot of time and effort, 'and some withdraw and some emigrate, and some transfer to be judges of the people's court'. Persons to serve the public without pay are not so easy to find. The case is not peculiar to Cape Verde.

I find it remarkable that these wage-workers are willing and even eager to serve. Every circumstance seems against such voluntary effort. All four of them are on construction work at the new airport down at Fajã d'Agua. How long to walk down in the morning? Well, maybe 45 minutes. And up again in the evening? Three hours, says one of them with a grin, 'or two if we're in the mood'. That makes at least 18 hours of walking down 670 metres and up again in a five-and-a-half-day week, for six days' pay at 105 escudos a day, while their foreman gets 165.* Who says Africans don't work?

These council members are cheerful about all this; after all, they are in regular employment. Two are Party members, while a third is a candidate for membership. Their council duties are various. They watch local produce prices so as to discourage speculation. They keep a list of unemployed so that there is order in the queue for such jobs as may turn up, mainly on soil-conservation work, municipal improvement, and the like. Most important, they have control of water from the pump at Campo Baixo, a pump which delivers from deep wells down the cliffside. As often in Cape Verde, perennially short of water, there has to be rationing. So the council sells water from 2 till 6 p.m., and watches the queue to see that workers who come late from down below are not deprived by others who come twice. The ration is 20 litres daily.

'We do it to avoid rows', says the secretary, and stresses the point. One chief aim of *poder local* is to get people concerned with the public interest. But another is to shelter the community from disputes and venoms, something that was never and indeed never could be done in the past. All power and initiative rested then with the local *administrador*. He was careful to take no notice until he had to, and then it was a matter for the police. Campo Baixo now is governed by its local council which has no police

* In 1986 the Cape Verdean escudo stood at 110 to the pound sterling.

but, instead, an available militia of twenty-two young men with cudgels, but 'they've really nothing to do'. The council's work of mediation is claimed to be effective, and there is little crime.

Those present have a proposal for the Brava Party secretary, with whom I have come to this encounter, and whom I had last met six years earlier at the first Party conference of Paúl. The councillors tell him that they lack experience. Yes, they have discussed this with the administration at Vila Nova Sintra, the little island capital where the plaque to Eugenio Tavares reflects an older history: but it's not enough. The schoolmaster member caps the point by saying that what they want is a seminar to improve their work. The committee operates all right and is accepted: but there are problems of knowing how best to do the work. A discussion ensues. There will be a seminar.

The Party is there to lead and advise and is looked to, as in this case, for what may be called civic education. At the beginning it had to do far more. In 1974 there had been only one Party member on Brava. Then Carlos Tavares, one of those released on May Day 1975 from Tarrafal, had come here and taken charge in a situation that was amazingly new and different. Gradually the Party had grown in numbers to its present membership on Brava of 120 members and fifty-one candidates with 15 per cent being women, rather more than the national average.

But its duties have narrowed with the formative years. A regular administration has been set in place. Now the Party on Brava is focused on its chief role as 'dynamizer', and organized in fifteen *grupos de base*. Other relevant statistics are available: the *Organisação da Mulher*, the women's organization, has 178 activists on the island in five groups, conducts three literacy classes for women, runs a nursery school in Vila Nova Sintra. . . .

One can watch this reality in as many meetings as one can attend. It is a reality that comes without rhetoric.

IV

This fabric of participation can be expressed in detailed numbers, and the extent of its 'coverage' is otherwise hard to grasp. Counting up all the men and women who are concerned in local councils, local tribunals, the Party itself, and the three organizations which serve specific interests of trade unions, women, and youth, I find in 1986 that they total about 60,000 persons, or about one in five of the whole Cape Verdean population. Of these 60,000, moreover, all but a handful are unpaid volunteers working 'in their own time'.

The number of local councils in 1986 is about 224, with eighty-six of them on the biggest island which is Santiago. Sant'Antão has fifty-one, Fogo thirty-nine, São Vicente sixteen, and the smaller islands have the rest. Roughly there is a local council, on average, for every 1300 souls. There are 255 local courts with some 1400 available magistrates; while the Party now has more than 6000 members. Another large contingent of activists gives time to the three mass organizations. Not included in the 60,000 are the officials of a State administration which is necessarily small for lack of means to pay for a larger one but also because mass participation works on its own initiative. It has no need to be administered; and, if administered, would cease to be mass participation.

How far, then, is the power of the State separated from the power of the Party? The Cape Verdean answer dates to an internal Party document of October 1975. 'At its upper level the State is, as it were, umbilically tied to the Party through executive fusion.' At the top, in short, the Party controls the State, and the State can do nothing without the Party. That is the inner sense and justification of this one-party State; and a corresponding responsibility of its leaders is to prevent Party control from degenerating into ossification. But in this respect the danger is also limited by two dominant factors: first, the Party 'down the line' has no executive power outside its own ranks, while, secondly, mass participation stands in the way of degradation.

Beneath the summit of authority there is thus no fusion of power.

> The intermediate and grass-roots levels of the Party have the duty to supervise, orientate and dynamize the actions of the State. But how? By giving orders? No. State administration receives its orders from its own senior executives . . . [The Party works] by active participation, [and] in every department of the State our militants are expected to be the best and most active, the most zealous and committed.

These Party volunteers work without pay.

All of them without pay? Almost all. I asked repeatedly about this interesting point. The island of Fogo, for example, has 31,000 people spread in small towns and hamlets around the great cone of its volcano. About 3 per cent, or about 1000 persons, are Party members in 1986 (of whom some 190 are women, again a proportion considered, at least officially, as deplorably low). Of all these, ten are full-time Party workers who receive a salary, while two others are on part-time paid Party work. I think these proportions are about average for each of the islands.

All this effort has had to be conjointly aimed at building statehood and nationhood. Olívio Pires remarks that this conjoint problem

has been little understood in Europe and America. In Europe, for example, the modern State had been generally the product of a nation, or at least of a national consciousness, which has already come into being. Yet here in Africa the case has generally been – and unavoidably – the reverse. The State has had to come into being before the nation.

And the damaging implications of this can indeed be seen in the fragility of new nation-States in Africa.

Olívio Pires:

At the start, as I've said, we had really nothing to build on. We saw that we should have to mobilize everyone who could be mobilized. Pedro Pires [Prime Minister in 1975 and after] defined our prospect during July 1975 when in one of his speeches, calling for unity, he said that 'our salvation as a people will come collectively, or not at all'.

And to meet the challenge of a confusion of external influences of one kind or another, we had in any case to promote a national consciousness. We further saw that to be able to do this we must act with an entire openness about whatever existed, and about whatever we proposed.

We had to carry our people with us in an enormous effort at self-realization and common purpose. It was completely obvious that any policy at the cost of the majority – a terribly impoverished majority in 1975 – would bring failure. There could be no case for trying to adopt – as Europe adopted for its self-development – the policies of capitalism: policies to benefit the few on the argument that later on they would benefit the many. We couldn't have accepted that. Even if we'd gone back on our pledge to end exploitation, we could never have made capitalism work. We were bound to look to the interests of the vast majority.

Such is the background to this Cape Verdean participation. It is a system in which, by the late 1980s, this whole society had become more or less involved. More or less: needless to say, the system is far from God-given, it still has to rely on human nature. Beyond the frailties of human nature, moreover, other problems arise. 'Even though the Party has no executive power', comments Olívio Pires, 'its position in the State' – defined by the independence Constitution of 1980 as being the guiding political force – 'and its prestige can produce problems. Problems, really, of political development.'

For example?

At the start, facing the void we found in 1975, our Party militants were asked to do whatever there had to be done – well, everything! It wasn't avoidable. So militants got used to doing rather than to steering. And steering, our proper work, is in any case always more difficult than simply doing the job yourself. If you do the job yourself, though, you cut into other people's chances of self-development.

But the criticism in Europe is that institutions of mass participation seem in practice, all too often, to be run by small groups in power. What about that?

Such minority influence may always be true, it seems to us – that's the human condition! Which are the political groups in Europe, I wonder, that aren't influenced by activists within them? Here it can be said that the Party imposes no answers. The Party argues and appeals and guides: beyond that, it's a question of political development.

Here in 1975 there was no political experience at all. So there wasn't any way, then, in which a majority could actually participate, could *know how* to participate. We'd come out of a long colonial night when no participation was as much as thinkable. But now – yes, now we've made irreversible conquests in promoting participation. Even if it's obvious that much remains to be achieved.

You've seen – its costs a lot to be a militant, it costs a lot! Duties you must walk to, hours there and hours back. Papers you must try to understand, even if you can barely read at all. Meetings! This system can ask too much of people – and yet without meetings you can't have participation.

That's an aspect of the contradiction in which we can't but be involved. To become developed in this modern world you have to be a technologized society: but to become a technologized society you have to be developed. Competing as we must with technologically advanced societies, we have to try to run a little faster than them. The necessary effort is tremendous.

Yet there are critics, sometimes friendly critics, who expect us to function as a society, as an economy, which has *already* gone through the necessary development. That kind of critique can be stimulating. But at other times all these various pressures from outside can seem intolerable, asking of us more than we can give, than anyone can give. As it is, we have laid foundations for an independent and decent future, no matter with what inadequacies. The institutions *work*.

We have gone a long way towards restoring human dignity in our islands, self-respect after an immense period when there wasn't any, when our people were denied even that they were a people. The old self-humblings are gone – such as when you'd pull off your cap in the presence of a person with power or wealth.

Three old men had in fact pulled off their caps the Sunday before, as I was driving with José Lobo from São Jorge dos Ornos. I'd asked José why they'd done that? He said he thought it was because the Bishop had a car like ours, 'and they'll have mistaken you for a Church dignitary'.

Olívio finds the story charming. And there are of course clerical opponents of the PAICV and its regime. 'They even run an opposition paper, the editor used to be a Party member. Now he's turned to outright opposition.' Olívio shrugs. 'But for what that paper's worth in terms of criticism, it exists.' As it happens I have read this periodical's latest issues, and find them vague, rhetorical, and all too clearly stemming from Rome.

'What we can say, further', Olívio continues, 'is that our people do not confuse State rules with Party rules.' It was understood that the Party should lead but not govern, or govern as little as possible, and in any case less and less. And the State, as executive government, should also govern as little as possible by handing down orders from above. 'Go and examine the work of our People's Courts, and see how it looks from there.'

V

In 1986 there are rather more than 255 *tribunáis de zona*, 'zonal courts', spread around the islands; and a majority of them, all of them of course unpaid, now have several years' experience. Proceedings are invariably open to the public. They have to be open to the public if the courts' functions are to be realized. The visitor may go to as many sessions as he likes. He may also arrange meetings with magistrates out of court hours.

I meet Pedro Gomes at a meeting with eight of the members of the local council (*comissão de moradores*) of Alecrim, a suburb of the city of Mindelo on São Vicente island. He is a municipal worker, middle-aged, greying a little at the temples, courteous though sparing of words as Cape Verdeans tend to be. A member of the first Alecrim council created in 1983, he is also a member of the newly-elected second council. He says it took more than a year for people to understand what the council was for. In colonial times everything had been decided by the *administrador* or perhaps his local side-kick, the *cab'chef*, 'and people just thought we were a new sort of *cab'chef*'.

The local tribunal had preceded the first local council of Alecrim, and the work of the two organs had at once become confused with each other. 'It took a lot more time,' says Pedro Gomes, 'to get it all straight.'

The Alecrim tribunal, these councillors say, likewise needed a year's work before it could bring itself to initiate a trial. Now, they say, it works rather well. But its punitive judgements, applied with short prison sentences or social labour or money fines, emerge as secondary in importance. First in importance, these councillors say, is reconciliation: overwhelmingly, as it appears, in cases of alleged defamation and bodily harm through drunken fights or minor uproars, cases of alleged theft being relatively rare.

The familiar problem, it seems, is to ensure that enough persons sit as magistrates and give enough of their time to it. This is often a great deal of time, because evidence in highly personalized cases tends to be lengthy. Yet it seems likewise clear that the courts are now relied upon and even found indispensable. There is the usual shortage of proper accommodation for courts, but the main weakness in 1986 lies probably in an undue predominance of men magistrates over women.

Looking at the work of these courts can give the visitor an entry to the intimacies of island life. A case I heard argued in a Sant'Antão tribunal concerned an offence usually punished by a fine: walking on irrigation dykes. Irrigated land is precious in this country with so little of it, and the damaging of dykes can be serious. 'This man', a peasant magistrate explained to me, 'was twice caught walking on a dyke. We fined him 300 escudos, that's as much as a third of the maximum we can fine.'

Appeals are allowed, but seem rare. Public opinion, very present as a local audience, is on the side of the courts, magistrates affirm, 'so long as we judges judge by conscience as well as by the letter of the law'. This attitude of acceptance and approval derives, as one sees, from the value people attach to the reconciliation of minor disputes – major crimes such as homicide are dealt with in professional courts – and from people's perception of their local magistrates as a means for achieving reconciliation.

This seemed to emerge repeatedly in the few cases I had time to follow. But Professor Boaventura de Sousa Santos, a Portuguese jurist who has made a detailed survey of this judicial system in Cape Verde, confirms it from a far wider and professional experience. Professor Santos examined many cases. Here is a single one, though I think singularly instructive, from the tribunal of Fonte Filipe, another suburb of Mindelo.

Cesario Moreira is in the dock. He is a stevedore aged forty-five, the unmarried father of seven children, and given to violence when drunk. He had previously knifed his neighbour Umberto 'for no reason I can remember, it was the *grog*'. The Fonte Filipe court had sentenced him to thirty days in prison but had reduced this to a suspended sentence, given his family responsibilities, and had bound him over to keep off the *grog* and behave himself. Drunk again, Cesario comes home one day and makes an 'uproar', *zaragata*, at which eventually the neighbours arrive. The Mindelo police are called. A court case ensues.

Long details, recriminations, explanations, as the court hears about this 'uproar'. Joana, Cesario's companion, had failed to send him his midday meal, though she and the kids only ate because he worked. 'So I stayed out till 9 but I came home with bananas on my shoulder, 10 kilos of bananas. But as I am telling you the truth I will say that I had fifteen *grogs* on the way home . . .' The chairman of the tribunal asks Joana if this was the first 'uproar' since Cesario was given his suspended sentence?

JOANA: It wasn't the first. He just has the habit of coming home with his problem. But I'm ashamed to go to the authorities [*autoridade*], so I've never gone.

CHAIRMAN [probing]: And are your neighbours satisfied with what goes on in your house?

JOANA: No, sir, our neighbours can't be satisfied with the uproars that he [the defendant] makes. I'm really ashamed before the neighbours.

The chairman agrees with her that the defendant's behaviour does seem undesirable. But the chairman is a man, after all, and asks if Joana isn't 'a friend of her children's father?'

JOANA [very upset]: A friend of that shameless fellow [*afronta*]? He's always in trouble. Who could stand this problem? Who? I'm ashamed.

CHAIRMAN: But isn't he worker? Doesn't he support the family when he earns?

JOANA: He does when he earns.

CHAIRMAN: With a working man who works, earns, supports the family, how can a woman be so hostile?

JOANA: Then why doesn't he stop his drinking, so's to keep out of trouble? The drink's what's wrong with him. Why doesn't he stop it?

Duly questioned, Cesario is penitent and blames the drink.

CHAIRMAN: Then why not give it up?

CESARIO: That's life.

He asks for a suspended sentence because he has children to support of whom six are under the age to work for themselves. But this time the court gives him thirty days in prison, having judged 'by the law and by our conscience'. Cesario, interviewed afterwards, finds the sentence just but regrettable. Likewise interviewed afterwards, the magistrates in question say that the public, on the whole, had been critical of their previous decision to reduce imprisonment to a suspended sentence, and equally against substituting a fine, because, they said, Cesario would simply repeat the offence.

So this time the court sent him to prison. But the magistrates were also his neighbours over many years. They had no faith in the remedial value of a prison sentence, 'but we'd really no alternative'. On the day after consigning Cesario to the calabooze, one of the magistrates on behalf of himself and the others went down to the port where Cesario normally worked, and drummed up contributions in money for Cesario's children.

9 Woman's place is . . .?

I

Generally, participation works and grows because people do in fact like to govern themselves. They like to feel they are moving ahead, keeping up with the times: changing – the words are those of Aristides Pereira – 'from an archaic to a modern society'.

But a proper scepticism may reply that in Africa over these years, depressingly often, people and above all rural people have found themselves pushed from above, have found this unjust or undesirable, and have simply withdrawn their loyalty. I doubt if there is any frontier in mainland Africa now, certainly in West Africa, across which otherwise law-abiding folk do not move illegally, or smuggle their goods, in more or less complete indifference to 'the national interest'. And they do this much as though the nationalism of the 'political class', increasingly an urban 'class', has become as alien or hostile as the old colonial rulers.

This failure of nationalism to carry peoples 'from an archaic to a modern society' has been variously explained. 'Senegal today, after a quarter of a century of national independence', Professor Boubacar Barry commented in 1985,

> is in profound economic, political and social crisis. This general crisis is the consequence of a policy of almost unbroken continuity with the colonial period, leading to continued rural impoverishment and to the reinforcement of a bureaucratic bourgeoisie: of a 'new class' which, by its illicit self-enrichment or political blindness, prevents the formation of a true national bourgeoisie outside the grip of international capital.

So the peasants revert to subsistence agriculture, refuse to repay debts or contract new ones, and look to the 'parallel trade' of smuggling. The rural world, says Barry, 'explodes with anger'.

The Republic of Guinea – ex-French Guinea, 'Guinea-Conakry' as distinct from Guinea-Bissau – won its independence in 1958 by 'mass mobilization and anti-colonial struggle . . . a remarkable

Like many of their sisters elsewhere, Cape Verdean women have had to cope with an all-pervasive male domination, a rasping and most tiresome *machismo* which persists in direct confrontation with the aims of national liberation. But times are beginning to change. Women are reaching out to new rights and responsibilities. (Photo copyright Augusta Conchiglia)

achievement [which] gave birth to a new state and nation', in the judgement of a Guinea scholar, Professor Lansiné Kaba, now teaching in America. But he goes on to say that the one party in question – the Parti Démocrate de la Guinée – became after independence a rigidly monopolist political bureau; and the political bureau soon became the helpless instrument of its secretary-general, President Sékou Touré; and Touré became in due course a bloodstained dictator. No one was moving anywhere in that 'one-man show' unless Touré pushed him; all too often, then, he moved into prison or a grave.

There spring to mind other examples where power has come out of 'the barrel of a gun', and the gun has been grabbed by men of paranoiac violence: Amin in Uganda, Bokassa in the Central African Republic, others elsewhere, until it can sometimes seem that an Africa of the warlords has engulfed the Africa of democratic promise. The one-party state, all too frequently, has become the no-party state, and the no-party state has proved so fragile that any upstart soldier could seize it overnight.

Could all this have been averted? There may be different answers. But a few points seem worth making in this context. One is that the struggle for anti-colonial independence was obliged by circumstance to take the road of nationalism. A second is that in taking this road the pioneers of independence were bound to expose themselves and their successors to every hazard of the colonial legacy and its economic implications and impositions. A third is that the 'archaic society' of the rural majority, however preferable that society may have been to the rural miseries of today, cannot be restored or created anew. If nothing else, the great famines of the 1970s and 1980s have proved that Africa must change, or Africa will die. The only issue of importance, now, concerns the finding of the means of change.

The relevance of all this to Cape Verde is partial but real. Whatever successes the Cape Verdean regime of independence has achieved, whether in its politics or other fields of action, all owe their dynamism to a popular acceptance. With whatever continuing doubts and hesitations, this people has willingly entered on a process of self-transformation. Here, as it has come about, even the most cautious sceptic will find no turning away from the new State, and no indifference to the new nation, on any scale which can 'set the clock back' to a para-colonial situation. This may be surprising, but this is what the evidence portrays.

'Elitism' can, of course, arise. If it arises, it can develop. If it develops, it can ruin participation. This is what must appear, in 1986, to have happened in Guinea-Bissau even while its President, General Nino Vieira, had had no such intention. The coup of November 1980 in Guinea-Bissau, rejecting union with Cape Verde and riding roughshod over democratic institutions so laboriously installed in years of struggle, has remained a vivid sore. 'What did it teach you?' I ask, in 1986, one of the veterans who came home in August 1974 (flying from Bissau to Cape Verde, as it happened, in the same plane as myself).

'It taught us to listen, listen still more carefully than we were doing then, listen very hard.'

What they listened and would listen to, in terms of people's claims, interests, anxieties and aspirations, will have appeared at least in outline during the course of this book, as well as the modes and approaches adopted by this Party in its listening. They concern a process of self-transformation in which, as may be expected, some aspects are easier than others, and a few, especially those relating to intimate habit and tradition, are extremely difficult. Among the latter the most difficult may also be the most necessary to the self-liberating process. I mean a large change in the status of women. The huge discriminations practised by Cape Verdean men against Cape Verdean women may well be a product of Cape Verde's distinctive history, as well as one of the general frailties of human nature. Today these discriminations appear as a deadweight which may even threaten to sink the ship of participation altogether, or, at least, reverse it to its starting-point.

A system of participation which proceeds without a growing acceptance of equal status and respect between the sexes is one that must be heading for the rocks. Little of any such acceptance on the part of men can yet be found, so far as I have seen, outside the practice of devoted Party members and some others who have wives with a good deal of education. This being so, it is fair to ask if this people really does wish for a system of participation? Or does this people merely want relief from poverty and backwardness within its traditional cultural limits, its *machismo*, its social irresponsibility? The irresponsibility has been, still is, impressive.

II

On one of my inland 'walking tours' I happened to visit an uncle of a Party leader, an emigrant living normally in Europe who comes back for holidays in the family home. We had moved off the track into a garden gained by a gate through a stone wall. Our host turns out to be a stoutish man of perhaps sixty, very sure of himself, exuding the successful emigrant's contempt for stay-at-homes. He gives us a good Cape Verdean welcome: hand clasps, laughter, a comfortable chair. In Europe, being dark of skin, he must be careful of his claims to importance; here he can happily display them.

His nephew teases him with affectionate questions which are also for my benefit. Naturally, they are about family matters, for this is a country of endless family gossip. It transpires that our host has twenty-one living children; 'or maybe it's more', he adds with great cheerfulness, 'you can't always keep count'. His father was thought to have had as many as sixty-three children. 'But again, it could have been more.' I recall that Amílcar Cabral's father Juvenal had scored about as many as that, and I remain puzzled.

Afterwards I ask my friend the nephew: 'But how do they support so many?'

'Oh they don't, they support some of them. As for the rest, there's always the mother.'

Hence a painful wound within this society. Its guarantee of continuity and social essence depend all the time on women. But its daily life is dominated by the wills or whims of men. This 'tradition', as it is rather too comfortably called, no doubt arose from the ancient dislocations of slavery. For slavery wrecked any balanced family structure and made social irresponsibility into a norm, even into a necessity. Then the long years of semi-slavery in forced labour prolonged and deepened the same dislocations. And the emigration of men, forced or voluntary, has left women to defend their lives as best they may. In different circumstances, the case has been general in most of Africa.

But women here became dual victims: victims of the archipelago's colonial misgovernment and ruin, and also victims of a male mastery, a rasping and most tiresome *machismo*, which even now, when things begin to be different, the visitor encounters every day. He also hears about it, for what is chiefly different in this respect is that now there are plenty of women who talk of it openly and frankly, though as yet they are still a small minority.

Up at Fajã de Marcos, a hill hamlet joined two years ago by cobbled road to the capital of Sant'Antão island, Joana Fonseca Modesto is local secretary of the *Organisação da Mulher*, the OM or Women's Organization of Cape Verde. In middle life, she is a person of handsome bearing, very much a woman with the charm of Cape Verdean femininity but with a tough peasant strength. Until lately a place of profound isolation, her hamlet is now in the midst of the movement of change, and Joana's local OM has thirty-three activists.

Joana considers the problems: perfectly typical, as I think, of these islands. Many of the older women have husbands, but nominally for the most part. She herself, with eight children, has not seen her husband for ten years and does not expect to see him. Few of the younger women have husbands but most have children. 'As there are no husbands, so there aren't any men to take responsibility for the children. It's us women who must do that, bring them up and work for them, even doing heavy labour in the fields.'

But why have women agreed to bear children when they know that the fathers will not necessarily, or even usually, recognize their fatherhood? Joana, like other women of whom I ask the same question, looks at me with a mingled pity and impatience: who is this man fallen from the moon? But she sets out to explain. What emerges, broadly, is that 'tradition' awards respect to women in the measure of their being attached to a man, or, as it may be, more than one man. Yet attachment to a man without the result of children has never been possible, so 'tradition' has taken it as axiomatic that a woman's self-respect goes with her having children, however fathered. The outcome has been a hallowed acceptance of a more or less complete sexual 'liberty' – read, irresponsibility – for men. Yet a corresponding 'liberty' for women, although an unavoidable corollary in this country of long-term emigration and geographically divided families, can still be the subject of carping gossip and the award of nasty reputations.

The cultural process now in train is entirely at odds with these 'traditions'. But not only the cultural process. In times when famine struck every twenty years or so, carrying off in a year or two a substantial fraction of the population, an unlimited production of children could be a necessary compensation. But today, with a regime which can and does provide against famine – conserving stocks of grain in State warehouses, for example, and in other more general ways – an unlimited production of children can threaten a social and economic disaster.

The Cape Verdean Minister of Health, Dr Ireneo Gomes, is a Brazil-trained physician and psychologist. He too speaks openly about these matters. Another product of the Mindelo lycée and its student nationalism, he likewise speaks from a long commitment.

With a demographic increase of around 3 per cent a year, on the present trend we shall have half a million people by 2000. And very soon after that we shall have more than double the number of people we have today. We have greatly reduced our rate of infant mortality since independence, so all the more must we now find ways of reducing our birth rate.

But this, he says, cannot possibly be easy.

There is the Church with its hostile attitudes to birth control. But perhaps more serious, and more difficult, there are habits derived from going abroad to find work. A man goes for a time, say for six months, and takes care to leave his wife pregnant so that, when he comes back, he'll know the child's his own.

Whenever, that is, he intends to recognize his fatherhood.

Men anyway tend to oppose birth control because they fear that their women may use it while they're abroad.

We certainly hope to get the birth rate down over coming years, and there are good prospects of success. But we can't try to do this 'from above': it's for men and women to decide for themselves.

What we *can* do, through the Party and our process of participation, is to act as dynamizers in getting the problem widely discussed and thought about, in trying to promote a greater individual responsibility. Tradition has made men irresponsible. And that's an attitude against which our organizations, including the Women's Organization, has so far made no real headway.

The spokeswomen of the Women's Organization – OM, *Organisação da Mulher* – speak to the same point. Much has been achieved, they insist, since independence. 'We have an enlightened Party and government', says their chairperson in 1986, Maria das Dores, 'and we have won enlightened laws. These laws advance and protect women's rights in marriage, divorce, inheritance, and in the condition of being an unmarried mother.' Legally, for example, daughters now inherit equally with sons, even if of unmarried origin. Legally, no man can any longer abandon his child without providing for it. Legally, every child must have a recognized father.

> The problems come in applying these laws. We are still plagued by the attitudes of male superiority, but it's part of the problem that those same attitudes have long since become women's attitudes as well. Years ago we had illusions about the possibility of women's liberation by changing men's attitudes. Now we know that we must and can work to change women's attitudes. It's what we've been doing since independence, and we've made some progress.

Continuing emigration raises other problems. There are more women in the islands than men.

> Another traditional attitude – women's too – holds that a man shouldn't be made to admit paternity if he doesn't want to. Women say: 'If he won't give his name to his child, it's not for me, who's the mother, to force him.' That's women's pride. It makes an attitude hard to change.

OM is one of the mass organizations of participation. In 1986 it has some 9000 members, only thirteen of whom are paid officials. Its spokeswomen say that its efforts are better welcomed in rural areas than in the towns. One reason for this, they say, is what gets known or believed in the towns about some versions of American feminism. 'That women should boycott men, for instance. Women here can only regard that idea as absurd. But our women in the villages don't get to hear that sort of thing. They come forward more easily to join us.'

A rough estimate of progress and resistance may be extracted from figures for women's participation. Out of the 6447 Party members and candidates for membership registered at the end of 1984, only 14 per cent were women. In the 255 people's courts, male magistrates outnumbered female magistrates, in the same year, by about six to one. The proportion of women in local councils is considerably higher, but there may be some doubt as to how far women's participation in council work is effective in practice. The newly-elected (third) People's National Assembly of 1986 has eleven women members against seven in the previous Assembly. But the proportion is no better, since the elected membership had been enlarged. 'And once more,' comments Maria das Dores, 'it is partly the fault of women. The initial lists of candidates presented 25 per cent of women. But fewer than 12 per cent were actually chosen.'

An intense effort, nationally, is being invested in a modernized and wide system of public education. This has had to be done against two large handicaps. One was a low rate of literacy in 1975, if much higher than in any other Portuguese colony. By the middle 1980s the illiteracy rate had been reduced to about 45 per cent, which still meant, in real terms, about 80,000 persons over the age of fifteen; and it was planned to reduce this again over the coming five years.

Below the age of fifteen the situation was already vastly different, for about a fifth of the whole population was at school by 1985, or double the number of pupils ten years earlier. In primary schools there is in 1986 a reasonable equality of numbers between boys and girls, but not yet at the secondary level. OM spokeswomen say that this is partly because of premature pregnancies when girls have to quit school, and partly because of parental prejudice against educating girls. 'But the secondary-level position is still better than at independence.'

A second large handicap in public education has been the legacy of Portuguese teaching aims and methods. These are said to have been rigidly bookish and elitist, little appropriate to the practical realism now required. Available history textbooks, as in other newly liberated colonies, were a mere reflection of the history of the colonizing power, a bland recounting of the blessings of imperialism. Maths and science texts were lacking or seriously out of date. Beyond these obstructions there was a manifest need to re-train teachers, and reshape syllabuses, for circumstances vastly different from those of colonial times.

A far-reaching reform of the system was on the stocks in 1986 but my own impression, for what it may be worth, is that much ground must be covered before any such reform can be effective. As in other African colonies, the educational system above the most elementary level was geared to the ideas and ambitions of Europe, so that students came out of African secondary schools with no real understanding of the realities and needs of their own countries. In a large sense, one may even say, they were mis-educated for useful life, and certainly for contented life. And this is a burden of 'unadaptedness' which cannot be quickly shifted. Listening to educators here, it seems at least that the burden is seen for what it is.

III

The regime's installation of a national health service, preventive in its priorities rather than curative, has clearly had large implications for the social relationships of women and men. 'Medicine for the people' is proving another factor of cultural change.

'In 1975', recalls Dr Gomes,

> there wasn't in Cape Verde so much as the bare notion of the meaning of a public health service, let alone of medical specialism in any of its branches. When I myself returned in 1974, for example, I was the first fully-trained psychologist ever known here. Nobody knew what a psychologist might be. Persons came to see me, claiming to be ill when there was nothing wrong with them, just to find out.
>
> There was an old asylum where disturbed persons were beaten, or treated with electric shocks and so on quite unscientifically. And in the outer islands, or the hamlets of the interior of our big islands, people hadn't so much as clapped eyes on a medical doctor. They used to call me 'Mr Nurse' – at least they knew what a nurse was.

A few more statistics are useful. There had been Portuguese military doctors for the garrisons here, but these had gone home at independence. In July 1975, the month of independence, the whole archipelago had a total of thirteen doctors, of whom eleven were Cape Verdeans, most of whom had come back late in 1974 or early in 1975. Ten years later, in 1985, there were 106 doctors; and all had emerged from a six-year training. In 1975 there had been one doctor for every 23,000 Cape Verdeans: in 1985 there was one for every 2300. The number of qualified nurses had increased from 140 in 1975 to 225 ten years later. And as with doctors, new recruits to nursing are continually in training.

Dr Gomes speaks of the extremely centralized system of the Portuguese.

> Narrowly curative, their system had concentrated all hospital facilities in two old buildings in Praia and Mindelo. Otherwise there were no hospital beds which deserved the name, and no laboratory technicians. But today we have a ratio of one laboratory technician for every 530 persons, while medical services are already provided in three new hospitals, seven health centres, fifteen pre-natal and infant-care clinics, and thirty-four general health clinics, with specialized services for malaria and leprosy.

Thanks to an insistent accent on preventive medicine, widely decentralized through the islands, the endemic disease of malaria no longer exists in the archipelago. 'Or at least', adds the prudent Dr Gomes,

> We have not had a single case in the last four years. What still exists is the mosquito, and now we have to eliminate that as well. Meanwhile we defend the archipelago against vector-carrying mosquitoes that may come by ship or plane. All arriving means of transport are sprayed, and at Sal and Praia airports [with air-links from the exterior] we maintain units who test for malaria in persons coming from infected zones abroad.

Child malnutrition, in Dr Gomes's opinion, remains the worst problem. Some 50,000 children, aged persons and chronic invalids, perhaps one-sixth of the population, continue in 1986 to receive free food supplied by the World Food Programme of the United Nations. This free food will continue to be vital. 'In general terms, however', comments Dr Gomes,

> we should like now to concentrate services on those who need them most – not treating as equal in need those who are really not equal: for example, the person with no more than four walls and the person with a little wealth of one sort or another. There are those who can pay something. Perhaps they should?

As it is, with a national health service widely installed, the rate of infant mortality has been cut from 108.6 per 1000 in 1975 to 73.5 per 1000 in 1985: 'and that is much below the average for our continent. But it's not being over-optimistic to affirm that we can get it down still further.' Life expectancy has meanwhile lengthened: roughly from 55.3 years for a man and 56.9 for a woman, in 1970, to 60.77 and 62.9 years, respectively, in 1985.

'Public hygiene? Yes, that's better. But we can't ask too much of people. Asking people to go out and clean the streets in their free time may be asking more than we should.' Public hygiene is a matter for the local councils and their volunteers. I think of those at Campo Bais, getting home in the evening after climbing 670 metres and a hard day's labour. 'Maybe', queries Dr Gomes, 'we need to reach the point where such work is paid for?'

Dr Gomes is another 'continuer of Cabral'. Reflecting on the future, he talks of the young in whom Cabral always saw the justification for the pain and effort of anti-colonial liberation.

> It's often said we're in a time of transition. No, it's a time of transformation, and there's a difference. We need to *disorganize* the old, the known, the familiar, just as much as we need to organize the new. In this country, where we are in process of discovering ourselves . . .

10 Land: trees: green renewal

I

During the tense middle months of 1974 when Sancho was expected down his mountain with furious intentions, the moderate and respectable of Mindelo and Praia were further alarmed by fresh slogans clandestinely painted on public walls. None of these messages from the night seems to have achieved the influence, whether of enthusiasm among the many or apprehension among the few, of *Nos Terra pa Nos Pavo!*: *Our Land for Our People*! The many, taking it also in the literal sense, expected nothing less. The few deplored it as another threat of dangerous extremism by *os meninhos malcriados*: 'the badly brought-up children' in the scornful term used by the moderate and respectable for the youthful activists, often lycée students or ex-students, of the movement of Cabral. I was not there at the time, but the evidence is copious.

The far-reaching reform of land tenure and usage had always been considered a prime task of liberation, and Cabral, as a skilled agronomist, had ensured that it should stand centrally in the long-term programme of the PAIGC. He saw it as essential to freeing productive potentials on the one hand, and to ending gross forms of exploitation on the other. But little was or could be securely known about the detailed realities of Cape Verdean agriculture as long as there was no seriously scientific research; and none was undertaken as long as colonial rule continued.

What had been understood by simple appraisal of the daily scene was that the ecology and rural economy of Cape Verde were sinking ever further into desert and decline. The old economy of trade of the sixteenth century was known to have given way to a largely subsistence agriculture based on maize and beans; while a total of about one hundred years in the four centuries since then

On these islands long bare of tree-cover, some nine million saplings were planted between 1977 and 1987, with further mass annual plantings in prospect. This seedling nursery on the island of Sant'Antão is one of many on the islands that meet the needs of this on-going programme of afforestation. (Photo copyright Augusta Conchiglia)

had been scored by famine and a terrifying mortality, against which this drought-stricken cultivation had proved helpless.

An ancient system based on slavery had thus made way for a system of tenure and production based on share-cropping and on cash-rent, but without any improvement in productive capacity or in land conservation. And so ingrained were the habits of this system that the peasants had come to accept it as though nothing better could be thinkable. Year after year they continued, and in the years following independence would still continue, to sow their maize and beans in the wan hope of rains in July and September that repeatedly failed to arrive. A common colonial comment on this repetitive tenacity was to put it down to 'peasant stupidity': fruitlessly, the peasants blindly did again what they had done before. That the colonial condition itself had induced a psychology of despair may be nearer the truth.

Then how could this same tenacity be used in service of a better agriculture, given the circumstances of the archipelago? Cabral and his companions had pondered the question. Cyclical drought was a manifest fact of nature that could not be changed. A maize-grain agriculture relying on the arrival of regular and timely rains could never be able to avoid times of disaster. All known history proved as much. Yet the understanding available even by the end of the colonial period 'allowed no alternative', in the words of the Cape Verdean agronomist João Pereira Silva, to the system in place, 'while the system in place had its logic and justification up to the 1970s, in that it functioned, although at the price of drastic falls in population through famine and through emigration'.

Some other Atlantic islands, for example some of the Canary Islands, might face much the same climatic problems but achieve a far stronger basis in fruit and horticulture; Cape Verde had simply continued as before. 'And if continuing-as-before was certainly a *via dolorosa* of fragile survival,' continues Silva, writing here in a retrospect of 1985,

> it was no less true that an alternative agriculture, based on irrigated horticulture and fruit, on rain-fed fruit, on stock-raising and timber – an agriculture in which cereal production becomes of secondary importance – must depend on a trading contact with the outside world. Only our independence of 1975 has made that contact possible for us.

The process of change and re-structuring would still have to be a long one, and its end-results assessable only in twenty years' time or more. Meanwhile it was imperative to begin. Beginning called first of all for solid information.

Initial scientific studies of the rural economy were launched in 1978. They revealed a grim reality. It was established that 39 per cent of all peasants, on average through the islands, owned no land at all; while another 30 per cent owned too little for bare subsistence and were thus obliged, if they could, to rent land from proprietors who, nearly always, lived in towns or in foreign countries. A few of these proprietors owned much land; most owned little; but all lived off the labour of an effectively landless peasantry.

Writing of this situation before land reform took hold, Silva comments that:

> The majority of Cape Verdean landowners receive revenues from the agricultural sector. They appropriate an important part of the surplus created by landless peasants. They consume this surplus outside the agricultural sector, and to that sector they contribute nothing.

He calls it a system of desertification, desert-making.

Having got to grips with this reality, the independent government set about trying to deal with it. Based on detailed surveys, a series of decree-laws was introduced in 1981. With the first of these – again quoting Silva, now Minister of Agriculture – 'the government nationalized the various large land-estates belonging to absentee owners and traitors'. This was a total of rather less than fifty persons or properties, but included most of the pockets of irrigated land.

> Later, sub-tenancy farming on new contracts of tenancy was forbidden, as was the further division of properties into plots of less than one hectare (2.2 acres) in the rain-fed zones, or of half a hectare (1.1. acres) in the pockets of irrigation. Measures were strengthened to allow rent reduction in time of bad harvest or crop failure.

The primary aim of this process, thus initiated, has been to end exploitation through share-cropping and leasehold, though by prudent advance from one small gain to the next while refraining from dramatic changes or expectations. Much effort has gone into persuasion and explanation, none at all into administrative use of force. At the end of 1985 Silva could hope that the system of share-cropping was accepted as belonging to the past, even if much still existed, and that tenure-by-leasehold should soon cease to be a dominant form of land use. The lines of advance were laid down, and were generally accepted, even if progress along them remained slow and difficult.

II

The reasons for the slowness and difficulty are among the complexities of the Cape Verdean scene. They vividly illustrate its peculiar attributes. They have little to do with any lack of peasant interest in land reform or perception of its value. Nothing in peasant meetings I have attended has been more discussed than the gains and problems of land reform, and its challenge to old habits and attitudes of mind. And while there must remain a fount of scepticism among peasants who have still to believe, inwardly, that 'their programme' is what is being applied, with one exception of 1981 there has been no movement of opposition or refusal.

Even the exception of 1981 was brief. Evidently stirred up by hostile emigrants still hoping to revive the perished fortunes of the little 'bourgeois groups' of 1974, such as UPICV, some peasants of the Ribeira Grande canyon in Sant'Antão came into town with cudgels in order to prevent, as they said, 'the theft of their land and stock' by this thing called land reform. One man lost his life in the ensuing uproar and two were wounded by the police in Ribeira Grande; but it was over almost as soon as it had started and no repetition followed. Those who set this uproar going had claimed that emigrants were to lose their land. But the land reform laws said that land will be taken only from those emigrants who have finally cut their links with the archipelago; and these laws have been kept.

Encoding the decree-laws which had set this process going, a basic law on agrarian reform was presented to the National Assembly in March 1982, and passed after debate which led to modifications. It came into application on 1 January 1983. At the end of the process, writes Silva, 'about 74 per cent of Cape Verdean peasants will have cast off the bonds of dependence which have bound them to one or more owners of land . . . and our agriculture will be based on a system of small peasant enterprise but integrated within various types of consumer and producer co-operatives'. Economic desertification will have ceased, and the process is then intended to move, if slowly, towards systemic co-operation.

The situation of 1986 showed that share-cropping had begun to be seriously reduced in the islands of Santiago and Fogo, where it has been the principal form of tenure; and the passage into use by leasehold was taking its place, with use by outright ownership (*posse util*) likewise taking shape on expropriated land or land otherwise held by the State. But no one who has ever attempted to look at the complexities of any land reform will be likely to imagine that neat statistics and conclusions can summarize its process of change. The process has been difficult to start; the process remains difficult to push forward.

Travelling in Santiago in 1986, we arrive at the small town of Santa Cruz: the Cape Verdean writer and social critic Manuel Delgado, and myself. Here is where a rough stone quayside gives uncertain shelter to sail-and-motor schooners which ply between Santiago and some of the smaller islands, but the town is chiefly dependent on artisan production and neighbouring agriculture.

We are met by the government official in charge, Arlindo da Sousa, a pleasantly efficient man in his thirties whom I had known in Sant'Antão during 1980; and we begin to discuss the local land reform. Does it exist? If so, what has it done? Arlindo clearly thinks the first question unnecessary, but is wry about the second Nobody, after all, is going to affirm that the land reform is an easy or rapid process.

Manuel Delgado's convictions, for his part, are passionately attached to the vision of a Cape Verde altogether better than the land of his childhood twenty years ago; but Manuel is a social critic who likes to stand on the ground of scepticism before allowing himself to look ahead. As Brecht remarked of the prime need in social change: 'First the square meal, then the ideal.'

We begin with a stout-hearted peasant, Domingos Correa, aged about forty-five. A share-cropper until 1984, Domingos now pays rent to his landowner, who resides in the neighbouring island of Maio. This landowner lives off the cash-rent – as, before, he lived off the rent-in-kind – paid by Domingos Correa, and by ten other former share-croppers, *parceiros* who are now *rendeiros*. Domingos approves of the land reform: the rent he pays in cash is worth less than the rent he used to pay in kind. But he has a problem.

The problem is, it seems, of a nature that is typical enough. Domingos is not only a lessee; he is also an informal bailiff who collects cash-rent from the other ten share-croppers on behalf of their and his landowner. But some of these other ten do not pay their rent. They do not refuse to pay it; they simply do not pay it. This worries Domingos, clearly a conscientious person. He wants to know how they can be made to pay the rent they owe?

A long discussion. The law says that lessees have to pay. Each must pay – and of course many do pay – according to the individual contracts drawn up between them and their landowners. This contract is a kind of bargain supervised by the local office of the Land Reform Commission. It provides for a rent that is in the favour of the new lessee, but even so there are those who do not pay.

I ask if this isn't therefore a matter for the local people's court? Domingos thinks that probably it should be, but seems unsure. Subsequent inquiries confirm that rent defaulters are in fact supposed to be taken before their local people's court and can, if recalcitrant, be expelled from the land they cultivate. But the issue, clearly, is difficult. Continued payment of rent to absentee landowners – living, mostly, in the towns – is widely resented, even if the level of exploitation is lower than it was before the reform. But the expulsion of defaulters is going to be far less popular.

In this case, I think, the Maio landowner will get his rents in due course, or most of them; but the trend of reform will go towards the gradual elimination of leasehold and thus of rent. All that will take time, as will the smoothing out of minor disputes such as currently on Fogo, where small landowners who grow coffee are at odds with peasants traditionally employed to look after the coffee bushes. The owners want to plant more land with their excellent coffee, the 'guardians' want to plant more beans and maize, while the Land Commission tries to find a compromise.

By 1986 the whole complex process of tenure reform had acquired a certain momentum. Already it was widely clear, especially in the pockets of irrigated land where land is passing into *posse util*, into outright individual ownership by he cultivators themselves, that the resultant plots are often too small to support their new owners. Beyond the transfer of tenure to the peasants lies an eventual perspective of productive co-operation. And this, in turn, implies the need for ecological improvement: for soil conservation, for better use of water, for trees.

III

The history of silence stripped these islands of their trees in times long past, mostly for wood for cooking fires; and its little towns were crouched even by the beginning of this century in landscapes of unrelenting desert. Surviving trees could be rare enough to be known by name, and cherished as ancient marvels.

Nobody seems ever to have replanted; except that colonial rule, here and there, made its erratic gesture to good sense and put down wells and laid out gardens of tropical delight, an acre here and half an acre there, tiny shelters of green and grateful shade within a flint-dry wilderness.

In this respect Cape Verde was merely ahead of the times. West Africa's mainland of today shows vast areas of ruined land that were tropical forest thirty or twenty or even ten years ago; and the ripping out of splendid hardwoods, mahogany and iroko and the rest, still continues apace. As the sands of the Sahara push southward the timber-strippers push northward. A whole rain-forest ecology is passing away. Leached and eroded soils take its place.

The rainfall pattern compounds the degradation even where, as in Cape Verde, volcanic soils retain a wonderful fertility. In rare times of rain, the barren hillsides of the archipelago are spread with green carpets that flourish for a week or so; but in usual times of drought or semi-drought these hillsides range in colour from a deadened grey to angry red and ochre. When the rains come they fall in tumult as though the skies had opened, and then the canyons briefly rage with pelting streams that bounce and race downward to the sea. Or so I am told, for I have never been here when abundant rains fell. Otherwise the islands can look as though rain has never fallen and never will fall.

But today there are trees, millions of trees, some of them at nine years old already making woodlands several metres tall. Planned reafforestation began in 1977, two years after independence, and proceeds annually. By 1985, some nine million trees had been planted, even though drought remained severe until that year; and between 70 and 75 per cent of these, according to the Cape Verdean forestry service, have taken with success. This annual planting continues. Already the bare hillsides around Praia, perhaps the most impressive example of this ecological restoration, are beginning to vanish beneath woodland cover.

A massive voluntary effort has enabled the foresters to get this done. It appears that seedlings, grown in special watered nurseries, must be planted in prepared holes whenever rain falls, or, when rain does not fall, with the help of mobile water tanks. So whenever rain has fallen, rarely since 1977 but even so now and then, volunteers have rushed from their places of work to plant seedlings in holes already dug. These volunteers have come from the mass organizations of participation – the trades unions, the youth, the women – as well as from local councils, government offices, and anywhere else that is organized or organizable.

Tree planting is planned to continue at a rough rate of 2 million young saplings every year for the foreseeable future; and the back-up in seedling nurseries, plant selection and specialized supervision is already well assured. So much may be seen even by an amateur forester like myself. Fogo the Volcano, for example, had planted 700,000 trees with success by 1985; and its plan provides for another 300,000 saplings each year, or sufficient to cover some 500 hectares (1100 acres) annually with a prospective success rate of 70 per cent. Brava, a much smaller island, had put in 150,000 saplings by the same year, so far covering 322 hectares (644 acres) with a corresponding plan of annual extension.

Having joined themselves to the world, Cape Verdeans have found the necessary plants and skills. They have found these especially in Arizona where, it seems, the climate and ecology are somewhat comparable and where the University of Arizona, at Tucson, has specialized in defending arid soils and conditions, and has come enthusiastically to the aid of the archipelago. Varieties of acacia – molissima, cyanophila, sanfelipe and others – have shown that they can prosper even where annual rainfall, as in most of Santiago Island, averages as little as 100 mm (7 inches) a year. They reach several metres in height within three or four years, continue to grow umbrella-like, and produce a useful 'fruit' which livestock can eat with advantage. Supplies of cooking firewood will become plentiful for the first time in centuries. Meanwhile the government has launched research into the provision of fuel-efficient cooking stoves for a people who must rely on wood for fuel.

At several points on Fogo and Sant'Antão the north-east trades strike ground above the 1300 metre (4264-foot) mark, and deposit their humidity. Here on the summit of Sant'Antão at Pico da Cruz, and on that of Monte Velho in Fogo, small forests of conifers and hardwoods are already in good existence. Begun in a small way during the last years of colonial rule, these forests are now being annually extended with pines and cypress, grevilha (silver oak), casuarina, ceratonia and other useful species.

The result is very grateful to the eye as well as to the ecology. In an hour or so the visitor drives up from hot and dry sea-level, climbing roads that serpentine and coil incredibly, into the chilly mist of Pico da Cruz or Monte Velho where the foresters wear stout jackets and rub their hands with the cold. Then he is glad to descend a little and inspect the new seedling-nurseries with their multitudes of plants in foot-long plastic sleeves of earth, wedged together in thousands and watered with a careful hand.

Water on Cape Verde is always too little save when the heavens open, and then it is too much; but nothing in the past was ever done, in any systematic way, to conserve it. In his bench-mark survey of ten years of achievement made in 1985, Aristides Pereira could report that soil- and water-conservation work since 1976 had already built 15,000 stone retaining-dykes or barrages across steep gullies and small canyons, had raised 20 million metres of earth-retaining-walls, and had thus added some 2,073,000 square metres of new rain-fed terracing available for cultivation.

Research into additional water resources, chiefly artesian, has so far revealed no likelihood of abundance, but is not discouraging. Fogo again dramatizes some of the natural problems here involved. Fogo has several reliable and even abundant springs of fresh water, but all of them emerge at the base of this huge volcanic cone, more or less at sea-level, and pumping to levels at least halfway up the 9000-foot cone is technically difficult but also expensive. Foreign aid money is being used for this purpose.

This old volcano of Fogo, erupting last in 1951 though in quite a pleasant way, sparing a church in its lava flow and thereby confirming God's occasional mercy in the eyes of all who were present or so it is said, does in fact offer a vision of what the future could be. Upwards from level to level, crops of many kinds can flourish in its volcanic soil: coffee, top-fruits, grapes and castor-oil are only four of them. Fogo can become a garden of food. Other islands, even the deserts of Sal and Boa Vista, can move with soil- and water-conservation in the same direction.

This means investment, and will continue to mean investment, most of which must come from continued foreign aid, given the necessarily narrow limits on local capital-formation. What has been able to be done so far is already a great deal more than a token of the difference between bad and good government. All forms of ecological first-aid and improvement – 'rural development' in the term used here – received one-third of all public investment in the ten years 1975–85, or twelve times as much as in the last colonial quiquennium of 1968–73. This is claimed, rightly I think, to have gone together with a considerably greater cost-effectiveness than was possible in colonial times of autocracy and despair; while the figures for these ten years take no account of the large voluntary effort, notably in tree-planting, which the regime has been able to evoke and sustain. This has been a decade, moreover, when other sectors made urgent demands, not least because the size of Cape Verdean towns has been rapidly expanding with correspondingly expanding needs. Here is one African country, one may think, which has got its priorities right.

IV

Travel round these islands can give a singular pleasure and surprise. Carlos Tavares wants to show me the fabled crater of Fogo within the summit of the cone. I have seen it before but that was in 1976, ten years ago. Has anything happened there since?

We traverse the furious roads of Fogo on a pearled azure morning, circling upward from its seaside capital of São Felipe. We round the great cone on its eastern side, with Santiago lost in the sea-mist of middle distance, and now below us there is the irrigated green of fruit gardens at Monte Ginevra. Fed by pumps lifting water from the base of the cone, Monte Ginevra is an emerald jewel in a blue and grey seascape, while up ahead is one of Fogo's twenty or so hamlets, a cluster of tufa-built houses within dry-stone garden walls. This is where the activist of the Women's Organization, who has hitched a lift, leaves us for her day's meeting with real or prospective local women-members; we shall pick her up again this evening.

At the thousand-metre mark we can pause and look down on slopes of mounded hillocks and small hills which are circled, circumcised, by ring-cuts one above the other to their summits: cuts which are ditches and low earthen dykes, lately built, to hold back rainfall and reduce erosion: whenever, that is, rain does fall. Driving upward again, we are out of the coffee belt and into the castor-oil belt; and the visitor ponders the thought that a dreadful medicine taken as a child – does anyone still take it? – might have come from Fogo. As a soldier stricken with dysentery in the valley of the Danube during World War Two, I was strangely sent supplies of castor-oil by parachute, and drank it in glassfulls with the desperate certainty, at once confirmed by dysentery's degrading thrust, that it could do no good at all. But I drank it all the same; and now I look at the castor-oil zone of Fogo and reach into forgiveness. It was scarcely Fogo's fault.

Well above the 1300-metre mark the road tops a shoulder-bone of the volcano and runs for a little space until suddenly it takes you round a cliff-hung corner and throws you into the Place of the Cauldron, Chã das Caldeiras, the vast crater itself.

The moment is worth coming a long way to experience. Before this corner you are on a high peak raised above ocean horizons: perched on a globe-revealing cloud, as it were, and easily able to imagine the whole of humanity out there in front of you. Then you are suddenly inside a monstrous container of gigantic slag that might be the churned-up leavings of a long artillery bombardment: except that what is here is no kind of mud but long-cold lava cast in tortured and fantastic clumps. Beside you the wall of the cauldron climbs sheer and jaggedly to a curtain-ridge 500 feet above, while there in the centre of the cauldron, dripping its petrified rivers of grit, goes up the inner core for another 2000 feet. You stop the car and get out and crane back your head, and still you cannot see the top of this volcano.

'One of these days', says Carlos, 'I am going to climb it.' The visitor has no such thought.

Ten years ago the road here was rough and unrepaired; now it is rough and well repaired. It snakes through the lava field to the hamlet of Chã das Caldeiras, a dozen or so houses set in little fields cleared of lava and laid with earth brought from wherever there is any. About 400 people live in this crater. I remember them from 1976, a population with blue eyes and long tawny hair, the picturesque descendants on their ancestral father's side, it is said, of a French nobleman who had fled here from the French Revolution of 1848. Few outsiders will have come to disturb the transmission of their Afro-Gallic features until, within recent memory, the road arrived. Even the innumerable mixtures of Cape Verdean appearance have no others quite like these.

Ten years ago there was nothing here of any public sense or

purpose. Now there is a primary school and a schoolmaster, a soccer pitch on black sand, a consumer co-operative, a local council, and a Party secretary; soon, they say, we shall have a people's court and we shall recruit a militia. It is not at all clear what the militia will have to do at Chã das Caldeiras, but everyone else has one.

Fogo Island secretary of the Party José Modesto, who has come to show us round, is tactfully proud of all this. I find him competent and direct. 'There is now no part of Fogo', he says, 'where the Party and our institutions of participation are not present and at work, even if some are still weak, especially the Women's Organization.'

Secretary Modesto has come with us to ask his own questions of people here as well as to help in answering mine. He considers that the best thing they've achieved 'is to change habits of work, to get away from the old attitudes of helplessness promoted by the charity-system of the colonial years'. It is what others have told me less coherently, peasants among them.

After the hamlet of Chã das Caldeiras our driver turns sharp left and heads for the foot of the cliff of the curtain-wall. Here, again suddenly, there are the buildings of a wine co-operative tucked into the cliffside, its vineyards in pockets out of sight. Its product is a strong country red of which Fogo, here and at one other place, makes about 10,000 litres annually and sells it to the towns of the archipelago. The person in charge is a woman who shows us new vats which hold vintages for the previous two years, and the bottling plant with rows of labelled bottles: *Vinho de Fogo Tinto*: *Co-operativa de Viticultores*. Ten years ago the wine-making was primitive, as I recall; now forty-two co-operative members work here, producing last year 6000 litres.

There may be other vineyards placed as strangely as this. What is strangest of all, here, is that this one is thoroughly organized. It is a solid piece of evidence in support of Secretary Modesto's claim. Later, I collect more evidence.

Altogether, in Fogo, about 4000 persons out of a total of 31,115 (census of 1980) are directly and regularly engaged in one or other of the means of mass participation. The 1050 Party members – with 194 women, which is slightly better than the national average – are organized in fifty-seven *grupos de base* spread around the cone and within the crater itself, 60 per cent of whose members are under thirty. The Fogo secretary of the Women's Organization,

Maria de Graça, who is twenty-nine and otherwise a school-teacher, has 775 members in seven *grupos de base*: while José Soares, who is secretary of the Youth Organization has 600 members (between fourteen and thirty) in forty *grupos de base*. Not yet enough, he says, but 142 new members were recruited last year. 'We explain the Land Reform. We play in bands and theatre groups. We argue against old habits of drinking and polygamy, above all against *caciquismo*', a plague which I interpret as 'boss-ism'. It would seem that Fogo secretary Modesto's claim for the pervasiveness of the institutions of participation is rather well based.

At the root of all these participatory activities one finds an effort to launch the work of economic development: a difficult effort, and for several reasons. Fogo's working population, for example, is reckoned at 14,500 persons: those, that is, who need work outside the subsistence sector. In 1985 only 5000 of these have such work, and therefore have wages. The rest must survive as they can from part-time work, family support, emigrants' remittances, and the hope that tomorrow will be better. What ground, in economic development, is there for any such hope?

V

A comprehensive picture of Cape Verdean economic development in its first decade can call on capacious materials, since this is a regime which takes care to explain itself, whether to its own electors in government reports presented to the National Assembly, in presidential summaries and retrospects, and in detailed meetings up and down the country, or to foreign donors of aid, whether these are governmental or non-governmental agencies. In this respect there could be no sharper contrast with the 'void' that existed in early 1975.

'The crude first problem', comments Adam Rocha, minister of industry and power in 1986 and one of a new wave of youthful leaders, men and women, who have come forward since the beginning of the 1980s,

> was that we really had no starting base to build on. No industrial base of course, but also no capital and certainly no capitalism. Incidentally, no statistics either. It couldn't be a question of changing from one system to a better; there wasn't any system to change from.

This is the same point that Olivio Pires and others have made, but from an economic viewpoint. 'There were some small shopkeepers,' Rocha continues. 'But we found no businessmen, no entrepreneurs – no one able to launch new enterprises or manage them if launched.'

Consequently it was the new State which was obliged to go into business, partly so that a private sector could be created in the wake of a State sector.

> We can affirm that State initiative here has stimulated private initiative, and that the second would never have appeared without the first. Even now we have demands from prospective entrepreneurs that the State should go in with them.

But this State's 'going into business', save in vital sectors of capital-intensive investment, is not a project which meets with any Party enthusiasm, convinced as this Party seems to be that every extension of bureaucracy means a reduction of participation. The drive is 'to get things going' among a people historically deprived of any initiative, and then to see what forms of economic co-operation can be made to emerge.

Small enterprises have been launched, as private ventures, as forms of co-operative, as mixed private-State businesses: in clothing, pharmaceuticals, shoes and such. State investment has gone into ships for fishing and cargo carriage, fish-refrigeration and allied projects aimed at building on Cape Verde's potentially valuable maritime position and background. Several major State projects have been launched in the sphere of port installations at Praia and Mindelo. At the latter, the development bank of the Organization of African Unity has financed a $40 million State investment in ship-repair and dry-dock facilities. The large hopes of successful earnings from this have been hit, for the time being, by world recession but should be realized in the longer run.

Most available aid and capital, not used for the import of essential foodstuffs, have gone into social infrastructure in a country which had hitherto possessed almost none at all. This has created, as we have seen, a widely decentralized health service, a far bigger schooling network, a basis for higher education, and the kinds of rural development sketched earlier in this chapter. Prime Minister Pedro Pires could report at the end of 1985 that investments realized in 1985 had been three times larger than in 1980, those for industry having risen from an insignificant 2 per cent of all investment in 1978–80 to 13 per cent in 1985. This put industrial investment into third place behind investment in rural development and investment in social infrastructure.

A round-table conference of all Cape Verde's many 'development partners', meaning aid-donors, was able to conclude late in 1985 that the country had 'succeeded in traversing successfully the initial stages of economic and social development despite all the unfavourable internal and external circumstances': no mean compliment at that time. Among 'the least developed countries', moreover, Cape Verde since independence has been 'unusually successful in maintaining a high positive *per capita* rate of growth and a substantial level of productive investment, while at the same time preserving the internal and external balances of the economy'. The donors added that they found this to be a remarkable achievement.

It was an achievement obviously threatened by the endemic fragility of this island economy so hugely bereft of immediately usable resources. Large annual imports of foreign food must continue for a long while ahead, and must be largely in the form of gifts even while steps are taken to reduce this dependence.

In another context, the import of productive goods has begun and expanded. President Pereira's ten-year summary of 1985 could note that 'imports of consumer goods multiplied by 6.4 times' between 1976 and 1982, 'but imports of machinery and equipment multiplied by 38.6 times'. This was still not much, given the almost zero starting point for imports of machinery and equipment; but it signalled the regime's determination to use foreign aid, for as long as it may remain available, for structural as well as emergency purposes.

Hardcore unemployment, inbuilt and inherited from the past, stood at rather more than 25 per cent of the employable population in 1985, and was capable of being seriously relieved only by continued emigration no matter what the regime might attempt in the near future. Yet the donor countries could also note, in 1985, an 'increasing self-reliance of the economy', a very positive factor reflected by a narrowing gap between gross domestic product and total domestic expenditure. The ratio between these two rose in fact from 48 per cent in 1977–78 to 67 per cent in 1984.

It would be easy to add more facts and figures, but 1986 was no doubt still too soon to demonstrate the irreversibility of an economic 'transformation from an archaic to a modern society'. What one saw in 1986 is that the process is *en route*, even while the transformation is still at an early stage. The direction of the march is posted, even while large claims and labels are eschewed. The regime holds to the promise of the Party of Cabral, declared so long ago in times of huge adversity, that it will end in a structural sense 'the exploitation of man by man': not therefore to build a capitalist society, but also not to claim that a socialist society can lie within conceivable reach. Meanwhile the accent is insistently egalitarian, and the 'line of march' perceived as the further building of a democracy of participation: a democracy of common purpose such as may be able to reach a life-giving hand into the most remote corners of these remote islands, and shape their future to a common good.

11 A country at peace

This book could be much longer, for the policies of independent reconstruction push out and ramify. In the full history of these years, moreover, many Cape Verdeans will be remembered for whom these pages have been able to find no space. Personal as well as historical reasons make me regret these omissions: to go no further, how forget a moment early in the 1970s – was it in 1972? – when, leaving the liberated zones of Guinea-Bissau after a long trek, and looking back from the canoe on the Cassine river at fighters of the PAIGC who had come to see me on my way, I saw the valiant Baro (Joaquim Pedro da Silva) waving his affectionate farewell. I have said nothing about Baro, from the island of Maio, and many others in this history; but the record that Cape Verdeans will write will remedy the injustice.

A longer book would not have altered the conclusions one could draw in 1986. Here was an African people which has found a way to save itself, which has shown how the poorest and most despairing of the legacies of foreign rule can be challenged and thrown off, and which so far has prevailed against every forecast of failure. Here was much that others may wish to think about.

Not that anyone in Cape Verde, I think, is likely to be heard crying triumph in the great gloom of the last years of our century: the problems now, and the problems for all the foreseeable future, remain both 'ample and complex' in the words of Aristides Pereira during his ten-year retrospective of 1985. Yet if poverty continues in Cape Verde, as it acutely does, this is no longer the poverty of despair; and the same is true of emigration. If discontents and frustrations likewise continue, they are a part of the general human condition: they are no longer the product of a hated system.

Bad setbacks have occurred and will no doubt occur again. So far, the most damaging has probably been the rejection of progress towards union by the Bissau coup-makers of 1980. This struck

After ten years of independence, Cape Verde had still to be at an early stage of building a viable and self-reliant society, of proving that 'Cape Verde is a possible country to live in'. There have been many achievements: but today *a luta continua*, the struggle continues . . . (Photo copyright Augusta Conchiglia)

hard at the basic concept of the Party of Cabral: that Cape Verde must find its destiny in Africa and not in Europe or America; and the blow was sorely felt. Not so much by the ninety or so who had gone through the liberation struggle on the mainland, and who 're-Africanized themselves' – the words are Dulce Duarte's – 'in that community of sacrifice': but for all those Cape Verdeans to whom the African continent had remained unknown and undesired, and for those Cape Verdeans 'who had lived there, in alienation, as the servants of Portuguese colonialism'. Yet while the Cape Verdean PAIGC felt itself obliged to become the PAICV, marking its separation from those in Guinea-Bissau who now rejected the project of union, Pereira and his companions began at once to forge new African links.

Already a member of the seventeen-country West African Economic Community, which it had joined in 1977, the regime embarked on an active diplomacy of multiplying contacts and shared obligations. Sticking to its principle of non-alignment in West–East rivalries and refusing all military or comparable commitments which might undermine this non-alignment, the regime took its place in the Organization of African Unity, assumed a leading role in the Sahel anti-drought committee, and, in the person of President Pereira, came forward as representative of the African group of 'Least Developed Countries'. The years of independence have indeed brought international recognition – Pereira in 1985 – 'of what to the eyes of many had appeared to be an absolute impossibility': recognition of Cape Verde 'as an independent state endowed with a politics that is serious, meditated and useful'.

This politics has enabled the regime to play a valued part in projects of various kinds, not least those of southern Africa and the struggle against apartheid in South Africa and against apartheid's external aggressions. If the regime continued to give transit-landing rights to South African Airways on Sal Island, this was a concession to its own poverty approved by the OAU and part of the general southern African dependence on certain crucial economic links with South Africa: links which, once apartheid is eliminated, can promise many benefits.

The regime has at the same time established its ideological and political independence. Conserving good relations with the USSR and other communist countries, it has fruitfully multiplied its contacts with the West. To Pereira's modest presidential quarters in Praia there come emissaries from every quarter of the globe.

Participation has begun to score its gains. These continue to collide with acute material shortages and, above all, with the painfully high rate of unemployment in towns such as Mindelo. But they do not collide with complacency at the top or with networks of corruption. In the conflict-ridden ex-colonial world of these terrible years, Cape Verde can be affirmed to have become a country at peace with itself.

Perhaps needless to say, this is not the same as affirming that Cape Verde has become a country at peace within itself. Participation may provide self-belief and confidence, and draw clear limits round the scope for careerism. But participation does not cancel out the past; and this remains a disturbed and anxious people still inwardly harassed by fearful memories and nagging doubts, pestered and distracted by old habits of the history of silence. The claws of self-depreciation are always at the margins of the space for confidence that has been cleared.

There is evidently much to be complained about. The PAICV of Praia, a capital now bursting at its seams for lack of housing, has lately started a journal of opinion, *Tribuna*, whose writers – Georgina Mello, Manuel Delgado, and others – are to the Cape Verde of independence very much what those of *A Voz de Cabo Verde* and *O Manduco*, long ago, were to the Cape Verde of colonial subjection: critics of conformity, awkward inspectors of the orthodox.

Issue 22 of May 1986 arrives as I work on this book. A front-page editorial entitled *A Fundamental Question* strikes at 'the outmoded mentality of some responsible cadres, whose methods of work exclude any kind of discussion or participation'. Such persons at the head of local Party groups, *grupos de base*, seem unaware of what they are at. Who can know or tell, from what they say and do, just how local Party groups may be useful?

> They have no faith in the ability of others. They are self-sufficient and authoritarian. They tolerate no opinions save those that praise them. They build their own psychological barricades against even the most constructive criticism. They take care to hide their mistakes and irregularities. They perpetuate wrong situations which could otherwise be mended.

Such complaints are real. They arise from human frailty, but also from the peculiar legacy of Portuguese colonial 'boss-ism', *caciquismo*: they point back to the deprivations of the colonial condition. And while it is true that the Cape Verde of 1986 had become a society that is viable and defendable for the first time in history, the outside observer may still be visited by the feeling that happiness, for many Cape Verdeans, is still somewhere else: in America or Holland, in Portugal or Brazil. World recession and the manifold benefits of independence may have questioned the old belief that 'real life must be over there: here we can only wait . . .'. But the old belief seems deep engrained.

Coming from ravages elsewhere in the world, the observer may further sense that what many Cape Verdeans may now greatly need, apart from a somewhat less spartan daily life, is to accept and realize their good fortune after never having known any: to realize and savour and enjoy it. Perhaps this begins to happen among the young, whose musical events are now a frequent festival of jazz and song; perhaps it is too much to ask of the old or middle-aged. The benefits of independence and the satisfactions that can flow from them still have to battle with the discouragements of doubt and deprivation, even when these no longer command the scene.

The regime is popular for every obvious reason but is careful not to commit the blunder of supposing that its own self-confidence can be a substitute for its people's self-confidence. It asks this people to forego old yearnings for 'somewhere else', to accept that Cape Verde is poor and will remain poor, but that a corresponding life-style need not be an unhappy one. Not everyone will respond. A leading militant says in 1986,

> There are those here who live and expect as though they were living and expecting in a different kind of country, in a rich country, in a country of limitless material possibilities. But we have to accept our destiny for what it really is.

The problem is not small. Speaking to the National Assembly in 1985, Prime Minister Pires appealed for 'a more dynamic vision of how to promote our cultural development', affirming that 'this is indispensable to our people in reinforcement of their identity, of their self-respect, of their confident integration in the general progress of mankind'. Big words, for once: but the point is very real.

The outside world, all too often, veritably tears itself to pieces in wrestling for 'more' even while, for many or even the majority, it fails to provide 'enough'. It is a kind of consciousness which can turn every sense of community upon its head, and make society despise itself. And all the influences that waft in here from outside, arguing their various nostrums of 'development', combine to urge the pull of 'more': just as if 'more', in and for itself, must remain the ultimate test of happiness.

To argue against that pull is not to preach the complacency of those who, not being poor, consider that the poor should rest content with their poverty. The continuers of Cabral, for their part, know all too well that 'the people are fighting for material benefits, to live better and see their lives go forward'. It remains that the so-called 'Third World', this immense sector of the globe so grossly disadvantaged by the existing 'economic order', has all too often victimized itself by concentrating on the sectional 'development of more' – more traffic jams, more personal profits, more greed if you like – rather than on the general 'development of enough'. Cape Verde certainly needs and means to get more of many good things; but that is not to say that its future has to be clamped into current philosophies which seem to measure developmental success by indices of a merely material growth, irrespective of the social matrix and balance within which such growth is expected to take place. No good prospect for the survival of these islands could lie that way. There will always be 'more' elsewhere, even while 'more' in that case has to go together with emigration, with exile and subservience.

What this regime can be seen to have done, within its first few years of independence, is to have demonstrated to this people, and for the first time in history, that their country can be a real home to them: possible and desirable as their own place in which to live and be at peace and decently prosper. With its stubborn and attractive optimism this regime has devised and installed sound public institutions where none of any such sort ever existed before: institutions which can guarantee the rule of law and respect for citizens' rights within a democratic structure. What it claims to offer within this guarantee is a system of participation which is also, and by its nature, an arduous process of self-discovery: a process, as it has seemed to me, somewhat like a tide in which each forward wave makes fresh ground until it falls and withdraws and is overtaken by the next.

That kind of process makes a challenge which can become

difficult and tiring but is not boring: a process, besides, in which a stiffly realist self-criticism can give assurance that the tide will not be reversed into stagnation. This means of course that much must continue to evolve, and that the scene outlined here is to be regarded as an elementary stage in this building of a viable society. It remains that the scene already differs vibrantly from the void of 1975.

The observer from afar questions his conclusions, being well aware that things go wrong as well as right, and far more easily and often: being well aware, besides, that good news from Africa is not what the world will easily believe. Yet in this case of Cape Verde, despite its modesty of size so patently a test case in this period of continental crisis and collapse, the observer stays with his conclusions. Here is a country with real solutions to the massive problems of post-colonial community. These are solutions to which the rest of Africa may usefully give heed and thought.

The weather in the world is bad, and will continue so. At least it will be prudent to expect as much. But in these storms it can be seen that the Fortunate Isles sail with a well-built ship and a steadfast crew. However unexpectedly, and at last, it may even be agreed that these islands deserve this name.

Appendix 1 Independence documents

Among documents concerning the liberation of the Cape Verde archipelago, readers may like to have the following extracts from three that were finally decisive.

1. Declaration of the Executive Committee of the PAIGC dated 16 May 1974, being the response of the PAIGC to initial feelers put out by the newly-formed Portuguese regime after the overthrow of the dictatorship in the previous month:

During the 17 years of its existence and especially since the beginning of our armed struggle for national liberation 11 years ago, our Party has never ceased to affirm its readiness to open negotiations with the Portuguese State . . .

[But] the rulers of Portugal, incapable of understanding the currents of thought and the political values universally accepted in our epoch, have maintained the most categorical rejection of all our proposals, and have unleashed and step by step intensified an unjust and barbarous war of genocide against our people. This has been the same rigid and inhuman attitude as that adopted by the Portuguese Government in Southern Africa where it has replied with war to the just claim of independence by our brother peoples of Angola and Mozambique . . .

[Now] in the new situation characterised by the irruption of democratic forces on the Portuguese political scene, the Executive Committee of the PAIGC submits to this new Portuguese political power the concrete proposal which follows here, and which can open the way to solving the conflict between our people and the Portuguese State.

This solution presupposes the total liberation of our people of Guiné [Guinea-Bissau] and Cape Verde. It can permit the establishment between our two peoples of a new relationship in the common interest and based on the principle of strict equality.

In the present phase of political and military evolution of our struggle and, generally, of the struggle against Portuguese colonialism in Africa, everything shows that this new relationship requires:

– Recognition of the Republic of Guinea-Bissau and of the right of our people in Cape Verde to self-determination and independence.

– Recognition of the same right of the peoples of the other Portuguese colonies . . .

Boé, Guinea-Bissau
16 May 1974

2. Agreement between the Portuguese Government and the PAIGC, dated 26 August 1974 (and signed in Algiers following initial negotiations in London a little earlier):

Article 1: Recognition *de jure* of the Republic of Guinea-Bissau, as a sovereign State, by the Portuguese State, will be made on 10 September 1974.

Articles 2–5 spelt out the practical implications of peace and Portuguese withdrawal from Guinea-Bissau: Portuguese military evacuation, measures of co-operation to be undertaken between the two States, and the forming of diplomatic relations, etc.

Article 6: The Portuguese Government reaffirms the right of the people of Cape Verde to self-determination and independence, and guarantees the realization of this right in agreement with the pertinent resolutions of the United Nations, also taking into account the expressed will of the Organization of African Unity.

Article 7: The Portuguese Government and the PAIGC consider that the accession of Cape Verde to independence, within the general framework of the decolonisation of African territories under Portuguese dominion, constitutes a necessary factor for a durable peace and sincere co-operation between the Portuguese Republic and the Republic of Guinea-Bissau . . .

Algiers, 26 August 1974, signed by

The Delegation of the Portuguese Government:

Mario Soares, Foreign Minister

António de Almeida Santos, Minister for Interterritorial Co-ordination
Vicente Almeida d'Eça, Naval Captain
Hugo Manuel Rodrigues Santos, Infantry Major

The Delegation of the Executive Committee of the PAIGC:

Pedro Pires, EC member, Comandante
Umaru Djalo, EC member, Comandante
José Araújo, EC member
Otto Schacht, EC Member
Lucio Soares, EC Member, Comandante
Luis Oliveira Sanca, Ambassador

3. Agreement between the Portuguese Government and the PAIGC, signed in Lisbon on 19 December 1974:

[Our] conversations have unfolded in an atmosphere of mutual understanding and perfect co-operation, and have reached the following agreement:

1. The Portuguese Government reaffirms the right of the People of Cape Verde to self-determination and independence in conformity with the Portuguese constitutional Law No. 7/74 of 26 July (1974), and with the pertinent resolutions of the Organization of the United Nations, taking also into account the expressed will of the Organization of African Unity.

2. The Portuguese Government and the PAIGC, conscious of the need to assure, under the best conditions, the transfer of powers to the future Independent State of Cape Verde, agree to establish the framework and calendar of the respective process of decolonization in terms of the following articles:

These articles provided for a Government of Transition consisting of a High Commissioner, equivalent to Prime Minister, and five other ministers, which government, having all executive powers, was to (a) conduct the general policy of the State of Cape Verde; (b) manage the economic and financial affairs of the State of Cape Verde; and (c) promote the democratization of the territory, notably through the substitution of colonial structures. The Portuguese President was to select and nominate the High Commissioner and two ministers of the Government of Transition, while three were to be nominated by the PAIGC.

Among other provisions, *Article 15* expressed the Portuguese Government's intention to form, with the future State of Cape Verde, 'bilateral agreements of active co-operation in all fields'.

Lisbon, 19 December 1974, signed by:

Delegation of the Portuguese Government:

Major Melo Antunes, Minister without Portfolio

Dr Mario Soares, Foreign Minister

Dr António de Almeida Santos, Minister for Interterritorial Coordination

Delegation of the PAIGC (CV):

Pedro Pires, EC member and Chairman of the PAIGC National Commission of Cape Verde

Amaro Alexandre da Luz, member of CV National Commission

José Luis Fernandes Lopes, member of CV National Commission

Appendix 2

Mass Participation (Participação Popular)

Extracts from documents presented to the Second Congress of the African Independence Party of Cape Verde (PAICV, created as the succcessor in Cape Verde of the PAIGC after the coup of scission made in Guinea-Bissau on 14 November 1980): June 1984:

Since its creation, the Party [in this reference the PAIGC, predecessor of the PAICV] established its fundamental aims as being the ending of foreign domination and the building of a new society both democratic and freed from the exploitation of man by man.

Yet the journey from a colonial society traumatized by a centuries-old subjection to a democratic society is not an easy one. It necessarily supposes a more or less long process in line with the development of productive forces and with the type of social relations established in the new society. It implies the individual and collective responsibility of the citizens . . .

In defining the nature of the regime to be installed after independence – a democratic regime based on the action of the masses in the management of its social, economic and cultural life as in the government of the Nation – the Party's programme has defined mass participation as the key-element in the construction of the State . . .

With the conquest of independence and the creation of the Cape Verdean State, there began the process of an ever greater involvement of the mass of the people in deciding its destiny.

It is within this framework that there arise, in the Cape Verdean political panorama, alongside the 'classical' institutions of power, the social organizations, whether of the masses or otherwise – such as JAAC (Amílcar Cabral Youth Association], Trade Unions, OM [Women's Organization of Cape Verde] and the Co-operatives – and the institutions of local power such as the residents' committees (local councils), zonal courts and people's militias, which combine to complete the Cape Verdean system of political power, and which enable the masses to act directly in the tasks that particularly concern them, or in the tasks of national interest . . .

The process will naturally meet with the most varied types of resistance. Old habits, old ideas, the remnants and the metamorphoses of colonial evils and vices such as authoritarianism, *caciquismo* (boss-ism), corruption and the trade in influence, bureaucratism etc., tend always to root and reproduce themselves and, therefore, stand in opposition to the means which enable the democratization of society.

It follows that, along with the conformism carried over from the past which discourages participation, there arise attitudes of rejection that may see in mass participation, and thus in the democratization of society, a threat to their continued privileges and positions, these often the product of inadmissible methods . . .

All such resistances and preconceptions are to be eliminated progressively but firmly, above all in the case of the agents of State power because these, through the weight they can exercise, would constitute serious obstacles to the initiated process of democratization of society . . .

The task of acting as principal dynamizer and organizer of mass participation belongs to the Party . . .

Notes on sources

The only serious study of the history of Cape Verde to be published in English up to the time when I undertook the present work is, so far as I am aware, a happily excellent translation and edition by Christopher Fyfe of one of the key works of the Cape Verdean historian António Carreira, *The People of the Cape Verde Islands: Exploitation and Emigration*, C. Hurst & Co., London (and Anchor, Connecticut), 1982 (*Migrações nas Ilhas de Cabo Verde*, Univ. Nova de Lisboa, 1977).

The recovery of Cape Verdean history up to the 1940s owes much to Snr Carreira, whose principal works are indispensable: notably, as well as the above, *Cabo Verde: Formação e Extinção de uma Sociedade Escravocrata (1460–1878)*, Centro de Estudos da Guiné Portuguesa, Bissau, 1972; *Cabo Verde: Aspectos Sociais*, Ulmeiro, Lisboa, 1977, but a second and enlarged edition of 1984 is to be preferred; *Documentos para a História das Ilhas de Cabo Verde e 'Rios de Guiné' (Seculos XVII e XVIII)*, Fundação Calouste Gulbenkian, Lisbon, 1983. Beyond the many fruits of his own researches, Carreira has shown himself a master of the classical Portuguese records, and quotes extensively from essential collections that are sometimes very hard to come by such as those of C. J. Senna Barcelos, *Subsídios para a História de Cabo Verde e Guiné*, Lisbon, 1899, and of António Brásio, *Monumenta Missionäria Africana (1342–1499*), Lisbon, 1952–85, 19 vols. André Donelha's *Descrição da Serra Leõa e dos Rios de Guiné do Cabo Verde*, Lisbon, 1625, has lately been republished in a handsome edition of 1977 by Junta de Investigações Científicas do Ultramar, together with an English translation.

Other useful re-editions of relevant classics include Raymond Mauny's edition (with translation into French) of Duarte Pacheco Pereira, *Esmeraldo de Situ Orbis* (*c*. 1506), Centro de Estudos da Guiné Portuguesa, Bissau, 1956; and António Brásio's edition of André Alvares de Almada (a sea-captain of the Island of Santiago), *Tratado Breve dos Rios de Guiné e Cabo Verde* (*c*. 1594), Editorial LIAM, Lisbon, 1964. Valuable additions to these contexts are in J. M. Blake, *Europeans in West Africa, 1450–1560*, Hakluyt Society, London, 1942, 2 vols. A recent commentary is in Walter Rodney, *A History of the Upper Guinea Coast, 1545–1800, Clarendon, 1970.*

Many stray references to the archipelago belong to the sailing-ship period of the eighteenth and early nineteenth centuries, sometimes in intriguing places. Charles Darwin arrived in the port of Praia on board HMS *Beagle* in 1831 and devoted the first page or so of his published *Journal of Researches* (1839, with later re-editions) to a description of the scene. He found that 'the neighbourhood of Porto Praya, viewed from the sea, wears a desolate aspect'; but in his *Diary* (Cambridge, 1933) he allowed himself a larger comment: 'Let those who have seen the Andes be discontented with the scenery of Santiago. I think its unusually sterile character gives it a grandeur which more vegetation might have spoiled. I suppose the view is truly African . . .' (p. 35). Nowadays there is a great deal more vegetation than in 1831 and the comment still rings true. Fifty years after his visit, in his autobiography, Darwin recalled Santiago as the place where he had first imagined that he too would write a book on geology. 'That was a memorable hour for me, and how distinctly I can call [it] to mind . . .' The book was going to be the *Origin of Species*. (See a sympathetic account by Alan Moorehead, *Darwin and the Beagle*, New York, 1969.)

For a useful bibliography, see J. M. McCarthy, *Guinea-Bissau and Cape Verde Islands: A Comprehensive Bibliography*, New York, 1977. But the relatively recent Portuguese archives offer disappointment, being scattered in places unknown, uncatalogued in places known, or in any case barred to access by an inexcusable fifty-year rule. It appears that large quantities of official documents on the African territories, including much written in confidence at the time, do in fact survive – three tons of such documents were mentioned in 1978 – but that long labour by qualified archivists now unavailable, as well as official permits now unobtainable, will be necessary before they can be consulted. See in this respect a woeful report in *O Dia*, Lisbon, 27 July 1978. As for other Portuguese colonies, this disgraceful situation means that the archival sources for practically the whole of the outright Fascist period from about 1930 remain silent or highly defective, while few officially permitted publications did anything useful to fill the void (but see References).

The USA Consulate in Praia that was opened in 1818 has materials up to 1898 available at the National Archives in Washington. In Cape Verde itself there are accessible municipal archives in Mindelo back to 1851, and other municipal collections on S. Nicolau, Boa Vista and possibly elsewhere. A national archive is now well housed in Praia under the charge of a trained Cape Verdean archivist, and was being catalogued in 1986. Collections of Cape Verdean newspapers and journals survive, and in this respect I have had the advantage of being able to read and quote from the work of the Cape Verdean historian Carlos Lopes Pereira (see References).

Several useful studies were also published during the later 'years of silence', among them that of Julio Monteiro Jnr, *Os Rebelados da Ilha Santiago de Cabo Verde*, Centro de Estudos de Cabo Verde, 1974. This treats of dissident peasants who defied authority in the 1960s and were persecuted for doing so. How far these dissidents were a Christian sect and how far a politically motivated current – Monteiro's account reminds one of the Watchtower or Kitiwala dissidents of Central Africa – remains under discussion. Early in the 1970s these peasants of northern Santiago evidently thought of Amílcar Cabral as 'Amílcar Christo'; but PAIGC activists recall that while the *Rebelados* 'accepted our PAIGC banner', they were unwilling or unable to give practical support. A few dozen evidently existed in the late 1980s and were in no conflict with the regime.

Independence brought a veritable explosion of Cape Verdean writing and publishing of many kinds. This happily continues, being further encouraged by a newly-created Instituto Caboverdeano do Livro. In this dimension I have been nourished by various papers and periodicals founded in or after 1975, notably *Nôs Luta* and *Voz di Povo* (both of Praia), *Voz de Revolução* (S. Nicolau), *Pâ Diante* (Sal), *Presença Cabo-Verdeana* (Lisbon), *Unidade e Luta* (Praia), *Tribuna* (Praia), and others mentioned in my references.

Foreign aid sources, notably those of the UN organizations and, for example, of Sweden's International Development Agency, possess a detailed documentation; and here I would like especially to thank Sigridúr Dúna Kristmundsdottir and Gísli Palsson of the Department of Anthropology of the University of Iceland for letting me have their report on *Cape Verdean Fishing Communities*, Rejkjavík 1984, fortunately in English. It seems particularly pleasing that one distant community of islanders should have come to the assistance of another, as Iceland has to Cape Verde.

Cape Verdean official documentation since 1975 is many-sided and readily accessible, as my references indicate. But the reader will have quickly seen that the story of the long struggle for independence, here set forth for the first time, has to rely in large degree on oral testimony; and for the opportunity to collect it, and crosscheck it, I am grateful to the patience and generosity of many Cape Verdean participants on that memorable scene. Their own historians will in due course complete this outline with the fuller details which its history deserves.

References
(by page numbers)

p. v José Saramago, *Jornal de Letras*, Lisbon, 5 May 1986.

Part One WHERE AND WHY?

p. 1: Jorge Barbosa (1902–71): Randall Leite (ed. with Eng. trans.) *Duas Linguas* . . ., Inst. Caboverdeano do Livro 1986, p. 21.

p. 3: I am likewise aware that Spanish custom calls the Canary Islands *Las Islas Fortunadas*, but national customs may be allowed to differ. Luis Camões sang in his *Lusiads* (Canto V) of Vasco da Gama and his men sailing past '*as Canarias ilhas que tiverem per nome Fortunadas* . . .', but I myself, with great respect for Portugal's heroic poet, will stick to my title. The Islands of the Hesperides were in any case the Islands of Cape Verde: where else in those waters were sumptuous damsels to be found?

p. 10: Of 1580, see A. Carreira, *Cabo Verde: Aspectos Sociais*, Lisbon, 1984 (2nd and enlarged edn), p. 17. Of 1610, same source. Carreira's works (see *Notes on Sources*) give a reliable and comprehensive account of the terrible droughts reported from early times. Luis Fonseca: interview in 1986.

p. 13: I have learned about the development of Cape Verdean Crioulo from *Mestre* Balthazar Lopes, to whom my thanks; relevant studies are also in M. F. Valkhoff (ed.), *Miscelânea Luso-Africana*, *Junta de Investigações Cientifica do Ultramar*, Lisbon, 1975, and Gulbenkian Foundation. For the markedly different Crioulo of Guinea-Bissau, see L. Scantamburlo, *Gramática e Dicionário Criol da Guiné-Bissau*, ed. Miss Italiana, Bologna, 1981.

p. 13: de Arpoare: see Carreira 1984, p. 20, quoting *Bol. Oficial* 7 of 1882. De Arpoare states that 30,000 died in the famine of 1864.

p. 14: Historians of the impressively large and cohesive New England community of Cape Verdean origin should refer to the records of this nineteenth-century US consulate.

pp. 16–17: The founding pioneers: here, as elsewhere, I am all too conscious that a brief account must omit names which a full Cape Verdean history of the struggle for independence will remember with vivid admiration.

p. 17: Olívio Pires: interview in 1986.

p. 19: The four great volumes of José Joaquim Lopes de Lima (member of the King's Council, deputy of the Cortes), covering all the Portuguese colonies, were published in Lisbon between 1844 and 1859, the first and second being of value in this context: *Ensaio sobre a Statística das Possessões Portuguezes.*

p. 19: For much of his life, Galvão was a colonial official and rose to be Inspector-General of Colonies at the end of the Second World War. A man of admirable sincerity, he then became a strong critic of Salazarist colonial policies, and was driven into political exile after suffering imprisonment in Lisbon. But the semi-official history which he wrote with Carlos Selvagem treads a careful path: see H. Galvão and C. Selvagem, *Império Ultramarino Português*, Lisbon, 4 vols, 1950–53.

Part Two THE HISTORY OF SILENCE

p. 21: Dulce Almada Duarte quoted this lament in her declaration to the Special Committee of the UNO: *Sobre a Situação do Povo de Cabo Verde*, June 1962: cyclostyled by PAIGC, Bissau.

1 Birth of a people

p. 23: R. Mauny, *Les Navigations Médiévales sur les Côtes sahariennes antérieures à la Découverte Portugaise (1434)*, Centro de Estudos Históricos Ultramarinos, Lisbon, 1960, early chs.

pp. 25ff.: See especially A. Carreira, *Cabo Verde: Formação e Extinção de uma Sociedade Escravocrata (1460–1878)*, Centro de Estudos da Guiné Portuguesa, Bissau, 1972.

pp. 31ff.: Dulce Duarte, 'A Dimensão cultural na estratégia de libertação nacional: os fundamentos culturais da Unidade Guiné-Dabo Verde', in *Continuar Cabral*, simpósio internacional Amílcar Cabral, 20–27 January 1983: published Praia, 1984.

2 A system of ruin

pp. 34–6: For proverbs I am especially grateful to Oswaldo Osório and Luis Fonseca, to whom my thanks.

pp. 37–9: A. Carreira, ed. and trans. C. Fyfe, *The People of the Cape Verde Islands*, Hurst, London; Archon, Connecticut, 1982, p. 108; p. 109 for Gov. Ribeiro; p. 113 for 'roped volunteers', those whom the local chiefs 'summarily ordered to be tied up and sent off "on contract" ', at the demand of the local Portuguese administration. The Portuguese original, whether cynical or scathing, was *voluntários de corda*. Later, after the

1920s, the term was dropped in favour of a distinction between *voluntários* and *serviçais* or *contratados*; but it often remained a distinction without a difference.

p. 40: Carreira has rescued these and other relevant statistics from the oblivion of archives chiefly in Lisbon: see especially Appendices in *The People of the Cape Verde Islands*, Hurst, London; Archon, Connecticut, 1982.

p. 43: Abilio Duarte: interviews in 1986.

pp. 44ff.: I am indebted to the Cape Verdean historian Carlos Lopes Pereira for his study of the early Cape Verdean press and its writers: *Alguns Aspectos da Resistência caboverdeana atraves de Meio Século de Imprensa, 1911–61*, Dept. of History, Univ. of Lisbon, 1985.

p. 45: Fontes de Pereira: see D. L. Wheeler, ' "Angola is Whose House?" ': in *African Historical Studies*, vol. II no. 1, 1969, p. 9.

p. 45: J. Ayodele Langley, *Pan-Africanism and Nationalism in West Africa 1900–45*, Clarendon, 1972, p. 133.

p. 46: The surprising case of 'Afro', Pedro Cardoso, is among the treasures recovered by Carlos Lopes Pereira, see *Alguns Aspectos da Resistência caboverdeana atraves de Meio Século de Imprensa, 1911–61*.

3 'But a day will come . . .'?

pp. 48–50. See D. L. Wheeler, *Republican Portugal*, Univ. of Wisconsin, 1978, various chapters.

p. 48: J. J. Gonçalves, *A Informação na Guiné, em Cabo Verde e em São Tomé e Principe*, Inst. Sup. de Ciéncias Sociais e Política Ultramarina, Lisbon, 1965, p. 302.

p. 52: British Embassy to FO: Public Record Office, London: 17420 (of 17 July 1933) in FO 371.

pp. 54–5: C-in-C South Atlantic to Admiralty: PRO C1705 in FO 371.

pp. 55–6: FO to Embassy Washington: PRO 24494 in FO 371. Atlantic Islands Project: I quote here from Premier and other papers cited by Martin Gilbert in vol. 6 of his biography of Churchill, *The Finest Hour*, London, 1984 (revised edn), at pp. 654 (footnote 3), 677, 933. Roosevelt's message to Churchill is quoted from John Colville, *The Fringes of Power*, London, 1985, p. 381.

p. 56: U-Boats in C. Verdean waters: see F. H. Hinsley, *British Intelligence in the Second World War*, HMSO, 1981, vol. 2, pp. 171, 179. See also Hinsley, 1984, vol. 3, pp. 231–2. DNI to Admiralty: PRO 26842 in FO 371.

p. 57: Consul to FO: PRO C2395 in FO 371.

pp. 57–8: Consul to FO in FO 371: e.g. especially C68520, C6573, C12813. Mario de Andrade, *Amilcar Cabral*, Paris, 1980, 16ff.

Part Three AGAINST THE ODDS

4 Beginnings

p. 63: Carreira, *The People of the Cape Verde Islands*, 1982, p. 125ff.

p. 63: See e.g. *Bol. Oficial da Col. de C. Verde*, nos. 5 and 17 of 1948, for the famine.

pp. 65ff.: Andrade, *Amilcar Cabral*, 45ff.

p. 69: da Cruz: the journal was *Mensagem*: see B. Davidson, *In the Eye of the Storm: Angola's People*, London, 1972, 157ff.

Cabral's radio talks: his own memoir, 'Texto de Amílcar Cabral', published posthumously in *Voz di Povo*, Praia, 18 September 1975.

p. 70: Aristides Pereira: interviews in 1986. I have had the honour of knowing him since 1961.

pp. 70–1: Abilio Duarte: interviews in 1986.

p. 72: Aristides Pereira: interviews in 1986.

pp. 73ff.: For the mainland struggle, see B. Davidson, *No Fist is Big Enough to Hide the Sky*, London, 1981, an enlargement of an earlier book, *The Liberation of Guiné*, London, 1969. The relevant bibliography, in Davidson, 1981, is considerable; see also bibliography in P. Chabal, *Amilcar Cabral*, Cambridge, 1983, p. 241.

p. 73: Maria Rodrigues Cabral: quoted here from P. Chabal, *Amilcar Cabral*, p. 49.

p. 74: Melo e Alvim to Cabral: in Andrade, *Amilcar Cabral*, p. 49.

pp. 75ff.: Luis Fonseca: interviews in 1986.

p. 77: Amaro da Luz: interview in 1986.

p. 78: J.Z. Soares: interview in 1986.

pp. 78–9: A. da Brito Cruz (Dul): interviews in 1986.

p. 79: Onésimo Silveira: for some of his poems, see M. de Andrade, *Na Noite Grávida de Punhais*, Lisbon, 1975, an indispensable 'thematic anthology' of African poetry in Portuguese. Silveira's poem here is on p 56.

p. 79: A. M. dos Santos: interview in 1986.

pp. 80–1: C. R. Lopes: interview in 1986.

p. 82: Pamphlet published for Cabral in 1960 by Union of Democratic Control, London (1914–64): *The Facts about Portugal's African Colonies*, from Cabral's French text in a translation by myself, the author using his pseudonym of Abel Djassi under which he was living at the time in Barnes and Mortlake, London. Reproduced in M. Wolfers (ed. and trans.), *Amílcar Cabral: Unity and Struggle*, London, 1980.

Dulce Duarte, 'A Dimensão cultural na estratégla de libertação nacional: os fundamentos culturais da Unidade Guiné-Cabo Verde', in *Continuar Cabral.*

p. 83: Dakar Party meeting: 'O Desenvolvimento da Luta em Cabo

Verde: Comunicado da reunião de quadres responsáveis', 17–20 July 1963: cyclostyled, PAIGC Dakar.

pp. 84ff.: Silvino da Luz: various interviews, chiefly in 1986.

pp. 87ff.: For a fairly detailed record of the war in 'Portuguese Guinea', and for the transformation of the latter into the Republic of Guinea-Bissau, see B. Davidson, *No Fist Is Big Enough to Hide the Sky*, Zed Books, London, 1981, reprinted 1984.

p. 90: T. da Sousa: see C. L. Pereira, *Alguns Aspectos da Resistência caboverdeana atravas de Meio Século de Imprensa, 1911–61*. Cabral's analysis: A. Cabral, *Unité et Lutte* (collected writings), Paris 1975, 2 vols: vol i, 150ff.

p. 92: Olívio Pires: interviews in 1986.

5 The struggle in the islands

pp. 93–8: Various interviews in 1986.

pp. 99–100: Lineo Miranda: interviews in 1986.

pp. 101–2: Pedro Martins: interviews in 1986.

p. 105: Prime Minister Pedro Pires: interviews in 1986.

p. 106: President Aristides Pereira: interviews in 1986.

p. 108: For these events in detail, see B. Davidson, *No Fist is Big Enough to Hide the Sky*.

6 The challenge of 1974

p. 109: Movimento das Forças Armadas em Cabo Verde: 'Estudo sobre a Situação Político-Economica em Cabo Verde', cyclostyled 7 November 1974.

pp. 111ff.: I am indebted to the PAICV, and especially to Foreign Minister S. da Luz, for providing me with originals or photocopies of these and other UDC and UPICV leaflets, mostly printed in Praia, 1974.

pp. 114–5: Osório: interview in 1986.

pp. 115ff.: I am grateful to General Vasco Gonçalves for generously helping me with written comments on the development of the Armed Forces Movement in Cape Verde.

pp. 116ff.: Among AFM documents which I have been able to consult, see especially motion of 11 October 1974 of the Associação dos Oficiais da Armada em Cabo Verde; motion of 1 November of the officers of the AFM in plenary; and *Estudo sobre a situação político-económica de Cabo Verde*, November 1974. For an authoritative overall review, written with the advantage of hindsight, see Vasco Gonçalves, 'Movimento das Forças Armadas, Projectos Políticos depois do 25 de Abril e Forças Armadas', in *Revista Critica de Ciencias Sociais*, Lisbon, May 1985.

p. 121: The letter to President Spínola conveyed the demands of 'militantes e simpatizantes da Ilha do Sal, reunidos em assembles geral', and was dated 24 November 1974. Copies of these remarkable letters to Spínola and Mobutu are in my possession.

p. 123: Press report: Gemini News Service, 18 October 1974, quoted here from *Africa Digest*, London, December 1974.

p. 123: Statement in AFM analysis of 7 November 1974, *Estudo sobre a situação politico-económica de Cabo Verde.*

p. 124: Pedro Pires: interviews in 1986.

p. 125: V. Gonçalves, 'Discurso proferido na cerimonia da independência de Cabo Verde', 1975.

p. 125: Now happily well preserved, the Praia archives began to be rescued by the British historian Christopher Fyfe when responding to an official invitation to visit, inspect, and advise on archives. A UNESCO grant then enabled a national archive to be fully and effectively established, and this in 1986 was in process of installation.

pp. 125–6: Interviews in 1986.

Part Four CONTINUING CABRAL

p. 127: Cabral: *Palavras Geráis*, 1975; Eng. trans. in Wolfers, *Amilcar Cabral: Unity and Struggle* (Trans. here is mine).

7 From the bare ground

pp. 131ff.: O. Le Brun, *Report* to UNESCO, No. FMR/SS/YTH/84/105, Paris, 1984.

p. 132: Olívio Pires: interviews in 1986.

pp. 133–4: Amid useful documentation on this period see: *Report* of the UN Secretary-General to the Economic and Social Council, *Assistance to Cape Verde* (21 September 1977); *ditto*, 18 July 1978 (A/33/167); and (French in my copy), *Assistance Demandée au PNUD* – in English UNDP – *par le Gouvernement du Cap-Vert pour la Période de 1978–81* (DP/GC/CVI/R.1 dated 8 September 1977). One should note in this context that the fiercely continuing drought of the early independence years, dating almost unbrokenly from 1969, had long been the subject of PAIGC publicity: see especially A. Cabral, *Sobre a Situação de Fome nas Ilhas de Cabo Verde*, Stockholm statement of 14 April 1971, which first alerted the world to the tragic condition of the islands, carefully concealed from public knowledge by the Salazarist regime: as noted by British Consul Sands of earlier droughts.

p. 134: Telegrams sent by 'Forças vivas mais representativas de S. Vicente' in wake of meeting at the Cine-Teatro Eden-Park, Mindelo, 6 June 1974.

pp. 135–7: There is a capacious and continuing documentation on *participação popular*, but in this context see especially *Documentos do II Congresso* (do PAICV): *A Participação Popular*, PAICV, Praia, June 1984, quoted here. And see Appendix 2.

p. 136: For *participação popular* in liberated zones of wartime Guinea-Bissau, I quote here from my own first-hand observations in 'Report on the Farther Liberation of Guinea-Bissau', *Socialist Register*, London, 1973.

p. 137: Lars Rudebeck: 'On the Class Basis of the National Liberation Movement of Guinea-Bissau': Dept of Political Science, University of Uppsala, May 1983. Retrospective: *A Participação Popular*, PAICV, Praia, June 1984.

p. 138: See *A Participação Popular*, PAICV, Praia, June 1984.

p. 138: Statement by Secretary-General Aristides Pereira at 3rd Congress of PAIGC, Bissau, 1977. Statement of 1980 by Olívio Pires, 'Sobre a Democracia Nacional Revolucionária', 1980, published by PAIGC Praia, Collecção 'Superação Político-Ideologica'.

p. 141: On the circumstances of the formation of the PAICV and its background, see especially documents relating to 1st congress of the newly-formed Party (Praia, 16–20 January 1981), and notably the introductory speech by Secretary-General Aristides Pereira: available in English, MAGIC papers, vol. II, no. 1, London, 1981.

pp. 141 and 161: Olivio Pires: interviews in 1986.

8 Launching participation

pp. 160ff.: PAIGC: *Sobre as Relações Partido Estado*, Praia, October 1975.

pp. 165–6: Boaventura de Sousa Santos: *A Justiça Popular en Cabo Verde*, Centro de Estudos Sociais, Univ. of Coimbra, 1984.

9 Woman's place is . . .'?

p. 167: Boubacar Barry, 'Le Sénégal 1960–80: Arachide, Bourgeoisie Bureaucratique et Sécheresse', in P. Gifford and Wm. R. Louis (eds), *The Transfer of Power*, vol. 2, New Haven and London, forthcoming.

p. 169: Lansiné Kaba, in P. Gifford and Wm. R. Louis (eds), *The Transfer of Power*, vol. 2.

p. 173: Dr I. Gomes: interviews in 1986, and *ibid. Principais Realizações durante Dez Primeiros Anos de Independência*, Ministry of Health and Social Affairs, Praia, June 1985.

pp. 173–4: OM spokeswomen: interviews in 1986.

10 Land: trees: green renewal

pp. 180ff.: All accurate information on Cape Verdean land ownership and proposals for changing it date from the early years of independence. See a detailed preview of the basis on which reforms were prepared: João Pereira Silva, 'The Rôle of Rural Institutions in Agrarian Transformation for Rural Development', paper for workshop at Arusha, Tanzania, 17–23 October 1983; *ibid.*, 'La Réforme Agraire au Cap Vert', Diplôme des Hautes Etudes Pratiques Sociales, Paris, n.d. but probably 1983; *ibid.*, 'A Agricultura Cabverdeana, as Secas e a Cultura do Milho', Praia, December 1985; as well as statistical and other materials archivally available in Praia. Among studies by visiting specialists those of Christian Sigrist and Gottfried Stockinger, also archivally available in Praia, are important.

p. 187: President A. Pereira, 'X Aniversário da Independência Nacional', Praia, 5 July 1985.

pp. 191–2: Adam Rocha, interview in 1986. For recent economic data see especially Prime Minister P. Pires, *Relatório de Execução do Programa de Governo, 1981–85*, Praia, November 1985; *ibid.*, *Programa de Governo 1986–90*; and debates of People's National Assembly, regularly printed, Praia. For a useful bird's-eye view of 1987, Lyse Doucet, 'Battling Against the Odds', in *West Africa*, London, 16 March 1987. She quotes from the *1985 Survey* of the International Monetary Fund, which wrote that 'despite a difficult terrain, an extreme paucity of natural resources, and a 12-year cycle of drought, Cape Verde has been relatively successful among small developing countries in maintaining a real rate of growth and a high level of generally productive investment'.

p. 193: (Second) Round Table of Development Partners, Praia, December 1986 (in two vols, cyclostyled, respectively of 80 and 50 pp.).

11 A country at peace

p. 197 Dulce Duarte, in *Continuar Cabral*, p. 222.

Thematic index

Aid, foreign sources, objectives
 donors' conclusions 133–4, 198, 218
 various donors 133
 World Food Programme 133
Armed Forces Movement (of Portugal: *Movimento das Forças Armadas*)
 contradictions within 115
 influenced by African movements 116
 initial approaches 106
 President Spinola ousted 120, 123
Armed Forces Movement of Portugal (in Cape Verde) 109
 development within 116–17
 support for PAIGC (CV) 117

Batuque 13, 53
Birth control *see* Family planning

Cabral, Amílcar
 assassination 104
 at United Nations (1962) ix
 at university 66–7
 Dakar meeting (1962) 83
 in Bissau (agricultural census) 73–4
 in London (1960) 82
 military strategy 88–9
 political analyses 89 ff.
 youth of 65
Caciquismo 138, 192
Canary Islands, contrast with 181
Cape Verde archipelago
 compass bearings 2
 dimensions 3
 early history 23 ff.
 population 5, 10–11
 prevailing winds 5
 slave system 25–6
'Colour prejudice', discussed 30 ff.
Comissões de moradores (local councils) 149 ff.
Creole culture 31

Deforestation 13, 37
Droughts *see* Famines

ECOWAS (Economic Community of West African States) 198
Education, public system of 175
Emigration
 after World War One 54
 elsewhere 41
 later 131
 to New England 40

Family planning 8, 173
Famines
 of 1580, 1610, 1927 10
 of 1864 38
 of 1900 38
 of 1911, 1916, 1921 38–9
 of 1941–2, 1947–9 54, 63
Frente amplo 118–19

Guinea-Bissau
 independence of 104–5
 rupture with 141

Health, public system 176

Industry: perspectives 192 ff.

Journalism, -ists
A Verdade 39
A Voz de Cabo Verde 44, 45, 48
Claridade 51, 89–90, 113
Eugenio Tavares 42 ff.
in Angola 45
José Lopes 44
Mocidade Africana 50
O Manduco 44, 46
Pedro Cardoso 46
Tribuna 119
Voz di Povo 214

Lançados (Tangomãos) 27
Land, traditional tenures 37
Land ownership pre-reform 181–2
Land reform 153, 182, 183 ff.
Landings project (from Cuba) 17, 91, 98–9, 103

Malnutrition 177
Morna 13, 34

National Assembly (of CV) 148
National Council of CV 107
Nativismo 45–6, 50
Non-alignment 134

Organisação da Mulher 159, 173–4

PAICV *(Partido Africano da Independência de Cabo Verde)*
foreign policy 198
membership 145, 150–1, 174, 191–2
origins 145
political principles *see* Participation
powers 147–8, 160
PAIGC (*Partido Africano da Independência de Guiné e Cabo Verde*)
actions in 1974 188 ff., 125
agitations of early 1970s 102–3
early developments in CV 75
founders and origins 69–73
launching in Guiné 72
Lisbon liaison 94–5
state model defined 138
with lycée students 84, 96–7
with port workers (Mindelo) 78, 93
Participation, mass socio-political (*participação popular*)
democracy dependent upon 141
development into local governmental forms 149, 150, 157–9
importance of 138 ff.
origins 135–6
overall involvement of population 159–160
programme 135
women's involvement in 167, 171–2
see also Appendix 2
Party systems discussed 140–1
Piracy in sixteenth century etc. 27–8
Population
contrasts with Transatlantic communities 31–3
formation of culture 11, 13
nature of culture 29
of islands 5, 29
origins 10–11
religions 13
Portugal
colonial policy 43
military dictatorship 19, 48
parliamentary republic 18
Salazar and *Estado Novo* 18–19, 48–50
Port workers (Mindelo) 78, 93
Proverbs 36

Reafforestation *see* Tree planting
Revolts
of Nhô Ambrosio 51
of slaves 14
Rebelados 210

'Sancho' 34, 53
Slavery in CV
as entrepôt system 26
numbers 25–6
origins 25

Tangomãos see *Lançados*
Tarrafal prison: politicals released 114–15
Tree planting 186–7
Tribunals, local (*tribunais de zona*) 149–50, 159, 163–6

UDC (Democratic Union of Cape Verde) 111
Unemployment 194
UPICV (People's Union for Independence of Cape Verde) 111–12

Water retention works 118
Wine 191
World War Two
  British invasion project 55
  Portuguese garrisons reinforced 57–8
  reports of famine 56–7

prosopography